ACCA Advanced Taxation: United Kingdom Reference

Copyright

Table of Contents

Copyright 2

Foreword 4

Advanced UK Tax System 6

    Foreign Trusts and Taxation.................................. 6

Overseas gains, related persons, exemptions 39

Inheritance tax complexities.............................. 70

    The basic principles of computing transfers of value.............. 74

    Trust Transfer Liabilities................................... 93

Overseas corporation tax complexities 102

Stamp taxes 149

VAT, Tax Admin, UK Tax....................................... 158

Tax Impact and Interaction 169

UK Tax Planning Strategies................................. 196

Professional skills.. 208

    Communication 208

Scepticism... 220

Commercial acumen 231

Employability and technology skills 240

Foreword

Welcome to the foreword of "ACCA Advanced Taxation: United Kingdom Reference." This comprehensive reference book aims to provide a clear and accessible guide to the advanced concepts and complexities of the United Kingdom's tax system. It is solely written for the candidates of ACCA Advanced Taxation United Kingdom variant, whose exams will be held from June 2023 to March 2024. Whether you are a tax professional, a student, or an individual seeking a deeper understanding of UK taxation, this book is designed to be a valuable resource tailored to your specific needs.

The table of contents presented above outlines the various topics covered from throughout syllabus in this book. From the advanced UK tax system to specific areas such as foreign trusts and taxation, overseas gains, inheritance tax complexities, and stamp taxes, each chapter delves into the intricacies of these subjects. Additionally, the book explores the basic principles of computing transfers of value, trust transfer liabilities, overseas corporation tax complexities, VAT, tax administration, and UK tax planning strategies.
In addition to the technical aspects of taxation, this book also emphasizes the development of professional skills necessary for success in the field. It covers topics such as communication, scepticism, commercial acumen, employability, and technology skills. These skills are essential for tax professionals to effectively navigate the complex landscape of tax regulations and provide valuable advice to clients.

Throughout this book, we have made a conscious effort to present the information in simple and accessible language. We understand that tax concepts can be daunting, and our aim is to break down complex ideas into easily understandable terms. Whether you are a beginner or an experienced tax professional, we hope that this book will serve as a valuable reference and enhance your understanding of advanced UK taxation.

We would like to express our gratitude to the authors and contributors who have dedicated their expertise and knowledge to make this book a comprehensive and reliable resource. Their commitment to providing accurate and up-to-date information is evident in the content presented within these pages.

Lastly, we would like to extend our appreciation to the readers. Your interest in advancing your knowledge of UK taxation is commendable, and we hope that this book will meet your expectations and serve as a valuable companion in your journey towards success in the ACCA Advanced Taxation United Kingdom variant exams, scheduled from June 2023 to March 2024.

We wish you an enriching and insightful reading experience with "ACCA Advanced Taxation: United Kingdom Reference."

Azhar ul Haque Sario

Advanced UK Tax System

Foreign Trusts and Taxation

The scope of income tax

Residence, domicile, and deemed domicile are important concepts in the UK taxation system that determine an individual's tax liabilities. Residence refers to where a person resides during a specific tax year, while domicile refers to their permanent home. Deemed domicile is a status assigned to individuals who have been resident in the UK for a certain period of time.

For income tax purposes, residents of the UK are generally taxed on their worldwide income, regardless of their domicile status. Non-residents, on the other hand, are only taxed on their UK income. This means that migrants to the UK or international students studying in the UK may pay less tax than UK citizens, as their residence and domicile status can affect their tax liabilities.

Domicile is distinct from residence, as it represents an individual's permanent home. It is not the same as residency, which can change from year to year. Domicile is particularly relevant for inheritance tax purposes, as individuals who are domiciled in the UK are subject to inheritance tax on their worldwide assets, while non-domiciled individuals are only subject to inheritance tax on their UK assets.

Deemed domicile is a status that can be assigned to individuals who have been resident in the UK for a certain number of years. Once deemed domicile is acquired, individuals are treated as if they were domiciled in the UK for inheritance tax and capital gains tax purposes. This means that their worldwide assets are subject to UK tax, regardless of their actual domicile status [3].

To illustrate the relevance of these concepts, let's consider a hypothetical case. James is an international student studying in the UK during the 2023-2024 tax year. He is originally from France and has been residing in the UK for three years. In this case, James would be considered a resident of the UK for tax purposes, but his domicile would still be considered as France. Therefore, he would be liable to pay tax on his UK income, but not on his foreign income. However, if James acquires deemed domicile status after residing in the UK for a certain number of years, his worldwide income would become subject to UK tax [1].

In conclusion, residence, domicile, and deemed domicile are crucial factors in determining an individual's tax liabilities in the UK. Understanding these concepts is essential for accurately assessing one's tax obligations and planning accordingly. It is always advisable to consult with a tax professional to ensure compliance with the current tax laws and regulations.

The remittance basis is a tax treatment available to individuals who are resident but not domiciled in the UK. It allows them to exclude foreign income and gains from UK taxation, as long as they are kept offshore [1]. To qualify for the remittance basis, individuals must be UK tax residents, classified as non-domiciled, and have foreign income or gains [2]. US expats are typically considered non-domiciled and can use the remittance basis [2]. However, there are drawbacks to using this basis, including the loss of allowances for income tax and capital gains exemption, as well as the requirement to pay a remittance basis charge [2].

To apply for the remittance basis, individuals need to complete the relevant form on a UK tax return [2]. The remittance basis is a flexible option that can be used for certain tax years and becomes chargeable after the eighth year of tax residence [2]. It is recommended for US expats with significant non-UK sources of income that they do not need to bring to the UK [2].

If you become a tax resident in the UK and have foreign income or gains during your stay, you will need to consider more complex tax rules. The UK aims to tax residents on their worldwide income and gains [3]. Examples of foreign income and gains include earnings from work performed in another country, profits from a business operating in another country, overseas rental income, and gains from selling overseas assets [3]. Non-UK domiciled individuals may also be able to claim overseas workday relief and the remittance basis of taxation, depending on their circumstances [3].

In summary, the remittance basis is available to UK resident individuals who are non-domiciled and have foreign income or gains. It offers the advantage of excluding foreign income and gains from UK taxation as long as they are kept offshore. However, there are certain drawbacks and requirements associated with using this tax treatment. It is recommended to seek professional advice to understand the implications and determine if the remittance basis is suitable for your specific situation.

A Beginner's Guide: Navigating through UK's Tax System as an Incomer or Emigrant

Introduction:
Grasping the intricacies of the UK tax system can be intimidating, particularly for those who are unfamiliar and are potentially arriving to, or departing from the UK. This point of this article is to deliver a complete summary of how tax in the UK operates, covering vital notions, rates, and obligations. In addition, a notional scenario will be discussed to visually explain the workings of the taxation system. Be informed that the details presented are pertinent to the tax year 2023-2024.

Demystifying the UK's Tax Structure:
Taxation in the UK is rooted in a residency-based system, implying that the tax one is charged relies on one's residency status. There are primarily three segmentation of individuals in terms for tax purposes: resident of the UK, non-resident, and non-domiciled resident.

UK Resident:
You'll be classified as a tax resident in the UK if you're present in the country for 183 days or above in each tax year, or possess a dwelling within its borders. UK residents are obligated to pay tax on a global level i.e. income and gains be it personal or sourced from diverse avenues such as self-employment, investment through property rentals and capital gains etc.

Non-Resident:
You'll fall into the non-resident category for taxation purpose in the UK should you live for less than 183 days within a UK tax year and do not have a UK residency. Tax is obligatory for non-

residents only on income originating from UK i.e. rental earnings realized within the UK boundary or job earnings.

Non-Domiciled Resident:
A non-domiciled resident, or more casually, non-doom, indicates the people who dues residency country outside the UK but still occupy the UK. They enjoy tax perks such as liability of tax on foreign income and gains only when sent to the UK. Nonetheless, non-dooms may opt to identify as domiciles in the UK for tax, in which case, they're answerable to worldwide tax.

Hypothetical Case Analysis - Personified by Mr. Smith:
Translating in terms of Mr. Smith's case, an individual intending to relocate to the UK and, assuming the role of a UK resident while working for a company within UK borders with earnings amounting to £60,000 in a financial year.
Delineating Income Tax:
In the UK, income tax follow levels of income for tax calculation, these thresholds are termed as tax brackets. Given is the layout for standard rates and income bands respectively for the 2023-2024:

Income that is devoid of tax - Personal Allowance: £14,000.
Basic Rate: 20% compensated on income ranging within £14,001 and £50,000.
Higher Rate: 40% taxed on income biased between £50,001 and £150,000.
Additional Rate: A further 45% for income exceeding £150,000.

In the occasion of Mr. Smith's annual earning declaration of £60,000, his earned income tax would equate:
Personal Allowance of £14,000 – 0 tax
The Basic Rate purview involves an income of £36,000 at 20% - £7,200.
Sum Total Income Tax: £7,200

National Insurance Contributions
Deferred from income taxes, UK workforce owes the 'National Insurance Contributions' too. It's a fraction of the employees' earning used for insurance purposes, varying in classification in accordance to the nature of the employee's work. Class 1 NIC's rates for 2023-2024 is down as below:

Employee's NICs: Earnings from £9,568 and £50,270 incurs - 12%.
Employer's NICs: On wage surmounting £9,568 the levy is — 13.8%.
Calculating Mr. Smith's salary using the aforementioned rate yields:
Earnings liable to NICs, £50,000 minus the NICs trigger point of £9,568 results in - £40,432. Imposing 12% on the total equates to - £4,851.84

Termination:
Imbibing information in terms of UK tax system while entering or exiting the region equips individuals for effective results. comprehending of residency status along flavoring oneself with income taxes rates and rules enables enforcement and allows the provision of informed portfolio resolutions. Thus, its undeniable support through an occasion of an assumed case model enabling limpid demonstration of nuance workings of UK tax mechanics. Documentarized, emphasize on counseling from tax subject matter authority surfaces at the pinnacle whilst considering regulation conformity in tax planning phase across assorted dimensions of financial management.

The UK tax system can be complicated when it comes to foreign earnings. If you are UK tax resident and you earn income or profits outside the country, you must consider the rules that apply to worldwide income and profits. This means that residents are also taxed on their foreign income and profits. Foreign income and profits include, for example, income from working abroad, profits from foreign companies, rental income from foreign real estate, profit from the sale of real estate abroad, interest on foreign bank accounts, pension income from abroad and other investment income from abroad. abroad [1].

The amount of UK tax on foreign and non-resident income can vary depending on whether the money or assets are brought into the UK. Non-UK residents who work in the UK during the first three tax years of their UK residence may be eligible for the Foreign Working Days Credit, which allows them to claim tax relief on wages paid and withheld abroad [1].

There are two tax bases in the UK: the tax base and the remittance base. The resulting basis obliges residents and non-resident persons to pay UK tax on their worldwide income and profits in the tax year in which they arise. On the other hand, the remittance basis allows non-residents to pay tax in the UK on foreign income and earnings only when they are brought into the UK. This can help avoid double taxation [1]. UK resident and permanent individuals are taxed on their worldwide income and capital gains. Non-UK resident taxpayers are generally only taxed on their UK income, but there are exemptions in certain situations involving UK assets or high value companies. Non-UK residents owning residential property in the UK are subject to capital gains tax of 28% [2].

Non-resident UK residents can choose to be taxed on remittances. This means that income and capital gains received outside the UK are only taxed when they are brought or used in the UK. Income taxes in the UK vary according to income, with higher income levels being higher. The dividend is taxed at the highest marginal individual rate with a dividend allowance of GBP 1,000 (GBP 500 from April 2024) [2].

It is important to note that people who do not live in the UK and have lived in the UK for at least 15 years are considered residents and can no longer claim the remittance basis. Former residents have a grace period of one year before their worldwide assets become subject to inheritance tax. HMRC closely monitors non-UK domicile requirements [2]. In summary, the UK tax system treats income from overseas differently depending on where you live and where you live. Residents are generally taxed on their worldwide income and profits, while non-residents are generally taxed only on UK income. The remittance basis allows non-residents to choose when they pay tax on foreign income and earnings. An understanding of the rules and expert advice are essential to ensure compliance with the UK tax system [1][2].

The OECD Model Treaty is very important to the UK tax system. It serves as a framework for the negotiation and implementation of bilateral tax treaties between countries. The purpose of these agreements is to eliminate double taxation and prevent tax evasion. In the UK, taxpayers benefit from model provisions when determining their income and capital tax obligations. For example, if a UK resident earns income from a foreign country with which the UK has an OECD tax treaty, they may be entitled to certain tax reductions or exemptions. This will help promote cross-border trade and investment by ensuring fair taxation.

To illustrate the application of the OECD model to the UK tax system, let's consider a hypothetical case.

Case: John lives in the UK and works as a consultant in an international company. In the 2023-24 tax year, he will receive a salary of £100,000 from the company's UK office and a further £50,000 in dividends from its overseas subsidiaries located in a country that has an OECD-based tax treaty with the UK.

Prerequisite: Determine John's UK tax liability for the tax year 2023-24 and identify any applicable treaty provisions. To calculate Jan's tax liability, we need to consider the tax rates and deductions for the 2023-2024 tax year. Assume the following prices and bonuses:

Personal allowance: £12,570
Base price: 20%
Higher price: 40 Additional prices: 45%
Dividend payment: £2,000
Dividend taxes: 7.5% (basic tax), 32.5% (higher tax) and 38.1% (additional tax)
First, let's calculate John's income tax on his salary:
Salary: £100,000
Personal allowance: £12,570
Taxable income: £100,000 - £12,570 = £87,430
Basic rate range: £50,270 (20%)
Higher tax: £37,160 (40%)
Income tax liability: (£50,270 * 20%) (£37,160 * 40%) = £20,054
Next, we calculate John's dividend tax rate:
Dividends: £50,000
Dividend payment: £2,000
Taxable dividends: £50,000 - £2,000 = £48,000
Basic tax on dividends: £48,000 * 7.5% = £3,600
Higher dividend tax: £0 (within the basic tax bracket)
Additional dividend tax: £0 (within the basic tax bracket)
Total dividend tax liability: £3,600
John's total tax liability for the tax year 2023-24 is therefore £20,054 (income tax) £3,600 (dividend tax) = £23,654.

We now examine the applicable provisions of the Treaty. As John received dividends from a foreign country with which the UK has a tax treaty based on the OECD model, the treaty may provide relief to avoid or reduce double taxation of the same income. This can be achieved through provisions such as a reduced rate of withholding tax or the exemption of dividends obtained abroad. To determine the specific provisions and their effect on John's tax liability, we must refer to the tax treaty between the UK and the relevant foreign country. The contract defines the conditions and requirements for the use of such benefits.

In conclusion, the OECD Model Double Taxation Agreement is very important for the UK tax system. It helps avoid double taxation, ensures fair taxation of individuals and businesses, and promotes cross-border trade and investment. Taxpayers like John benefit from tax treaty provisions based on the OECD model that can help reduce their tax liabilities and remove barriers to international economic activity.

Understanding Double Taxation Relief in the UK Taxation System

Introduction:
The UK taxation system has provisions in place to prevent individuals from paying tax twice on the same income, known as double taxation relief. This article aims to explore the concept of double taxation relief, its relevance to the UK taxation system, and provide a hypothetical case to illustrate how it works.

What is Double Taxation Relief?
Double taxation relief refers to agreements and provisions that prevent individuals from being taxed twice on the same income or property. It can occur when income is taxed at both the corporate and personal level, or when individuals have income sources in different countries [3]. Double taxation relief aims to alleviate the burden on taxpayers and promote international trade by avoiding the duplication of taxes.

Double Taxation Relief in the UK:
The UK has bilateral double tax conventions with several countries to mitigate the impact of double taxation on estates, gifts, and inheritances [2]. These conventions ensure that individuals are not taxed by both the UK and another country on the same property or gift. In cases where there is no specific double taxation agreement, individuals may be eligible for relief under Unilateral Relief provisions [2]. Under Unilateral Relief, UK law determines the location of the asset and provides a credit against Inheritance Tax for the tax charged by another country on assets in that country.

Calculating Double Taxation Relief:
To understand how double taxation relief works, let's consider a hypothetical case for the tax year 2023-2024:

Case Scenario:
John, a UK resident, receives rental income from a property he owns in France. The rental income is subject to tax in both the UK and France. The tax rate in France is 20%, and the tax rate in the UK is 25%.

Calculation:
Step 1: Determine the taxable income in each country.

John's rental income in France: £10,000.
Tax payable in France (20%): £10,000 * 20% = £2,000.
Taxable income in the UK: £10,000.

Step 2: Calculate the tax relief available.

Determine the tax payable if the income was solely taxable in the UK.
Tax payable in the UK (25%): £10,000 * 25% = £2,500.
Deduct the tax already paid in France from the UK tax payable: £2,500 - £2,000 = £500.

Result:
John can claim double taxation relief of £500, which is the amount of tax paid in France, against the UK tax payable on the same income.
Conclusion: Double taxation relief plays a vital role in the UK taxation system by ensuring that individuals are not unfairly taxed multiple times on the same income or property. Through bilateral double tax conventions and Unilateral Relief provisions, individuals can avoid or reduce the impact of double taxation. Understanding the provisions of double taxation relief is essential for individuals with income or assets in multiple countries, as it can help optimize their tax liabilities and promote international trade.

Disclaimer:
The hypothetical case provided in this article is for illustrative purposes only and does not constitute tax advice. Tax calculations

and relief availability may vary based on individual circumstances and specific tax laws. It is advisable to consult with a qualified tax professional for personalized advice related to double taxation relief and other tax matters.

References:

[1] The UK has 'double taxation agreements' with many countries to try to make sure that people do not pay tax twice on the same income.
[2] If both the UK and another country charge Inheritance Tax, you could avoid or reclaim the tax through a double taxation convention.
[3] Double taxation refers to income taxes paid twice on the same income source.

Income from employment

In the UK, share option and share incentive schemes have specific tax treatments. Share options granted to employees are generally subject to income tax and National Insurance contributions (NICs) when exercised. The taxable amount is the difference between the market value of the shares at exercise and the exercise price. Employers are also liable to pay employer NICs on the taxable amount. However, if the share options are granted under an approved scheme, such as an Enterprise Management Incentive (EMI) scheme, they may qualify for tax advantages [1].

Under an EMI scheme, employees can receive share options with favorable tax treatment. When the options are exercised, the employee is only liable for capital gains tax (CGT) on any increase in the share value since the grant date, rather than income tax. The tax rate for CGT depends on the employee's annual income and the amount of the gain. Additionally, EMI schemes offer the possibility of a 10% tax rate on the sale of shares acquired through the scheme, subject to certain conditions being met [2].

Share incentive schemes, such as Save As You Earn (SAYE) and Share Incentive Plans (SIPs), also have tax advantages. Under SAYE, employees can save a regular amount of money over a specified period, which can be used to purchase shares at a predetermined price. The income tax and NICs liability arise when the shares are acquired, based on the difference between the market value at that time and the price paid. However, if the shares are held in a SAYE plan for at least five years, any gains made on their subsequent sale are free from income tax and NICs [3].

SIPs provide a tax-advantaged way for employees to acquire and hold shares in their company. Employees can purchase partnership shares through deductions from their pre-tax salary, which are then held in a tax-efficient employee trust. Any dividends received on the shares are exempt from income tax, and if the shares are held in the plan for at least five years, any gains made on their sale are also exempt from income tax and NICs [3].

In summary, share option and share incentive schemes in the UK have different tax treatments. Approved schemes like EMI can offer favorable tax rates, while schemes like SAYE and SIPs provide tax advantages based on the length of time the shares are held. It is important for both employers and employees to understand the tax implications of these schemes and seek professional advice if needed.

In the UK taxation system for the time 2023- 2024, lump sum bills are subject to duty treatment grounded on certain rules and regulations. The duty treatment of lump sum bills depends on colorful factors similar as the nature of the damage, the taxpayer's particular circumstances, and the applicable duty rules. One academic case that can be considered is a taxpayer entering a lump sum payment as a withdrawal benefit. Let's assume that Mr. Smith, aged 65, has worked for a company for 40 times and is now retiring. His employer's pension scheme offers him the option to admit a lump sum payment of £ 300,000.

Under the UK duty rules for 2023- 2024, lump sum pension payments are subject to duty. still, there are certain duty reliefs and allowances available to taxpayers. The duty treatment of Mr. Smith's lump sum damage will depend on whether it's considered a taxable or non-taxable damage.

In general, if the lump sum payment is entered from an approved pension scheme, a portion of it may be duty-free while the remaining portion may be subject to income duty. The duty-free portion is generally determined by applying a specific formula grounded on the taxpayer's continuance allowance and the quantum of the lump sum payment. Any quantum exceeding the duty-free portion will be subject to income duty at the taxpayer's borderline rate.

In Mr. Smith's case, let's assume that his continuance allowance is £. Grounded on the formula, the duty-free portion of his lump sum payment can be calculated as follows duty-free portion = (Continuance allowance/ Value of pension rights) x Lump sum payment Using the assumed values, the duty-free portion would be duty-free portion = (£/ £ 600,000) x£ 300,000 = £ 750,000. Thus, £ 750,000 of Mr. Smith's lump sum payment would be duty-free, and the remaining£ 150,000 would be subject to income duty. It's important to note that the below computation is a simplified illustration and doesn't consider other factors that may affect the duty treatment, similar as the existent's particular allowance and any other sources of income. also, duty rules and allowances may change over time, so it's essential to relate to the specific duty rules for the applicable duty time and seek professional advice if demanded. In conclusion, the duty treatment of lump sum bills in the UK depends on colorful factors and is subject to the specific duty rules for the given duty time. Taxpayers entering lump sum payments should precisely consider the applicable duty rules, seek professional advice if necessary, and insure compliance with their duty scores grounded on the specific circumstances of their case.

In the UK, a personal service company (PSC) is a type of business structure used by individuals to provide services to clients. Basically, it is a joint stock company through which an individual entrepreneur operates. By using a PSC, the entrepreneur benefits from certain tax benefits, such as lower tax rates and more flexible dividend payments.

However, providing services through a single point of contact has specific tax consequences. One of the biggest concerns is the IR35 legislation, which aims to prevent "undercover work". This means that if a contractor is regarded as an employee other than in name, they will have to pay Earned Income Tax (PAYE) and National Insurance Contribution (NIC) as if they were an employee. To determine whether a contractor falls within the scope of IR35, HM Revenue and Customs (HMRC) considers a number of factors, including the level of control the client has over the contractor, the right of subrogation and the nature of the employment relationship.

If a contractor is considered to be within IR35, they will have to pay income tax and NICs on the income they receive from the PSC as if they were an employee. This means that they do not benefit from the lower tax rates and dividend payments of the single contact points.

We calculate the tax liability of a hypothetical case, considering the following scenario:

John is a software developer who runs his personal services company, ABC Ltd.
In the tax year 2023-24, ABC Ltd had total income of £100,000. After deducting the £10,000 of allowable business expenses, the company's pre-tax profit is £90,000.
Now let's calculate John and ABC Ltd.'s tax liability under the UK tax rules for 2023-2024:

Corporate income tax:
The annual corporate income tax rate is 19%.
ABC Oy has to pay corporate income tax on its pre-tax profit.
ABC Ltd.'s corporation tax liability is £90,000 x 19% = £17,100.

Dividends:
John can withdraw dividends from ABC Ltd as a way of raising money.
Dividends are taxed differently than ordinary income. In the tax year 2023-2024, the dividend taxes are as follows:
Basic interest: 7.5%
Higher interest: 32.5% additional interest: 38.1%

John can choose how much of the remaining after-tax profit he wants to distribute as dividends.

Personal income tax:
When John takes a salary from ABC Ltd, it is subject to income tax and credit cards.
Salary is treated as earned income under the PAYE system.
The tax rates and thresholds for the tax year 2023-2024 are as follows:

Personal allowance: £12,570 (tax free)
Base price: 20% (up to £50,270)
Higher price: 40% (£50,271 - £150,000)
Premium: 45% (over £150,000)
John's personal tax liability depends on how much he takes from ABC Oy, considering his other income.
It is important to note that UK tax rules are subject to change, so it is advisable to consult a qualified tax professional or use the latest HMRC guidance when calculating tax liability in a particular case.

Income from self-employment

Changing the accounting date can have implications for UK taxpayers under the 2023-2024 tax rules. When a change in accounting date is made, it may affect the timing of income recognition and the calculation of taxable profits. It is important to note that the change must be notified to HM Revenue and Customs (HMRC) within the specified time frame.

For example, let's consider a hypothetical case of a sole trader named John who runs a small business in the UK. Until now, John has been preparing his accounts on a year-end date of 31st December. However, due to a change in business circumstances, John decides to change his accounting date to 30th June.

To change his accounting date, John must follow the rules set out by HMRC. He needs to inform HMRC in writing, stating the new accounting date and providing valid reasons for the change. In this case, John could cite reasons such as aligning his accounting period with the seasonal nature of his business or better matching his accounting period with his cash flow.

Once the change is approved by HMRC, John will need to prepare accounts for a transitional period, covering the period between his old year-end (31st December) and the new accounting date (30th June). This transitional period will be treated as a "short period" for tax purposes.

When calculating taxable profits for the transitional period, John will need to apportion his income and expenses based on the number of days falling within each accounting period. This apportionment ensures that the profits for the transitional period are calculated fairly.

It is important to note that changing the accounting date can have implications for tax payments as well. If the change in accounting date results in a longer or shorter accounting period, it may affect the timing of tax liabilities. For instance, if John's new accounting date results in a longer accounting period, he may have to make larger tax payments spread over a longer period. On the other hand, if the new accounting date results in a shorter accounting period, John may have a reduced tax liability for that year.

In conclusion, changing the accounting date can have implications for UK taxpayers. It is essential to notify HMRC within the specified time frame and follow the guidelines set out by HMRC. When changing the accounting date, taxpayers need to apportion income and expenses for the transitional period and consider the potential impact on tax payments. Seeking professional advice from a tax advisor or accountant is recommended to ensure compliance with the UK tax rules for the 2023-2024 tax year.

Note: The information provided is based on UK tax rules for the 2023-2024 tax year. For accurate and up-to-date information, it is advisable to consult the official HMRC website or seek professional advice.

In the UK, if a company transfers a business to another company and incurs trading losses, there are relief options available for such losses. These losses can be offset against other gains or profits within the same accounting period or carried forward to future periods [1].

To claim relief for trading losses, the losses should be included in the Company Tax Return. If the company has a group relationship with another company, they can choose to offset certain losses against the profits of other group members [1]. However, there are restrictions on the amount of carried forward losses that can be offset against profits from April 2017 [1].

Alternatively, a trading loss can be carried back to offset against profits from a previous 12-month period, but certain conditions must be met for this option [1].
It's important to note that losses can be carried forward indefinitely until they are used against profits from the same trade in a future tax year [2]. However, there is a time limit of 4 years from the end of the tax year in which the losses were incurred to use them [2].

Now, let's create a hypothetical case to illustrate how these relief options for trading losses following a business transfer would work under the UK tax rules for the year 2023-2024:
Assume that Company A transfers its business to Company B in the tax year 2023-2024. Company A incurs trading losses of £100,000 in this transfer.

Option 1: Carrying forward losses

Company B can choose to carry forward these losses and offset them against future profits. Let's say in the subsequent year, Company B makes a profit of £150,000. They can offset the carried forward losses of £100,000 against this profit, resulting in a taxable profit of £50,000.

Option 2: Group relief

If Company B has a group relationship with Company C, which also makes a profit of £100,000 in the same accounting period, Company B can offset its losses against Company C's profits. In this case, Company B can transfer £100,000 of its losses to Company C, reducing Company C's taxable profit to zero.

Option 3: Carrying back losses

If Company B meets the conditions for carrying back losses, they can choose to offset the losses against profits from a previous 12-month period. Let's assume that in the tax year 2022-2023, Company B made a profit of £80,000. They can carry back the losses of £100,000 and offset them against this profit, resulting in a taxable loss for that year of £20,000.

These are just a few examples of how relief options for trading losses following a business transfer can be utilized under the UK tax rules for the year 2023-2024. It's important to consult with a tax professional to understand the specific rules and requirements based on your unique situation.

Optimizing Annual Investment Allowance Allocation for Related Businesses in the UK

Introduction:
The allocation of the annual investment allowance (AIA) between related businesses plays a crucial role in optimizing tax benefits in the United Kingdom. By strategically distributing the AIA, businesses can maximize their capital expenditure deductions while ensuring compliance with the UK tax rules for the 2023-2024 tax year. This article explores the concept of AIA allocation, provides a hypothetical case study, and offers insights into how businesses can make informed decisions to optimize their tax positions.

Understanding the Annual Investment Allowance:
The AIA is a valuable tax relief measure provided by the UK government to encourage investment in fixed assets. It allows businesses to deduct the full cost of qualifying capital expenditures from their taxable profits in the year of purchase. The AIA is subject to an annual limit, which determines the maximum amount eligible for relief.

Allocation Strategies for Related Businesses:
When multiple businesses are related, careful consideration is required to determine the most tax-efficient allocation of the AIA.

Here are some strategies to optimize the allocation:

Assessing the Total AIA Limit:
The total AIA limit for related businesses depends on their relationship and the period under consideration. To determine the maximum AIA available, businesses should calculate the combined qualifying capital expenditures of all related entities.

Identifying Qualifying Expenditures:
It is crucial to identify and segregate qualifying expenditures that can benefit from the AIA. These may include investments in machinery, equipment, commercial vehicles and computer software. By focusing on eligible assets, companies can maximize their use of AIA.

Balanced use:
To optimize the allocation of AIA, companies should assess the expected investment needs of each relevant entity. By allocating

AIA based on forecasted investments, companies can ensure optimal use of emergency aid across the group.

Hypothetical case study:
Consider a hypothetical group of related companies: Company A, Company B, and Company C. The group's total eligible investment is £1,500,000 in the tax year 2023-24. Each company anticipates the following investments:

Company A: £800,000
Company B: £600,000
Company C: £400,000

To optimize the AIA distribution, the team should consider the following approach.

Target AIA proportionally:
The share of AIA can be distributed proportionally based on the planned investments of each company. In this case, Company A would receive 53.33% (£800,000 / £1,500,000) of the AIA, Company B 40% (£600,000 / £1,500,000) and Company C 26.67% (£400,000).

Transfer of unused AIA:
If the company does not fully utilize the AIA granted to it, it can transfer the remaining emission rights to another company in the group. This allows for further optimization and ensures that AIA is fully utilized. Conclusion:
Optimizing the allocation of the annual investment compensation between related companies is an important aspect of maximizing tax benefits in the UK. By carefully estimating the total AIA limit, identifying eligible expenses and balancing usage, companies can ensure that the allowance is determined in the most tax-efficient manner. A hypothetical case study shows how companies can strategically allocate AIA based on expected investments. However, it is very important to consult tax professionals and refer to the UK tax rules for the tax year 2023-2024 to ensure AIA compliance and accurate allocation.

Property and investment income

Together held resources are a common event within the UK, particularly among hitched couples and commerce accomplices. When two or more people mutually claim a resource, they share the proprietorship rights and duties similarly. This implies that each party has a rise to say within the administration of the resource and is entitled to a break even with share of any wage created from it. In any case, there are charge suggestions that come with together held resources.

For illustration, let's consider a speculative situation in which a married couple together possesses a rental property within the UK. The property creates a rental pay of £30,000 per year. The couple chooses to part the salary similarly between them, with each companion accepting £15,000. In this case, both life partners are capable for detailing their share of the rental salary on their charge returns.

Accepting both life partners are fundamental rate citizens, they would each be obligated for wage assess at a rate of 20% on their share of the rental wage. This implies that each life partner would owe £3,000 in pay tax on their share of the rental wage. In any case, in the event that one life partner could be a higher rate citizen, they would be at risk for wage charge at a rate of 40% on their share of the rental wage over the essential rate restrain.

In differentiate, on the off chance that one companion claims all the rental pay and the other companion does not pronounce any wage, this seem raise a ruddy hail with HMRC. Agreeing to HMRC's property income manual, where two or more people mutually possess a property and get rental wage, the salary ought to be part similarly between them unless there's a substantial reason to do something else. In case one companion claims all the rental pay without a substantial reason, this might be seen as charge avoidance and may result in punishments and intrigued charges.

In conclusion, it is imperative for people who together hold resources to get it the charge suggestions of their proprietorship course of action. It is additionally imperative to take after HMRC's rules with respect to the announcing of salary from together held resources to maintain a strategic distance from any potential issues with the charge specialist. By working with a qualified assess proficient, people can guarantee that they are compliant with UK charge law and are maximizing their assess productivity whereas minimizing their charge risk.

1. UK Tax assessment Framework: Outline and Standards

The UK tax assessment framework could be a complex system of laws and controls that govern the collection and organization of charges within the Joined together Kingdom. It is outlined to guarantee that people and businesses contribute their reasonable share towards open consumption, such as healthcare, instruction, and framework advancement. The UK tax framework is based on the rule of dynamic tax assessment, which implies that people with higher livelihoods are subject to higher assess rates.

The most sorts of charges within the UK incorporate pay charge, national protections commitments, value-added assess (VAT), enterprise charge, and capital picks up assess. Each assess has it possess set of rules and controls, which are intermittently overhauled to reflect changes in financial conditions and government arrangements.

2. UK Charge Rules 2023-2024: Key Changes and Upgrades

The UK assess rules for the year 2023-2024 present a few key changes and upgrades that influence the assess treatment of reserve funds salary. These changes are pointed at guaranteeing a reasonable and effective assess framework whereas advancing financial development and speculation.

One noteworthy alter is the presentation of a modern reserve funds pay tax band. Beneath the unused rules, people with reserve funds pay up to £5,000 will be qualified for a 0% charge rate. This implies that the primary £5,000 of reserve funds salary will be tax-free. Be that as it may, any investment funds wage over this edge will be subject to the appropriate charge rates.

Another imperative alter is the modification of the assess rates for reserve funds salary. The unused charge rates for the year 2023-2024 are as takes after:
- Essential rate citizens: 20% charge on reserve funds wage
- Higher rate citizens: 40% assess on investment funds pay
- Extra rate citizens: 45% assess on reserve funds salary

These assess rates apply to the parcel of investment funds wage that surpasses the £5,000 tax-free limit.

3. Assess Treatment of Reserve funds Pay: Definition and Cases

Reserve funds salary alludes to the pay produced from different sorts of investment funds and ventures, such as intrigued on bank accounts, profits from offers, and rental pay from property. The charge treatment of reserve funds wage depends on a few components, counting the sort of salary, the individual's assess status, and the pertinent assess rules.

In common, reserve funds wage is subject to salary charge. Be that as it may, the charge treatment may change depending on whether the pay is paid net of charge or net of assess. When investment funds salary is paid net of charge, it implies that the charge has as of now been deducted at source, and the person gets the pay after charge. On the other hand, when reserve funds salary is paid net of assess, it implies that the person gets the salary some time recently charge, and they are dependable for detailing and paying the charge on their charge return.

The charge treatment of reserve funds salary paid net of assess is moderately direct. Since the assess has as of now been deducted at source, the individual does not ought to report the income on them assess return or pay any additional charge. The net sum gotten is considered the ultimate sum of pay for assesses purposes.

For case, let's consider a speculative case where an individual receives £10,000 in investment funds pay from a bank account. The bank has as of now deducted £2,000 as salary assess, and the individual gets the remaining £8,000. In this case, the person does not require to report the £10,000 as income on their charge return. The £8,000 gotten net of charge is considered the ultimate sum of wage for charge purposes.

4. Speculative Case: Calculation of Assess on Investment funds Salary

To advance outline the assess treatment of investment funds salary paid net of charge, let's consider a theoretical case utilizing the UK assess rules for the year 2023-2024. It would be ideal if you note that all values and scenarios in this case are accepted for illustrative purposes as it were.

Suspicions:
- Individual's add up to pay: £50,000
- Reserve funds pay paid net of assess: £10,000
- Tax deducted at source: £2,000

To calculate the assess liability on investment funds wage, we got to consider the individuals add up to pay and the appropriate assess rates. In this case, the person falls beneath the fundamental rate taxpayer category, as them add up to wage is underneath the higher rate edge of £50,270.

The primary step is to deduct the tax-free reserve funds pay edge of £5,000 from the whole investment funds salary. In this case, the assessable investment funds pay is £5,000 (£10,000 - £5,000).

Following, we apply the essential rate assess rate of 20% to the assessable reserve funds income. The assess risk on the investment funds wage is subsequently £1,000 (£5,000 x 20%).

Since the charge has already been deducted at source, the person does not have to be pay any extra assess on the reserve funds pay. The net sum gotten (£8,000) is considered the ultimate sum of pay for assesses purposes.

5. Conclusion: Understanding the Assess Treatment of Reserve funds Salary within the UK

In conclusion, the assess treatment of investment funds wage paid net of charge within the UK is moderately clear. When reserve funds salary is paid net of assess, it implies that the charge has as of now been deducted at source, and the person gets the wage after assess. The net sum gotten is considered the ultimate sum of pay for charge purposes, and the person does not get to report the pay on them assess return or pay any extra charge.

The UK charge rules for the year 2023-2024 present a modern reserve funds wage assess band, where the primary £5,000 of investment funds salary is tax-free. Any investment funds wage over this edge is subject to the pertinent assess rates, which are

20% for essential rate citizens, 40% for higher rate citizens, and 45% for extra rate citizens.

In a theoretical case, we calculated the tax liability on reserve funds pay paid net of charge utilizing the UK charge rules for the year 2023-2024. The calculation involved deducting the tax-free investment funds wage edge from the entire investment funds salary and applying the significant assess rate to the assessable reserve funds salary.

Salary from trusts and settlements is a critical point to get it within the setting of UK tax collection. For the most part talking, in case you get salary from a trust or settlement, you may be at risk to pay salary assess on that income. However, the sum of charge you may ought to pay will depend on a number of components, such as the sort of believe or settlement you're a recipient of, the sum of wage you get, and your by and large wage assess position.

One of the key things to get it around salary from trusts and settlements is that it is treated in an unexpected way to other shapes of pay for charge purposes. This is often since trusts and settlements are lawful courses of action that are outlined to hold resources on sake of recipients, and so the income that emerges from these courses of action is considered to be isolated from the wage of the person recipients.

When it comes to calculating the amount of pay charge that you just will ought to pay on your pay from trusts and settlements, there are a number of diverse variables that will ought to be taken under consideration. One of the foremost critical of these is the sort of believe or settlement simply are a recipient of. For case, in the event that you're a beneficiary of an optional believe, at that point the trustees will have the watchfulness to choose how much salary you get, and so this will ought to be taken into consideration when calculating your tax obligation.

Another imperative figure to consider is the sum of pay merely get from the believe or settlement. The more pay you get, the higher your tax liability will be. In any case, there are also certain remittances and reliefs that you just may be entitled to, such as the individual remittance and the profit remittance, which can aid diminish your charge risk.

To demonstrate how salary from trusts and settlements is taxed in practice, let us consider a speculative case. Envision that you simply are a recipient of an optional believe, which has produced salary of £50,000 within the assess year 2023-24. The trustees have chosen to disseminate £20,000 of this wage to you as a recipient.

Expecting merely have no other wage within the charge year 2023-24, your charge obligation on the £20,000 of wage from the believe would be as takes after:

Individual remittance: £12,570
Assessable salary: £7,430 (£20,000 - £12,570)
Assess rate: 20%
Wage assess risk: £1,486

So, in this situation, you'd have to be pay £1,486 in salary assess on the £20,000 of salary you gotten from the believe. In any case, it is worth noticing that this calculation is based on a number of suspicions, and there may be other variables that might influence your assess obligation.

In conclusion, understanding the pay charge position of believe recipients is an imperative portion of overseeing your funds within the UK. By taking the time to get it the rules and controls around pay from trusts and settlements, you'll be able guarantee that you simply are paying the right sum of charge on your income, and that you are expanding any stipends and reliefs merely may be entitled to.

The comprehensive computation of taxable income and the income tax liability

Assignment of the individual stipend to distinctive categories of pay alludes to how the tax-free pay edge is dispersed among different sources of wage. Within the UK, the individual stipend is the sum of salary a person can win some time recently they begin paying wage charge. For the charge year 2023-2024, the standard individual remittance is £12,570 [1].

When it comes to diverse categories of wage, the individual remittance is connected to each source independently. For case, on the off chance that a person has wage from numerous sources such as business, self-employment, state benefits, and annuities, the individual remittance can be designated proportionately to each category of pay. This implies that the tax-free edge can be utilized over all the distinctive sorts of pay an individual receives.

To demonstrate this, let's consider a theoretical case. John could be a UK inhabitant who gains a compensation of £30,000 per year from his full-time work. He moreover wins £5,000 per year from a part-time independent gig. In this situation, John's add up to salary is £35,000.

Since John's salary surpasses the individual stipend of £12,570, he will be at risk to pay salary charge on the sum that surpasses the edge. In this case, John's assessable salary would be £35,000 - £12,570 = £22,430.

Presently, let's calculate John's pay charge obligation based on the charge rates for the charge year 2023-2024. The UK salary charge framework works on a dynamic premise, meaning that diverse parcels of income are subject to distinctive charge rates.

For the assess year 2023-2024, the essential salary charge rate is 20% for salary between £12,570 and £50,270. Any wage over this edge is subject to the higher rate of 40%.

In John's case, his assessable salary of £22,430 falls inside the fundamental salary assess rate band. Hence, he would pay 20% charge on this sum.

Charge payable = 20% of £22,430 = £4,486

So, based on the given situation, John's wage assess liability for the charge year 2023-2024 would be £4,486.

It's important to note that usually a disentangled case and does not take under consideration other components such as charge credits, findings, and stipends that will apply to an individual's particular circumstances. It is continuously fitting allude to">to allude to with a charge proficient or allude to the official UK assess rules for precise and personalized charge computations.

Within the United Kingdom, the salary charge position of the wage of minor children is subject to certain rules and directions. By and large, in case a child is beneath the age of 18 and wins wage, it is treated as the child's salary for assess purposes. Be that as it may, there are special cases to this run the show.

One critical special case is known as the "parental settlement" run the show. This run the show applies when a parent or gatekeeper gives resources to a child and those resources produce salary. In such cases, the pay is treated as the parent's salary for charge purposes, not the children. This run the show is in put to anticipate guardians from moving their salary to their children in arrange to diminish their claim charge risk.

Another exemption applies to wage earned from work. On the off chance that a child is utilized and wins pay, it is treated as the child's pay and subject to wage assess. Be that as it may, there are certain confinements on the sort of work that children can lock in in and the number of hours they can work.

It is imperative to note that the pay assess rules for minor children can be complex, and it is prudent to look for proficient counsel to guarantee compliance with the directions. Legitimate charge arranging can help minimize the assess risk and guarantee that the child's wage is overseen viably.

Theoretical Case:

Let's consider a theoretical case to demonstrate the pay tax position of the pay of minor children within the UK for the assess year 2023-2024.

Sarah, a 16-year-old understudy, works part-time at a nearby grocery store and wins £5,000 per year. Moreover, she has a few speculations that create £2,000 in salary every year.

Based on the common run the show, Sarah's work pays of £5,000 will be treated as her wage for assess purposes. Subsequently, she will be at risk to pay wage tax on this sum.

In any case, the wage from her speculations can be subject to the parental settlement run the show. In case Sarah's guardians given the reserves for these speculations, the salary would be treated as their pay for charge purposes. Hence, they would be dependable for detailing and paying assess on this pay.

It is critical for Sarah's guardians to keep appropriate records and documentation to bolster the truth that the speculations were supported by them and not by Sarah herself. This will help guarantee compliance with the charge rules and anticipate any potential issues with HM Income and Customs.

In rundown, when it comes to the pay assess position of the pay of minor children within the UK, it is critical to consider the particular circumstances and appropriate rules. Looking for proficient counsel and legitimate charge arranging can help guarantee compliance and optimize the charge position for both the child and their guardians or gatekeepers.

[1] https://www.gov.uk/income-tax/taxfree-and-taxable-state-pensions
[2] https://www.gov.uk/income-tax/taxfree-and-taxable-state-pensions

The use of exemptions and reliefs in deferring and minimizing income tax liabilities

Unlocking opportunities: the start-up investment scheme and the corporate investment scheme in the UK tax system

Demonstration:
The UK tax system offers various opportunities for individuals and businesses to invest in promising projects while enjoying tax benefits. Two such schemes are the Seed Enterprise Investment Scheme (SEIS) and the Enterprise Investment Scheme (EIS). In this article, we explore these systems, their rules and regulations, and how they can provide opportunities for investors and entrepreneurs alike.

Understanding the Initial Investment Scheme (SEIS):
SEIS was launched in 2012 to encourage investments in start-up and venture companies. The aim of the system is to support start-ups by offering tax incentives to investors. To qualify for SEIS, a business must meet certain criteria, such as being less than two

years old, having less than £200,000 in assets and having fewer than 25 full-time employees.

Investors participating in the SEIS scheme can receive various tax benefits. They can claim income tax relief of up to 50% of the sum invested, but up to a maximum of £100,000 per tax year. In addition, it is possible to be exempt from capital gains tax (CGT) if SEIS shares have been held for at least three years.

Researching the Enterprise Investment Scheme (EIS):

The Enterprise Investment Scheme (EIS) complements SEIS by providing tax incentives for investment in risky small and medium-sized enterprises (SMEs). Launched in 1994, the EIS encourages investment in companies that are out of the start-up phase but still need financing for growth.

To qualify for EIS, a company must meet several conditions, such as having fewer than 250 full-time employees and not being listed on a reputable stock exchange. EIS investors can claim an income tax reduction of up to 30% on their investments, subject to certain restrictions. In addition, they can defer CGT on profits from other investments by investing the amount in an EIS-eligible business.

Hypothetical Case Study: Tax Accounting for SEIS Investment:

Consider a hypothetical case illustrating the tax treatment of a SEIS investment for the UK tax year 2023-24. John, a British taxpayer, decides to invest £50,000 in a SEIS-eligible company. He is entitled to a 50 percent tax credit. He can therefore claim £25,000 in tax relief in the tax year in which he invests.

Assuming John's annual tax liability is £30,000, his tax liability will be reduced by £5,000 after claiming SEIS relief. If John has held the SEIS shares for at least three years, the capital gain on the sale of those shares will be exempt from CGT. Conclusion:

The Seed Enterprise Investment Scheme (SEIS) and Enterprise Investment Scheme (EIS) offer attractive opportunities for investors and entrepreneurs in the UK. These schemes encourage investment in start-up and high-growth companies and offer tax benefits to investors.

By understanding the rules and regulations related to SEIS and EIS, individuals can make informed investment decisions while benefiting from tax incentives and exemptions. The hypothetical case study presented here demonstrates the potential tax benefit of investing in a SEIS compliant business.

As the UK tax year 2023-24 approaches, it is vital to keep up to date with the latest guidance and seek advice from tax professionals to maximize the benefits of these investment schemes. By unlocking the potential of SEIS and EIS, investors can promote the growth and success of innovative companies by receiving favorable tax treatment.

Unlocking the Potential of Venture Capital Trusts: A Creative Exploration of UK Taxation System

Introduction:
Venture Capital Trusts (VCTs) offer a unique investment opportunity for individuals seeking to support and benefit from the growth of innovative companies. In this article, we will dive into the rules surrounding investments in VCTs and explore their implications within the UK taxation system. Through a hypothetical case study, we will demonstrate the application of UK tax rules for the tax year 2023-2024, shedding light on the potential benefits and considerations when investing in VCTs.

Understanding Venture Capital Trusts:
Venture Capital Trusts are investment vehicles that provide capital to early-stage companies with high growth potential. These companies are often seeking funding for research and development, expansion, or other business activities. By investing in VCTs, individuals indirectly support these companies while also gaining tax advantages.

Tax Benefits of Investing in VCTs:
The UK government offers attractive tax incentives to encourage investments in VCTs. One such benefit is income tax relief. Investors can claim income tax relief of up to 30% on the amount invested in VCTs, subject to certain conditions. For example, an individual investing £10,000 in a VCT can potentially reduce their income tax liability by £3,000.

Dividend Tax Exemption:
Another advantage of investing in VCTs is the exemption from dividend tax. Generally, dividends received by individuals are subject to income tax. However, dividends received from VCT investments are exempt from income tax, providing a tax-efficient way to generate income.

Capital Gains Tax Exemption:
Investors in VCTs may also benefit from capital gains tax (CGT) exemption. When selling or disposing of VCT shares, any capital gains realized may be exempt from CGT. This exemption further enhances the attractiveness of VCT investments, as it allows investors to potentially enjoy tax-free gains.

Hypothetical Case Study: Maximizing Tax Benefits with VCTs
Let's consider a hypothetical scenario for the tax year 2023-2024 to illustrate the application of UK tax rules in relation to VCT investments.

Case Study Instructions:

Individual A invests £20,000 in a qualifying VCT.

Individual A is a higher-rate taxpayer with an annual income of £70,000.

The VCT provides income of £2,000 and a capital gain of £5,000 at the end of the tax year.

Using the UK Tax Rules 2023-2024:
Based on the given scenario, Individual A can claim income tax relief of £6,000 (30% of £20,000) on their VCT investment. This reduces their taxable income to £64,000 (£70,000 - £6,000). Additionally, the £2,000 income received from the VCT is exempt from income tax. Therefore, Individual A's taxable income remains at £64,000.

Furthermore, the capital gain of £5,000 realized from the VCT investment is also exempt from CGT. This means that Individual A does not have to pay any tax on the capital gain.

Conclusion:
Venture Capital Trusts offer investors an exciting opportunity to support innovative companies and potentially enjoy tax benefits. By understanding and applying the rules related to investments in VCTs, individuals can make informed decisions and optimize their tax positions. The hypothetical case study showcased the potential tax advantages of investing in VCTs, highlighting the importance of considering such investments as part of a comprehensive tax planning strategy. As the UK taxation system evolves, it is crucial to stay updated with the latest rules and regulations to make the most of these investment opportunities.

In simple terms, the threshold level of income refers to the minimum income amount below which the tapering of the pensions annual allowance does not apply. This threshold determines whether an individual is subject to a reduction in their annual pension allowance based on their income level.

Now, let's dive into a creatively formal writing style to explore this concept further. Imagine you're sitting down with a cup of tea, discussing the UK taxation system and its intricacies.

The UK taxation system is a complex web of rules and regulations that determine how much individuals and businesses must contribute to the country's public funds. One important aspect of this system is the pensions annual allowance, which sets a limit on the amount of money one can contribute to their pension fund while still receiving tax relief.

However, this allowance is subject to tapering for individuals whose income exceeds a certain threshold. The tapering of the pensions annual allowance means that for every pound earned above the threshold, the annual allowance is reduced by a certain percentage. This reduction can significantly impact the amount of tax relief an individual is entitled to receive on their pension contributions.

To put this into perspective, let's consider a hypothetical case. Meet John, a hardworking individual with a steady income. In the tax year 2023-2024, John's income reaches £200,000. He also contributes £20,000 to his pension fund.

Based on the UK tax rules for that year, the threshold level of income below which tapering of the pensions annual allowance does not apply is set at £150,000. Since John's income exceeds this threshold, his annual allowance will be subject to tapering.

The specific tapering rules for the 2023-2024 tax year state that for every £2 of income above £150,000, the annual allowance is reduced by £1. Therefore, John's income is £50,000 above the threshold, so his annual allowance will be reduced by £25,000 (£50,000 divided by 2).

As a result, John's adjusted annual allowance for pension contributions will be £15,000 instead of the full £20,000 he originally planned to contribute. This means that only £15,000 of his pension contributions will receive tax relief, while the remaining £5,000 will be subject to tax.

This hypothetical case illustrates the impact of the threshold level of income and the tapering of the pensions annual allowance under the UK tax system. It highlights the importance of understanding these rules and planning one's finances accordingly to optimize tax benefits and retirement savings.

In conclusion, the threshold level of income determines whether the tapering of the pensions annual allowance applies. If an individual's income exceeds this threshold, their annual allowance will be reduced based on specific tapering rules. This can have significant implications for individuals' tax relief on pension contributions, making it crucial to navigate the UK taxation system with knowledge and planning.

Overseas gains, related persons, exemptions

The scope of the taxation of capital gains

Within the UK, autonomous tax assessment suggests that each companion is dependable for them possess assess issues and assess liabilities. This implies that each life partner will have their claim individual remittance, assess groups, and charge rates pertinent to their salary [1]. Exchanges between companions, such as endowments or legacy, are for the most part excluded from charge as long as they meet certain conditions. For illustration, exchanges between life partners who are living together are ordinarily absolved from legacy tax [1].

To demonstrate the charge suggestions, let's consider a theoretical case. John and Sarah are a hitched couple living within the UK. John wins £40,000 per year, whereas Sarah gains £30,000 per year. With the autonomous tax assessment framework, each of them will be saddled independently based on their pay.

For the tax year 2023-2024, the individual allowance is £12,570. This implies that the primary £12,570 of John's wage isn't subject to pay assess. As a result, John's assessable wage is £27,430 (£40,000 - £12,570). Based on the current assess groups and rates, John will be saddled at 20% on the parcel of his wage between £12,570 and £50,270.
Sarah's assessable salary will be £17,430 (£30,000 - £12,570), and she will moreover be taxed at 20% on her wage between £12,570 and £50,270.

Be that as it may, it is imperative to note that this is often a streamlined illustration and does not take under consideration different charge findings, remittances, and reliefs which will be appropriate to John and Sarah's circumstance. It is continuously prescribed to look for proficient exhortation or counsel the official HM Income and Traditions (HMRC) site for precise and up-to-date data with respect to person assess circumstances [1].

In conclusion, beneath autonomous tax assessment, each companion is dependable for their claim charge undertakings and assess liabilities. Exchanges between life partners, such as endowments or legacy, may be excluded from charge beneath certain conditions. It is critical to get it the particular rules and controls of the UK charge framework and look for proficient exhortation to guarantee compliance with the tax laws [1].

Note: The data given is based on the UK assess framework as of the tax year 2023-2024. Assess rules and controls may alter over time, so it is imperative allude to">to allude to the official HMRC site or look for proficient counsel for the foremost precise and up-to-date data with respect to tax assessment within the UK.

Residence, domicile, and deemed domicile are important concepts in the UK taxation system, particularly in relation to capital gains tax. Let's break down each concept and understand their relevance.

Residence refers to where an individual resides in a specific tax year. It is determined based on the amount of time spent in the UK. If someone is a resident in the UK, their worldwide income and gains are generally taxable, including capital gains. However, non-residents are generally not liable for capital gains tax in the UK, with some exceptions [1].

Domicile, on the other hand, refers to the place that an individual considers their permanent home over their lifetime. It is an important factor in determining tax liabilities, including capital gains tax. If someone is resident and domiciled in the UK, their worldwide income and gains, including capital gains, are taxable. However, migrants who come to the UK for at least six months but do not intend to stay permanently typically become resident but keep a non-UK domicile. In such cases, their foreign income and gains, including capital gains, are not subject to UK tax [1].

Deemed domicile is a concept that applies to individuals who were born in the UK with a UK domicile of origin but have acquired a domicile of choice in another country. From April 6, 2017, deemed domicile rules were introduced for individuals who have been resident in the UK for at least 15 out of the previous 20 tax years. Under these rules, individuals are treated as deemed domiciled in the UK for all tax purposes, including capital gains tax. This means that their worldwide income and gains, including capital gains, are taxable in the UK [1].

Now, let's consider a hypothetical case to understand how these concepts apply to capital gains tax in the UK for the tax year 2023-2024.

Suppose John, a UK resident and domiciled individual, sold a property during the tax year 2023-2024 and made a capital gain of £100,000. As a resident and domiciled individual, John's worldwide income and gains, including capital gains, are taxable in the UK. Therefore, he would be required to report the capital gain of £100,000 in his UK tax return and pay capital gains tax on it.

Sarah, a non-resident individual, also sold a property during the tax year 2023-2024 and made a capital gain of £100,000. Since Sarah is not a tax resident in the UK, her foreign income and gains, including capital gains, are not subject to UK tax. Therefore, she would not be liable to pay capital gains tax in the UK on the £100,000 capital gain.

It's important to note that the specific details and tax rates may vary based on the individual circumstances and the tax laws in force for the tax year 2023-2024. Seeking professional advice from a tax advisor or accountant is recommended to ensure compliance with the UK tax rules and regulations [1].

In conclusion, residence, domicile, and deemed domicile play a crucial role in determining the tax liabilities, including capital gains tax, for individuals in the UK. Understanding these concepts is important for individuals to accurately report their income and gains and fulfill their tax obligations.

The remittance basis is an alternative tax treatment available to individuals who are resident but not domiciled in the UK [1]. It allows them to exclude foreign income and gains from UK taxation as long as these funds are kept offshore [3]. To qualify, you must be classified as non-domiciled and have foreign income or gains [3]. However, the remittance basis is not available to those deemed domicile in the UK [1].

While the remittance basis offers benefits, there are drawbacks to consider. You will lose allowances for income tax and the annual capital gains exemption [3]. Additionally, you may be required to pay a remittance basis charge and keep complex records [3]. Foreign tax credits may also be lost [3].

To apply for the remittance basis, you must claim it through a UK tax return if your unremitted foreign incomes and gains exceed £2,000 [3]. The remittance basis is free for the first seven tax years of residence, but a charge applies starting on the eighth year [3].

Hypothetically, let's consider a case where an individual named John is a US expat residing in the UK. He has significant non-UK sources of income that he doesn't need to bring to the UK [3]. John has been a UK resident for three tax years and decides to claim the remittance basis for the first time in the 2023-2024 tax year.

To calculate his tax liability, John would need to determine his total foreign income and gains that are remitted to the UK. Only these amounts would be subject to UK taxation [1]. He would also need to consider any relevant rules and obligations for remitting foreign income and gains [1].

It's important for John to keep detailed records of his remittances and consult with a tax professional to ensure compliance with the UK tax rules [3]. By utilizing the remittance basis, John can minimize his UK tax liability while benefiting from his non-UK sources of income [3].

The UK tax system can be relatively straightforward if you only have income and gains from UK sources during your stay in the country [1]. However, things become more complex if you become a tax resident in the UK and have foreign income or gains. The aim of the UK tax system is to tax residents on their worldwide income and gains. This includes various forms of foreign income and gains such as earnings from work done abroad, profits from running a business overseas, rental income from properties outside of the UK, gains from selling or giving away foreign assets, interest on savings in foreign bank accounts, overseas pension income, and other overseas investment income.

If you are a non-domiciled resident, the amount of tax you pay on foreign income and gains depends on whether you bring the money or assets into the UK. There are specific tax relief options available for non-domiciled individuals who come to work in the UK. The tax basis of taxation differs depending on your residence and domicile status. The arising basis means you pay tax on worldwide income and gains in the year they arise, regardless of whether you bring them to the UK. On the other hand, the remittance basis allows you to choose to pay tax on foreign income and gains only when they are brought to the UK [1].

When it comes to foreign currency gains or losses, the simplest type is realized in respect of foreign currency holdings. Taxpayers may have foreign currency holdings that can result in gains or losses [2]. The design and drafting of income tax laws related to business and investment income in the UK consider both individuals and legal persons. Special rules are commonly provided for taxing this type of income, particularly regarding the tax base, timing of income recognition, and collection of tax. Timing rules are crucial as they must navigate the differences between financial accounting and taxation. The characterization of income as business income is significant in determining whether it is classified as such, and this definition may overlap with employment for tax purposes. It is important to coordinate the definitions of employment and business to avoid double taxation.

In cases where double taxation occurs, the UK provides relief. For example, pursuant to paragraph 4 of Article 24, the United Kingdom grants a foreign tax credit for U.S. tax imposed on such gains [3]. Double taxation relief ensures that individuals or entities are not taxed twice on the same income or gains in different jurisdictions, promoting fairness and avoiding economic inefficiencies.

Hypothetically speaking, let's consider a case study for the UK tax year 2023-2024. Suppose Mr. Smith, a UK tax resident, has a rental property in Spain from which he earns £10,000 in rental income during the tax year. Additionally, he sells shares in a French company, resulting in a capital gain of £20,000. Mr. Smith also has a savings account in Switzerland, earning £5,000 in interest during the year.

As a UK tax resident, Mr. Smith is subject to UK tax on his worldwide income and gains. Therefore, he must declare the rental income from Spain, the capital gain from France, and the interest income from Switzerland on his UK tax return. The tax rules for foreign income and gains will apply, considering any available relief or exemptions.

If Mr. Smith chooses to use the arising basis of taxation, he will pay tax on the rental income, capital gain, and interest income in the tax year they arise, regardless of whether he brings them to the UK. Alternatively, he may opt for the remittance basis, paying tax on foreign income and gains only when he brings them to the UK.

To avoid double taxation, Mr. Smith may be eligible for various relief options, such as foreign tax credits or a tax treaty between the UK and the relevant foreign country. These mechanisms ensure that Mr. Smith is not taxed twice on the same income or gains in different jurisdictions.

In conclusion, the UK tax system considers the taxation of foreign income and gains for tax residents. It aims to tax residents on their worldwide income and gains, including various forms of foreign income and gains. Different tax rules apply depending on the individual's residence and domicile status. Relief options are available to prevent double taxation, ensuring fairness and avoiding economic inefficiencies in the global tax landscape.

Considerations regarding capital gains tax implications are crucial for individuals migrating to or departing from the UK. Those exiting the UK may still have an obligation to pay UK tax on any capital gains achieved through the selling of assets. Several contributing factors would determine this, including the individual's residential status and the type of asset sold.

Conversely, those relocating to the UK could potentially be liable for capital gains tax on any sold assets during their residing period, particularly if they are recognised as UK tax residents. It's worth noting that capital gains tax calculation is done based on the escalated value of the asset from the time it was purchased up until its selling point.

Take the hypothetical scenario of John, an American citizen. he moved to the UK in 2023 and became a tax resident of the UK. A year later, he liquidated some US shares that had cost him $10,000 in 2020; they had appreciated to $15,000 by 2024. Being a UK's tax resident at the time of sale, he may have to bear the UK's capital gains tax on his profit margin.

Concerning the specific amount John should anticipate paying for the capital gains tax, it rests on his total income that is eligible for tax for that year, as well as the duration within which he kept the shares. Generally, the opportunity to get lower rates on capital gains tax is available to those who hold assets over longer time frames.

One should also consider that different asset types may be taxed at differing capital gains tax rates. The sales of residential property leading to gains, for instance, might face stringent capital gains tax as compared to other types of assets.

A Comprehensive Guide to UK Taxation on Gains from Disposal of UK Land and Buildings for Non-Residents

Introduction:
The UK taxation system imposes Capital Gains Tax (CGT) on gains from the disposal of UK land and buildings for non-residents. This article aims to provide a clear understanding of the UK tax rules for non-residents and offers a hypothetical case study to illustrate the application of these rules.

Overview of Non-Resident Capital Gains Tax:
Non-residents who have sold or disposed of UK property or land are likely required to submit a non-resident Capital Gains Tax return. The charge for Capital Gains Tax on UK property or land covers both direct and indirect disposals. Direct disposal refers to selling or disposing of UK property or land directly, while indirect disposal refers to selling or disposing of an asset that derives 75% or more of its gross value from UK land.

Residential and Non-Residential Property:
The scope of the charge for Capital Gains Tax includes various types of property. UK residential property encompasses buildings suitable for use as a dwelling, while non-residential property

includes commercial property, agricultural land, forests, and other property not suitable for residential use.

Entities Subject to Capital Gains Tax:
Several entities are chargeable to Capital Gains Tax, including non-resident individuals, UK resident individuals meeting split year conditions, personal representatives of non-residents, non-resident partners, and non-resident trustees. Special rules apply for jointly owned properties and for giving UK property to a spouse, civil partner, or charity.

Reporting and Paying Capital Gains Tax:
Non-residents must report and pay Capital Gains Tax for disposals of UK property or land within specific deadlines. The reporting process differs for direct and indirect disposals. Even if non-residents have no tax to pay or have made a loss on the disposal, they must still report it to comply with the tax regulations. Online reporting is the preferred method, but a paper form is available for those unable to report online.

Hypothetical Case Study:
Let us consider a hypothetical case involving Mr. Smith, a non-resident individual who recently sold a residential property in the UK. The property was purchased in 2018 for £300,000 and sold in 2023 for £400,000, resulting in a gain of £100,000.

Under the current UK tax rules for the tax year 2023-2024, Mr. Smith would be required to report this gain by submitting a non-resident Capital Gains Tax return. The gain of £100,000 would be subject to Capital Gains Tax, with the applicable tax rate determined by Mr. Smith's income tax band.

Conclusion:
Understanding the UK taxation system for gains from the disposal of UK land and buildings is crucial for non-residents. This comprehensive guide has provided an overview of the rules and regulations surrounding non-resident Capital Gains Tax, along with a hypothetical case study to illustrate their application. It is essential to consult with a tax professional or refer to official HM Revenue and Customs guidance for specific tax advice and calculations based on individual circumstances.

Under the UK tax system, a partner in a partnership might become liable for a chargeable gain when a partnership asset is disposed of. If the partnership sells or transfers an asset profitably, the partner may be taxed on their share of this gain. Using a hypothetical scenario involving a partnership in the property business, where the partnership decides to sell property, earning a substantial profit, each partner could be taxed based on their share of the gain, reflecting their ownership stake in the partnership.

To figure out the chargeable gain, partners must identify their share of profit according to their partnership agreement or corresponding documents. Thereafter, the partner's share of the gain attracts capital gains tax at rates that apply in the 2023-2024 tax year.

Not all partnership asset disposals will lead to a chargeable gain as certain exemptions and reliefs might mitigate or dismiss the tax liability. For example, exempt asset disposals, like some personal belongings or assets used for personal use, may relieve the partner from tax on the gain.

Sometimes, to accurately figure out their chargeable gains, partners may need to provide additional details on their tax returns, such as profit-sharing agreements, disposal specifications, and any claimed exemptions or reliefs. It's wise for partners, facing difficulty calculating chargeable gains or complex tax situations, to consult HMRC or a tax adviser for accurate advice specific to their situation to ensure adherence to UK tax rules.

In summary, when a partnership asset is disposed of, a chargeable gain may be raised upon a partner. Partners must compute their gain share, factoring in the partnership's profit-sharing scheme and any fitting exemptions or reliefs. For intricate tax matters, consulting a professional is advisable for adherence to UK tax regulations.

Capital gains tax and trusts

Transferring property into a trust can have significant implications for capital gains tax in the UK. The tax treatment depends on the type of trust and the circumstances of the transfer.

In a revocable trust, where the grantor retains control over the assets, there is no immediate tax consequence. The grantor continues to be responsible for any capital gains tax if the property is later sold. However, if the trust is irrevocable, the tax liability may rest with the trust itself.

When a property is sold from a trust, the grantor is generally subject to capital gains tax on any profits made from the sale. The tax is calculated based on the difference between the sale price and the property's market value at the time it was transferred into the trust.

To illustrate the tax implications, let's consider a hypothetical case. John transfers a property worth £500,000 into an irrevocable trust. Five years later, the property is sold for £700,000. The capital gains tax is calculated by deducting the property's market value at the time of transfer (£500,000) from the sale price (£700,000), resulting in a gain of £200,000.

For the tax year 2023-2024, the capital gains tax rate in the UK is 20% for higher-rate taxpayers. Thus, John would be liable to pay £40,000 in capital gains tax on the gain of £200,000.

It is important to note that tax rules and rates can change, so it is always advisable to consult a tax professional or HM Revenue and Customs for the most up-to-date information and guidance regarding capital gains tax on property transfers into trusts in the UK.

Consider a situation wherein a trust's property is fully transferred to a beneficiary, it's crucial to acknowledge potential capital gains tax requirements. In the UK, this tax represents the amount payable when one sells an investment, which is determined via growth achieved from the sale. Thus, there will likely be a capital gain if the trust's property has accumulated value since its inception, and the capital gain signifies the difference between the property's present market value and its initial buying price upon transfer to the beneficiary.

Let's imagine a fictional scenario. Suppose the trust procured a property in 2010 worth £200,000. By 2023, the property's market value has increased to £400,000. When the beneficiary receives full ownership of the property, they are considered to have acquired it at the present market rate of £400,000.

Calculation of capital gains tax requires establishing the profit made from the sale of the property. In this situation, the gain equals £400,000 (current market value) minus £200,000 (purchase price), equaling £200,000. Nonetheless, an Annual Exempt Amount reduces taxable earnings annually. For tax year 2023-2024, this amount is pegged at £14,300, making the taxable gain (the profit minus the Annual Exempt Amount) £185,700.

Capital gains tax rates hinge on one's income tax bracket, set at 10% for basic taxpayers whilst those with a higher rate pay 20%. Hypothetically, if the beneficiary comes from the former category, their capital gains tax for this gain (£185,700) will be 10% - equaling £18,570.

However, tax guidelines and rates are prone to adjustment – it's sufficiently advised to engage a tax professional or seek insights from the up-to-date tax law for reliable and up-to-date data.

The basic principles of computing gains and losses

<u>Deciphering Linkages Among Individuals, Entities and Tax Outcomes Stemming from Transfers Within the UK's Tax Framework</u>

Introduction:

Comprehension of intricately linked individuals or entities—referred to as connected persons—and the related tax outcomes is essential in taxation law. This piece will explore the concept of these 'connections' within the UK's tax framework especially where capital gains tax (CGT) is involved. We will apply these notions to a theoretical case to demonstrate how the UK's taxes work in the 2023-2024 tax period. We will be setting out on a comprehension-expedition to untangle certain complexities within the UK tax framework, especially those affecting 'connected-person' transfers.

Underlining Connections for CGT Objectives:

A 'connected person' could be an individual or an organization in a close professional or personal relationship with another, causing a possible sway in their financial decisions or work. When it comes to CGT, pertaining relationships could sway transfers of assets or holdings between involved parties. Under legislative directives in the UK, connected persons reflects certain categories, from spouses and close relatives, to civil unions.

Consequences of Transfers Among Connected Individuals:

Asset or property transactions between connected individuals may lead to tax liabilities, mainly from CGT. The proceeds of such transfers are either seen as market value transactions or fully-exchanged ones by the UK tax platform, which calls for any gains or losses due to transactions to be included and subjected to CGT.

Take for instance, John hopes to grant a house he owns to his sister Sarah as a present. The local tax guidelines as of 2023-2024 would see this kind act as an act of disposal for CGT purposes. To calculate any mandatory CGT overview, the property's market value during transfer time draws immediate interest. Then proceeds to tax based on any gain that John potentially receives, relying on the transfer according to the 2023-2024 financial year's CGT tariffs and allowances.

Take account that dispatch menu between collaborating people can trigger other tax components like inheritance tax (IHT) or the stamp duty land tax (SDLT). However, this analysis will focus on attributions related to the Capital Gains Tax.

Conclusion:

When operating within the UK tax framework, understanding connected persons and their implications is invaluable. As it relates to CGT, transactions among interconnected people naturally submit to market value hereby risking capital gains tax. Through studying a hypothetical tax scenario, we've looked into the UK tax system laws for 2023/2024 financial year. Entities or individuals immersed in hard monetary transfers should solicit advice from a competent UK tax system specialist or ones extensively skilled in national taxation legislation. These professionals provide advice with due tailor-fit adaptations responding to individuals personalized being to yield compliance that abides by profuse, changing tax regulations.

The UK tax system, in the 2023-2024 tax year, significantly considers the dates of disposal. These refer to when an asset is sold off or disposed, ultimately affecting the payable tax. The tax principles dictate that disposal time is the determinant of the tax year when the asset's gain or loss is officially acknowledged. That implies if the asset disposal takes place before the tax year concludes, it will be factored into the calculation for the current year tax. Conversely, if disposal occurs after the tax year ends, then the gain or loss will apply to the subsequent tax year. Hence, it is critical to clearly contemplate the disposal dates to strategize tax plans efficiently and lessen tax obligations.

In UK tax regulations, capital losses have a poignant impact during the year of death. When someone dies, all assets are usually transferred to their heirs or sold. Knowing how capital losses are applied in the year of death is crucial, especially in case an asset sale results in loss.

The UK tax system allows the use of capital losses to offset any capital gains that arise in the same tax year. If a deceased person had capital gains from asset sales, any capital losses can be utilised to lower the total tax due. But, only up to £3000 of capital losses can be taken off against other income types, such as employment income, during a tax year.

Should these capital losses surpass £3000, then the extra losses can be deferred to subsequent years and used to counter future capital gains. Nonetheless, it is vital to realise that capital losses can only be deferred for a specific period. In the UK, these losses can be deferred indefinitely until they are exhausted or until the asset is sold.

Imagine a theoretical scenario. Death overtakes someone possessing two assets; Asset A and Asset B. They sell Asset A at a £5000 loss, and Asset B at a profit of £8000. During the year of death, Asset A's capital loss can offset the capital gain from Asset B, resulting in a net capital gain of £3000 (£8000 - £5000).

If the deceased had other income types, including employment or rental income, then the remaining £2000 of loss (after subtracting the £3000 net gain) could be offset against that income, thereby lowering the entirety of tax due for the year of death.

For assurance of adherence to the specific rules and norms underlying the UK tax system, consulting with a tax advisor or competently qualified individual is crucial. Since tax laws and rates may shift annually, it is essential to keep track of the current information declared for the fiscal year 2023-2024.

Wrapping up, capital losses are instrumental in the year of death for offsetting capital gains as well as diminishing total tax liability. If they go beyond the permissible deduction limit, it's possible to defer them for future application. For sound tax planning and compliance, gaining knowledge of the laws and requirements around capital losses in the expiry year, as per the UK tax law, is crucial.

Gains and losses on the disposal of movable and immovable property

In the UK taxation system, a part disposal refers to the sale or disposal of only a portion of a property or asset. This can occur when an individual sells a part of their land while retaining ownership of the remaining portion. It is important to understand the tax implications of such transactions.

When it comes to small part disposals of land, the rules can be complex. In general, the amount chargeable to Capital Gains Tax (CGT) depends on the proportion of the land disposed of. To calculate the gain, you would need to determine the original cost of the entire property and allocate a proportionate cost to the part being disposed of.
For example, let's consider a hypothetical case where John owns a piece of land that he purchased for £200,000. He decides to sell a

small portion of the land for £50,000. To calculate the gain on this part disposal, John would need to determine the proportionate cost of the land being sold. If the portion being sold represents 20% of the total land, the allocated cost would be £40,000 (20% of £200,000).

Next, John would subtract the allocated cost from the sale proceeds to calculate the gain. In this case, the gain would be £10,000 (£50,000 - £40,000). This gain would then be subject to CGT at the applicable rates for the tax year 2023-2024.

It is important to note that these calculations can become more complex if there have been previous part disposals or if there are other factors involved. Consulting with a tax professional or referring to the latest UK tax rules for the specific tax year is recommended to ensure accurate compliance with the regulations.

In the UK taxation system, determining the gain on the disposal of leases and wasting assets involves following the rules set out by the UK tax laws for the year 2023-2024. According to Section 603 of the TCA 1997, if an asset is tangible movable property and considered a wasting asset, it is generally exempt from Capital Gains Tax (CGT), except when it is used for specific purposes [3]. To calculate the gain on the disposal of leases, it is important to consider the market value rule specified in the tax laws. When a taxpayer is subject to a deemed disposal of assets moving in or out of the tax system, the market value of the disposal should be applied [1]. This means that the gain will be determined based on the difference between the market value of the lease at the time of disposal and its original cost or value.

For wasting assets, the tax rules provide specific exemptions and guidelines. A wasting asset is one that has a limited lifespan or is expected to significantly depreciate in value over time. In general, such assets are exempt from CGT [3]. However, it is essential to ensure that the disposal of wasting assets meets the criteria set out in the tax laws to qualify for the exemption.

To illustrate the application of these rules, let's consider a hypothetical case. Suppose a taxpayer owns a lease on a commercial property that was acquired for £100,000. After using the property for several years, the taxpayer decides to dispose of the lease in the 2023-2024 tax year. At the time of disposal, the market value of the lease is estimated to be £150,000.

Using the market value rule, the gain on the disposal of the lease would be calculated as the difference between the market value (£150,000) and the original cost (£100,000), which is £50,000. This gain would be subject to CGT, unless any applicable exemptions or reliefs apply.

It's important to note that this is a simplified example and specific circumstances may require additional considerations or adjustments. Consulting with a tax professional or referring to the official UK tax legislation for the year 2023-2024 is recommended to ensure accurate calculations and compliance with the tax rules.

The Treatment of Assets Damaged, Lost, or Destroyed: Including Capital Sums Received

Introduction:
In the realm of taxation, the treatment of assets that have been damaged, lost, or destroyed is a crucial aspect to understand. It not only affects individuals and businesses but also plays a significant role in the overall tax liability. In this article, we will explore the UK taxation system's approach to handling such situations, with a focus on the tax year 2023-2024. Additionally, we will delve into hypothetical case scenarios and apply the relevant UK tax rules to provide a comprehensive understanding of this topic.

Treatment of Damaged, Lost, or Destroyed Assets:
When an asset such as property, machinery, or equipment suffers damage, loss, or destruction, it can have a substantial impact on its value and usability. The UK tax system recognizes this and provides guidelines on how to account for such situations.

Capital Sums Received:
In certain instances, when an asset is damaged, lost, or destroyed, individuals or businesses may receive compensation in the form of capital sums. These capital sums aim to mitigate the financial loss incurred due to the asset's damage or loss. It is important to consider the tax implications of such receipts.

Taxation of Capital Sums Received:
Under the UK taxation system, the treatment of capital sums received for damaged, lost, or destroyed assets is subject to specific rules and regulations. These rules determine whether the capital sums received are taxable or exempt.

Ordinary Trading Assets:
For individuals or businesses who hold assets as part of their ordinary trading activities, the receipt of capital sums due to damage, loss, or destruction is generally subject to income tax. The capital sums received are treated as income and should be included in the relevant tax computation.

Capital Assets:
In the case of capital assets, such as investment properties or shares, the tax treatment varies. If the asset's disposal would have generated a chargeable gain for capital gains tax (CGT) purposes, the capital sum received is treated as a disposal consideration. It is then considered when calculating the CGT liability.

Non-Taxable Receipts: There are instances where the capital sums received are not subject to taxation. For example, if the capital sums received are considered as compensation for personal injury or death, they are generally exempt from income tax and CGT. However, it is important to consult the specific tax rules and seek professional advice to ensure compliance.

Hypothetical Case Scenario:
To illustrate the practical application of these rules, let's consider a hypothetical case. John, a self-employed contractor, owns a van used for his business activities. Unfortunately, the van is severely damaged in an accident and is beyond repair. John receives a capital sum from his insurance company as compensation for the loss.

In this case, as the van is an ordinary trading asset, the capital sum received by John will be treated as income for income tax purposes. He will need to include this amount in his tax computation for the relevant tax year, following the guidelines provided by the UK taxation system.

Conclusion:

The treatment of assets damaged, lost, or destroyed, including capital sums received, is an important aspect of the UK taxation system. Understanding the rules and regulations surrounding this topic is crucial for individuals and businesses to ensure accurate tax compliance. By applying the relevant UK tax rules to hypothetical case scenarios, we have shed light on the practical implications and provided insights into the treatment of such situations. Remember, seeking professional advice is always recommended to navigate the complexities of the UK tax system effectively.

Negligible value claims can have significant tax effects for investors in the UK. When the value of an investment falls to a negligible amount, you may be able to claim a capital loss for tax purposes. This loss can be offset against any capital gains you have made, reducing your overall tax liability [1].

To make a negligible value claim, you need to demonstrate that the investment is now of little or no value. This can be a complex process, as it requires evidence and documentation to support your claim. You should gather information such as financial statements, market data, and any relevant correspondence with the company [1].

Once your claim is accepted by HM Revenue and Customs (HMRC), you can use the loss to reduce your taxable income in the year the claim is made. The loss can be carried forward and offset against future capital gains, or even carried back and offset against gains from previous tax years [1].

It is important to note that the tax treatment of negligible value claims can vary depending on the type of investment and the specific circumstances. Furthermore, the rules and regulations governing tax in the UK can change from year to year. Therefore, it is crucial to consult with a qualified tax advisor or accountant who has up-to-date knowledge of the UK tax system and can provide personalized advice based on your situation [1].

In conclusion, making a negligible value claim can have a significant impact on your tax liabilities in the UK. By properly documenting and supporting your claim, you may be able to offset the capital loss against gains and reduce your overall tax burden. However, it is essential to seek professional advice to ensure compliance with the latest tax regulations and to maximize the benefits of making such a claim [1].

Gains and losses on the disposal of shares and securities

Grasping UK Taxation System's Rights Issues and Small Part Disposal Rules

Introduction:
In the intricate workings of the United Kingdom's taxation structure, it is essential to understand how rights issues and small part disposal rules are handled. This article aims to clarify in detail these elements, highlighting their impact and importance. Moreover, we'll talk through a theoretical case focusing on the UK tax regulations for the fiscal year 2023-2024 to demonstrate the practical usage of these aspects.

Understanding Rights Issues:
A rights issue is essentially a tactic companies utilize to raise additional funds, giving existing shareholders the right to buy extra shares at a fixed price. This enables the company to boost its monetary status and finance growth projects. Existing shareholders receive first refusal to acquire additional shares in correlation with their existing equity, ensuring their share of ownership remains intact.

Tax Treatment of Rights Issues:
The taxation treatment of rights issues tends to be elaborate when viewed from a taxation perspective. This treatment varies depending on whether the shareholder chooses to invoke their rights or auction them in the market. If a shareholder takes up the company's offer and buys additional shares, the acquisition cost of these shares is incorporated into their initial cost base. Consequently, the future sale of these shares is subject to capital gains tax (CGT), relying on the updated cost base.
However, if a shareholder opts to immerse their rights in the open market, the capital earned from the sale is regarded as a capital receipt. The shareholder may be faced with CGT on the disposal of these rights, depending on their cumulative capital increases for that fiscal year.

Understanding Small Part Disposal Rules:
The intent of small part disposal rules is to make the tax treatment of minor disposals easier to understand. These rules come into play when a person makes a small part sale of their shares or securities. In the context of rights issues, the small part disposal rules get activated in a scenario where a shareholder opts to sell their rights rather than use them.

As per the small part disposal procedure, the disposal of rights from a rights issue is handled as a separate disposal from the original shares. This translates to gains or losses from the sale of rights fixed separately and subject to CGT. The flexibility offered by the rules allows shareholders yearly exempted amount towards any benefit accrued from the rights disposal.

Theoretical Case Study:
To ascertain the application process of the UK taxation commissions decided for the term 2023-2024, take the hypothetical instance. A shareholder, Mr. Smith is offered rights to purchase supplementary shares in Company X. The companies granting of additional shares at £10 for every five shares held.

Scenario 1: Invoking Rights

Mr. Smith invoked his rights and acquires an additional 100 shares. He will pay £1,000 for these additional shares (100*£10), adopts his cost base. Later, when Mr. Smith sells the shares, benefits or losses will get calculated considering the cost base of £1,000.

Scenario 2: Disposing of Rights

Conversely, Mr. Smith sells these rights; he gets £500 from selling 100 preferences (acceptable £5 per right). Here, the £500 acquired is regarded as a capital receipt and may attract CGT, interpolating Mr. Smith's total capital increase for that taxation term.

Conclusion:

For shareholders steering through the United Kingdom's taxation system, it's critical to comprehend the functioning of rights issues and small part disposal rules. The tax impact changes subject to whether the shareholder chooses to invoke or sell the rights, and the rules attached to small part disposal present more possibilities. Upon applying these regulations to a theoretical situation, we've delved into their effective application according to the UK tax rules intended for the term 2023-2024. As taxation laws remain subject to transformation, shareholders and investors must maintain abreast of these rules.

A qualifying corporate bond (QCB) is a type of security that meets specific criteria, such as being denominated in sterling and lacking provisions for conversion into another currency. On the other hand, a corporate bond that does not meet these criteria is considered non-qualifying. The distinction between QCBs and non-QCBs is significant because QCBs are exempt from capital gains tax (CGT), while non-QCBs are not. When it comes to the disposal of QCBs in exchange for cash or shares, there are capital gains tax implications to consider.

In the UK, the tax treatment of QCBs is more favorable compared to non-QCBs. QCBs are exempt assets, meaning that their disposal does not give rise to any chargeable gain or allowable loss for capital gains tax purposes [1]. This exemption provides a tax advantage to investors holding QCBs, as they can dispose of these securities without incurring capital gains tax liabilities. However, it is important to note that outside of the capital gains tax regime, there may be other tax consequences to consider [1].

The recent court case of N Trigg v HMRC shed light on the factors that determine whether a security is classified as a QCB or a non-QCB. The court ruled that a clause allowing redenomination of bonds does not disqualify them as QCBs [3]. This case highlighted the significance of the structure of loan notes received in determining their tax treatment.

To understand the tax implications of the disposal of QCBs in exchange for cash or shares, let's consider a hypothetical case. Suppose an individual, John, acquired QCBs in the tax year 2023-2024. He decides to dispose of these bonds and receive cash in return. In this scenario, since QCBs are exempt from capital gains tax, John will not be liable for any capital gains tax on the disposal of his QCBs [2].

However, if John had received shares instead of cash for his QCBs, the capital gains tax implications would vary. When QCBs are exchanged for shares, the disposal is treated as if John had disposed of the QCBs for their market value in cash and then immediately used that cash to acquire the shares [1]. In this case, John would be liable for capital gains tax on any chargeable gain arising from the disposal of his QCBs.

The computation of the capital gains tax liability would involve calculating the chargeable gain by deducting the acquisition cost of the QCBs from their market value at the time of disposal. The chargeable gain would then be subject to the prevailing capital gains tax rates and allowances for the tax year 2023-2024 [1].

In conclusion, qualifying corporate bonds (QCBs) are a type of security that meets specific criteria, such as being denominated in sterling and lacking provisions for conversion into another currency. QCBs enjoy a tax advantage as they are exempt from capital gains tax. However, the tax treatment of QCBs can vary depending on the structure of the loan notes received. When disposing of QCBs in exchange for cash or shares, individuals should consider the capital gains tax implications and consult the relevant tax rules and regulations applicable in the UK for the tax year 2023-2024 [1][2][3].

Navigating Tax-Efficient Options for Business Redesign, Rebuilding, and Merging in the UK

Introduction:
The intricate realm of tax often leads corporations to consider redesigning, rebuilding, and merging as means to fine-tune their structures and performance. Such moves can streamline processes, enhance effectiveness, and cultivate cost-effectiveness. Nonetheless, comprehending the tax outcomes and pinpointing optimum tax-saving possibilities can be a tough task. In this write-up, we will explore the British tax system, examine hypothetical scenarios, and keep you enlightened on the tax-saving alternatives given the scenario.

Understanding the UK Tax System:
The British tax system operates under a variety of guidelines determining how entities and individuals are taxed. These

directives periodically undergo alterations, hence, for our discussion, the taxation for the fiscal year 2023-2024 will be taken into consideration.

Case Study: Hypothetical Scenario:
Consider a UK-based manufacturing entity, Company X, aiming to realign its activities. The aim is to explore the most tax-efficient scenarios to reduce tax burdens and amplify its overall financial scenario.

Option 1: Merging or Combining:
Company X might consider merging with another entity, incorporating the assets, liabilities, and activities into one unified unit. This could be planned as exchange of undertakings or share-by-share.
The advantage of a share-for-share exchange is the potential to swapping their stakes in the newly merged entity without initiating any tax event, thus temporarily postponing capital gains tax until the equity is eventually sold.
Alternatively, shares can be exchanged for undertaking, but this induces a tax event with any capital gains on disposing of stakes being subject to tax implications. However, strategic planning around available alleviations and abatements could minimize this tax hit.

Option 2: Dividing Company or Spin-off:
Another efficient possibility includes parting a subsection of the business off into its individual entity through redistribution of equities to the existing stakeholders or by directly selling the respective subsection of the business.
Company X might choose to delegate certain division into a newly found entity, benefitting with a pleasant flexibility to manage diverse sections independently. Tax-wise, planning and qualifying for potential tax reliefs might make this a tax-neutral event.

Option 3: Restructuring via Share Buybacks:
Company X has also opened the option to reform via buying back its own equities. These buybacks can harness and redirect residual funds to stakeholders and consolidate the stakes.
From a tax aspect, the tax effects of revisiting share purchases extensively depend on the type of transaction- capitation recipience or income recipience subjected tax. Capital recipiences

usually deal with capitation gain tax and income micro transections invite income tax. Availability of entrepreneurs' discounts can fade the actual tax burden.

Conclusion:
Examining tax consequences is key when business systems are undergoing alteration, resettlement, or mergers. In Britain, many tax options are reachable including business combinations, divisions, and stock buybacks with varying treatment. However, deliberating upon risks around tax regulatory constraints and consequences, execution and decisions reflecting 2023-2024 will result in maximizing tax benefits.
In circumstances like Company X, most efficient pathways could be discerned by analyzing individual aims and situations.
Companies are strongly advised refer to professional advisors and make practical decisions within the limitations of legal procedures that not only allows entities to deepen their performance, reduce tax burdens but also establish long strategies towards success in dynamically changing British taxation boundaries.

Enhancing Relief for Capital Losses on Shares in Non-listed Trading Companies through the UK Tax System

Introduction:
Encouragement for investment and entrepreneurship is promoted through various exemptions and reliefs within the UK tax system. This includes relief for capital losses on shares in non-listed trading firms. Within this article, the idea of capital losses will be explained and how it can be beneficially used as will the specific relief offered for losses endured on shares in non-listed trading firms. We'll also utilize a hypothetical example to shed light on the application of UK taxation rules for the 2023-2024 tax year.

Understanding Capital Losses:
Simply put, a capital loss arises when an asset is sold for less than its initial purchase price. Such losses can be set against capital gains to decrease the total tax that an individual is obligated to pay. Capital gains refer to the profits obtained from selling assets like investments, property, or shares. By using capital losses, taxpayers can effectively lower their taxable capital gains.

Relief for Capital Losses on Shares in Unquoted Trading Companies

The UK taxation system realizes the significance of assisting businesses, particularly those in their initial developmental phase. There is a particular relief for losses that investors encounter on shares in non-listed trading firms to stimulate investment in these businesses. This relief usually goes by the names Entrepreneur's Relief (ER) or Business Asset Disposal Relief (BADR) and fosters entrepreneurship and risk driveness.

With ER/BADR, a decreased rate of 10% is offered on Capital Gains Tax (CGT) for qualifying gains, given they meet some criteria. This relief pertains to an individual who has managed to hold a minimum of 5% of the general share capital and voting rights for at least a biennium prior to disposing of the shares.

Hypothetical Case Study:
We'll present a hypothetical case as a means to demonstrate the procedure for the relief for capital losses on shares in non-listed trading businesses. Think of John, a UK citizen who yields taxable income, who made a £50,000 investment in an unlisted trading firm, ABC Ltd., in April 2022 and unfortunately, due to fiscal issues on the part of the company, sold his shares for £20,000 in June 2023, thus dealing with a capital loss worth £30,000.

As per the 2023-2024 tax year UK tax regulations, John could set off his capital loss on his capital gains in that same fiscal year. In an event where John racked up £40,000 as gains from selling off another asset, he could use his £30,000 loss to bring down his £40,000 gain to a taxable capital increase of £10,000 (£40,000 - £30,000).

Furthermore, John would have to pay a 10% CGT (on his taxable increase of £10,000) as opposed to the normal rate if his fulfilment of the norms to be eligible for Entrepreneur's Relief/Business Asset Disposal Relief is assumed. This way, his CGT LIABILITY would be £1,000 (£10,000 × 10%).

Conclusion:
The relief for capital losses on shares in non-listed trading firms offers taxpayers chance to balance losses against gains, adjusting their tax liability. Coupled with incentive offerings for early-stage firms' investors and entrepreneurs, the UK tax system supports economic augmentation innovation. Developed knowledge about

and good use of these reliefs can considerably favor taxpayers while encouraging to active participation in unpredictable and ever-changing business world.

The use of exemptions and reliefs in deferring and minimizing tax liabilities arising on the disposal of capital assets

Enterprise Investment Scheme (EIS) reinvestment relief is a tax relief available in the United Kingdom that allows individuals to defer capital gains tax (CGT) on the sale of an asset if they reinvest the proceeds in qualifying EIS shares. This relief encourages investors to support smaller, riskier companies by providing an incentive to reinvest their gains.

To illustrate this concept, let's consider a hypothetical case. Suppose Mr. Smith sells a property in the tax year 2023-2024 and realizes a capital gain of £100,000. Normally, he would be liable to pay capital gains tax on this amount. However, if Mr. Smith decides to reinvest the gain in qualifying EIS shares within a certain timeframe, he can defer the capital gains tax liability.

Under the EIS reinvestment relief, Mr. Smith can defer the capital gains tax on the £100,000 gain until he disposes of the EIS shares or the shares cease to qualify for EIS relief. This means that he can potentially defer paying the tax for a significant period, allowing his investment to grow.

It's important to note that reinvestment relief does not exempt Mr. Smith from paying capital gains tax altogether. Rather, it provides a deferral of the tax liability until a later date. When Mr. Smith eventually sells the EIS shares, he will be liable to pay capital gains tax on the gain made from the disposal of those shares.

The reinvestment relief is subject to certain conditions. The amount reinvested in EIS shares must be equal to or less than the amount of the capital gain. Additionally, the shares must be issued within a specified time period, usually within the tax year in which the gain arises or the following tax year.

In conclusion, the Enterprise Investment Scheme reinvestment relief is a valuable tax relief that allows individuals to defer capital gains tax by reinvesting the proceeds in qualifying EIS shares. This incentive encourages investment in smaller, riskier companies and supports economic growth. However, it is crucial for investors to understand the eligibility criteria and comply with the relevant rules and regulations to benefit from this relief.

SEIS reinvestment relief is a tax benefit for individual investors in the UK. This relief rewards those who reinvest capital gains obtained from the sale of assets into SEIS qualifying businesses aimed at boosting support for high-risk early-stage enterprises by offering tax incentives. The relief component allows investors to drop their capital gains tax liability by half of the reinvested amount when they reinvest their capital gains. With the annual cut-off cap at £100,000, a maximum tax reduction of £50,000 can be achieved.

Investors wanting to benefit from SEIS reinvestment relief need to make sure the company they reinvest in satisfies SEIS eligibility. The company in question should be initiating a new qualifying trade, fulfil the risk to capital condition and issue ordinary full-risk shares without a redemption feature and devoid of any special rights. Another essential condition requires the firm to execute the SEIS funds within a three-year timeframe for launching a qualifying trade or facilitating research and development.

A better understanding of SEIS reinvestment relief can be gained through a hypothetic illustration. Let's take John, residing in the UK, who gains a capital increase of £200,000 from selling an investment in 2023-2024 fiscal year. In lieu of incurring capital gains tax on the entire gains, John selects to reinvest £100,000 into a company meeting SEIS qualification, getting a 50% deduction on his capital gains tax liability leading to a savings of £50,000.

Although, SEIS reinvestment relief comes with definite constraints. The risk of potential revocation of tax relief exists if funds are withdrawn or if satisfying SEIS qualification isn't attained in the demanding period. This might necessitate repayment of previously enjoyed tax savings.

Ultimately, SEIS reinvestment relief offers UK investors, a lucrative tax relief motive supporting the backing of early-scale, high-risk companies. Through reinvestment in SEIS_Participating firms, investors can reap capital gains tax liability reductions generously saving a substantial sum of money. It is pivotal, however, that investor conformity with business SEIS eligibility prerequisites is affirmed along with adherence to proper stipulated regulations guaranteeing the endurance of provided tax relief.

Business Asset Disposal Relief (formerly known as Entrepreneurs' Relief) is a tax relief scheme in the UK that aims to support entrepreneurs by offering reduced capital gains tax rates on the sale of qualifying business assets [3]. This relief allows individuals to pay a lower rate of Capital Gains Tax (CGT) when selling their business or certain business assets [1]. To be eligible for this relief, there are specific criteria that need to be met. Firstly, the individual must be a sole trader or business partner and have owned the business for at least two years. The same conditions apply if the business is being closed. If selling shares or securities, the individual must be an employee or office holder of the company, and the company's main activities must be in trading. Additional rules apply if the shares are from an Enterprise Management Incentive (EMI). If the shares are not from an EMI, the business must be a 'personal company,' and the individual must have at least 5% of shares, voting rights, and entitlement to profits or disposal proceeds. If the company issues more shares and the individual's shareholding falls below 5%, they may still claim the relief by electing to be treated as if they sold and re-bought their shares [1]. The relief can be postponed by completing the relevant forms or writing to HMRC. If the company stops being a trading company, the relief can still be claimed if shares are sold within three years [1]. If selling assets lent to the business, the individual must have sold at least 5% of their part of a business partnership or shares in a personal company and owned the assets for at least one year. Trustees may also qualify for the relief when selling assets held in the trust [1]. The benefits of Business Asset Disposal Relief include reduced capital gains tax rates (10% compared to standard rates of 10-20%), encouragement of entrepreneurship and innovation, attraction of foreign investment, enhanced financial flexibility for business owners, and facilitation of business succession planning [3]. Overall, Business Asset Disposal Relief provides a valuable tax incentive for individuals looking to sell their business or certain business assets, helping to foster entrepreneurship and support economic growth in the UK.

The UK tax system has an important feature called 'incorporation relief' that benefits taxpayers transitioning their businesses from unregistered formats to limited companies. This allows a tax-free transfer of business assets to a limited company. As per UK tax laws effective between 2023 and 2024, this relief can be claimed only when certain factors, such as transferring business assets in exchange for shares in the recipient company and a legitimate business restructuring rather than missing taxes, are in place.

The process to calculate this relief is shown below. Visualize Mr. Smith who functions a profitable sole owner company decides to set his business as a limited company. The business assets are valued at £500,000, which Mr. Smith puts into the limited company in return for complete shares. The relief is figured out by comparing the market value of the business assets to the base cost of the shares received. Thus, when the business assets market value supersedes the shares base cost, the difference will accord for relief.

In Mr. Smith's case, let's assume the shares' base cost with Mr. Smith is £200,000. Since the £500,000 worth of business assets are much more significant than the share receipt base cost (£200,000), the leftover £300,000 is unleashed for relief incorporation. Successively, Mr. Smith can claim relief on the transfer of his business assets, hence circumventing immediate taxation on the remaining £300,000. Consequently, the tax liabilities will be deferred until future actions such as the sale or disposal of shares.

However, it's important to understand the intricacy relating to the calculation of incorporation relief, so it's suggested for taxpayers to seek professional advice to ensure alignment with the UK tax laws and regulations. In conclusion, putting into action the incorporation relief when transferring an unincorporated business to a limited company is exceedingly crucial for taxpayers in the UK. By adhering to the defined prerequisites and accurately computing the relief, taxpayers can put on hold their tax liabilities and maximize their earnings potential from a tax point of view.

Understanding Capital Gains Tax Implications in Variation of Wills in the UK

Introduction:
In the United Kingdom, it is essential to understand the implications of capital gains tax when it comes to the variation of wills. This article aims to provide a comprehensive overview of the UK taxation system in relation to capital gains tax, using the rules for the tax year 2023-2024. We will explore a hypothetical case scenario and analyze the relevant tax rules to gain a better understanding of how capital gains tax applies to variations in wills.

Understanding Capital Gains Tax:
Capital gains tax is a levy imposed on the profit realized from the sale of capital assets, including investments and personal use items [1]. In the context of variations in wills, capital gains tax becomes relevant when inherited assets are disposed of or transferred. It is important to note that capital gains tax only applies when an investment is sold, and it is applicable to capital assets such as stocks, bonds, cryptocurrencies, jewelry, and real estate [2].

Taxation of Inherited Assets:
When someone dies, tax is typically paid from their estate before any money is distributed to the heirs [3]. In the case of inherited assets that are subject to capital gains tax, the tax liability is determined based on the market value of the asset at the time of inheritance. If the asset is subsequently disposed of or transferred, any increase in its value from the date of inheritance may be subject to capital gains tax.

Hypothetical Case Scenario:
To illustrate the application of capital gains tax in the variation of wills, let's consider a hypothetical situation. John inherits a property from his late father, who passed away in the tax year 2023-2024. The property has a market value of £500,000 at the time of inheritance.

Capital Gains Tax Calculation:
Suppose John decides to sell the inherited property after a few years, when its market value has increased to £600,000. To calculate the capital gains tax liability, we need to determine the

gain realized from the sale. In this case, the gain would be £100,000 (£600,000 - £500,000).

Capital Gains Tax Rates:
The tax rates for long-term capital gains in 2023-2024 are 0%, 15%, or 20%, depending on the income of the individual [2]. To determine the applicable tax rate for John, we need to consider his overall income and the gain from the sale of the property. Let's assume John falls into the 20% tax bracket due to his income level.

Tax Liability Calculation:
As John is in the 20% tax bracket, the gain of £100,000 from the sale of the property would be subject to a capital gains tax rate of 20%. Therefore, John's capital gains tax liability would amount to £20,000 (£100,000 x 20%).

Conclusion:
Understanding the capital gains tax implications of the variation of wills is crucial when dealing with inherited assets in the UK. By considering the rules and rates applicable in the tax year 2023-2024, we have explored a hypothetical case scenario and calculated the capital gains tax liability for John in our example. It is important to consult with a tax professional or seek expert advice to ensure compliance with the UK taxation system and make informed decisions regarding inherited assets.

Inheritance tax complexities

The scope of inheritance tax

The concepts of domicile and deemed domicile are utilized in the UK to figure out an individual's inheritance tax liability. Domicile refers to the country deemed as a permanent home by an individual, regardless of their birthplace or current location. Deemed domicile is a legal term given to individuals with a lengthy stay in the UK.

Inheritance tax is charged on everything a deceased person owned, like property, money and other possessions. In the UK, an inheritance tax rate of 40% applies to anything over £325,000, though there are some potential reductions and exemptions.

Those domiciled in the UK face inheritance tax on all their assets, no matter their location. In layman's terms, a UK-domiciled person who owns assets in another country is going to be taxed in the UK for those assets. But those without a UK domicile are taxed only on their UK assets.

Individuals that have stayed in the UK for 15 out of the last 20 tax years are deemed domicile, treating their worldwide properties as if they were in the UK for tax purposes.

Let's review these concepts by envisaging a hypothetical example featuring John, a US nationality living in the UK for two decades. He owns a UK property worth £500,000 and a US property worth $1 million, in total he has £1.5 million worth in assets.

If John's domicile is the UK, the £1.5 million worth assets will be subject to inheritance tax, meaning he would face a tax liability of £400,000, given the 40% rate. Yet if John is not domiciled in the UK, only his £500,000 UK property would be counted for tax, which sends him below the £325,000 threshold, making him exempt from paying inheritance tax. Treated as if he is domiciled in the UK, the £1.5 million worth assets would mean he'll pay the inheritance tax of £400,000 if he's deemed domiciled.

In the long run, it's worth analyzing domicile and deemed domicile thoroughly when dealing with inheritance tax liability. Understanding one's own status of domicile and each country's specific regulations on your belongings is crucial. It's worthwhile to seek expert advice to avoid overpaying on your inheritance tax.

Properties that fall under the category of "excluded property" refer to specific assets that are not subject to the UK's inheritance tax when they are owned by someone not domiciled in the UK. Inheritance tax planning considers the critical role of excluded property, as it offers individuals the opportunity to arrange their assets to decrease their inheritance tax obligations.

Examples of such properties are as follows:

International Real Estate: Real estate in foreign lands, be it residential or investment property, is generally classified as excluded property. Thus, it isn't regarded in the UK's inheritance tax bracket, even with owners domiciled within its borders.

Assets Placed in Foreign Trusts: An asset that an individual placed in a trust set up outside the UK might be tagged as excluded property, meaning that it's free from the inheritance tax, as long as specific conditions are met.

Foreign Currency Bank Accounts: Generally, funds found in foreign currency bank accounts, regardless of them being lodged in UK banks, fall in the excluded property cadre. They are thus immune from the inheritance tax.

Life insurance Policies: The product of life insurance policies, especially when held in trust or if the payout goes to a beneficiary not living in the UK, is usually not counted under the UK inheritance tax.

However, keep in mind that navigating excluded property rules is complicated. Therefore, acquiring professional tax advice is advisable for adherence to tax regulations within the UK.

The tax implications based on the geographical positioning of assets in the UK could vary widely. Comprehending how diverse tax regulations connect to various asset classifications and their respective places is cardinal. Diverse regimes such as income tax, capital gains tax, and inheritance tax are imposed on both individuals and companies throughout the UK. Determining the whereabouts of assets plays a crucial role in concluding whether they are possessed inside or across borders. If the assets are stationed within the UK, they usually come under UK taxation. In the case of offshore assets, the specific tax rules mostly depend on individual circumstance.

For instance, if a person owns a property in the UK, the income generated from rental gets subjected to income tax. The profit made through the sale of the property must cover capital gains tax. When dealing with international assets, such as overseas real estate or financial commitments, understanding tax obligations can prove to be challenging. To tackle tax evasion, UK imposes standardized tax procedures. Under these rules, foreign assets and revenue must be disclosed to concerned tax authorities like the HMRC, which stands as the UK benchmark organization.

HMRC has been stepping up its vigilance on tax evasion by enforcing mechanisms such as the Common Reporting Standard (CRS), allowing for increased communication and sharing of information about asset tax responsibilities including inheritance. As a rule, when a person dies, the total wealth owned by them at that point gets calculated to estimate the value for inheritance tax. However, certain incentives and reliefs designed to offer relief from the burden of inheritance tax are available. Concessions related to property transfer to a spouse or civil partner, and business premises and rural landholdings relief are instances that have noticeable tax ramifications.

Understanding the varying tax regulations for differing classes and locations makes it of primary importance. Ensuring compliance with these rules is crucial to avoid any penalties and assure the fulfillment of tax responsibilities by both individuals and corporations. Having the expertise of a capable tax advisor or getting guidance from HMRC may be beneficial to comprehend asset tax obligations effectively.

"Gifts with reservation of benefit" pertain to instances in which a person gives away something of value but still reaps some advantages from it. In Britain, specific taxation regulations apply to these gifts. As per the UK taxation system of 2023-2024, they are not recognised as genuine gifts for tax considerations. Instead, they're managed as though the person giving the gift retains ownership. Consequently, it's worth endures in their wealth for inheritance tax issues. Additionally, any revenue or benefits coming from the asset are subject to income tax payments. For instance, imagine John owns a pricey artwork which he gifts to his daughter, Emma. However, he maintains the artwork displayed in his domicile and enjoys its beauty as if it were still his possession. In this example, the gift constitutes a reservation of benefit, implying the artwork's inclusion in John's inheritance tax. Furthermore, any resulting income from the artwork like rent money or proceeds from sales will incur income tax. To steer clear of any potential tax consequences, it's crucial to thoroughly grasp and comply with UK tax regulations governing gifts with reservation of benefit.

The basic principles of computing transfers of value

Understanding Valuation Principles in the UK Tax System and Associated Property Laws

Introduction:
Determining the monetary value of assets and properties is a significant component of UK's taxation process. This document aims to relay a detailed comprehension of UK's tax system's valuation principles and associated property laws for tax year 2023-2024. Exploring pertinent legislation and presenting a fictitious case study, the report will illustrate how these principles and rules apply.

The Basics of Valuation:
Valuation governs the process of estimating the financial worth of an asset or property. Taxation related valuation principles in the UK are chiefly dictated by laws and guidelines put forward by Her Majesty's Revenue and Customs (HMRC). These necessary principles encourage consistency, impartiality, and precision in evaluation of assets' value.
Market Value Definition:
Various assets' financial worth for taxation is established beginning with market value. Market value is defined as the price a property could fetch in an open market, with a willing seller and buyer. It is crucial to establish this value considering current market conditions and comparable sales data.

Legal Valuations:
Some assets, particularly land and buildings, may have value defined by statutory law. For inheritance tax, the merit of land could be assessed on its agricultural or development worth, rather than its market value. An in-depth understanding of specific valuation laws for diverse asset types is necessary.

Requirement of Expert Opinions and Proper Documentation:
Professional values, such as chartered surveyors or accosted appraisers, often undertake valuations due to their specialist knowledge and skills in estimating complex asset value. It is vital, moreover, that valuation documents, including supporting

evidence, methodology applied, and underlying assumptions are meticulously kept.

Rules for Property:
Key to the valuation process are diverse laws applicable to property under the UK tax system. Applying relevant taxation rests on recognizing the precise nature and application of a property. Important laws to consider include:

Capital Gains Tax (CGT):
CGT applies when an asset that has increased in worth is sold, disposed of. The initial and final valuation of this asset assists with computing the capital gain. Distinct allowances and exceptions may apply based on asset type and other factors.

Inheritance Tax (IHT):
IHT is applied to the accumulated wealth of a person upon their death. Establishing the asset value of the estate is vital for the correct assignment of the IHT. Specific allowances or exceptions may apply based on the nature of the assets.

Stamp Duty Land Tax (SDLT):
SDLT is a tax imposed on property or land purchases in the UK. The valuated property guides the SDLT rate that will apply. These rates will vary based on purchase value and buyer circumstances. First-time buyer exceptions may be an additional circumstance to consider.

Valuation Example: Assuming House Sale Capital Gains:
Our sample situation is named 'John,' who bought a house in 2010 for £300,000, and he sells it in 2023 for £500,000. To ascertain his tax debt under the CGT laws, John must clarify the profit made on the property employing valuation principles, valuations are required, and potentially data comparison acquired from 2010 and 2023. These-hypothetically determine the worth 2010 as £350,000 and 2023 as £550,000.
His CGT liability is calculated by taking a difference of the two totals, resulting in an achieved £200,000 on selling the house. Subtracting from that the annual CGT exemption (£14,000 in 2023-2024FY) equals £189000—he owes for taxation - a possibly adjusted sums upon finalization from the adequate CGT rates.

Conclusion:
Assessing microeconomic value in the UK uniformly with properties and for purposes of tax regulation would be difficult without general property law and valuation principles. It's vital for those to be correctly assessed for an encompassing application. Heeding these principles where and when required ensures no avoidance or miscalculations - ultimately guided by advice when professional information is attained.

Taxpayers should advise professional aid needed or take particular notice laws in place from H.M.R.C. Observing these enables the complex rules and regulations for property value considerations within the tax law requirements.

Business Property Relief (BPR) and Agricultural Property Relief (APR) are important components of the UK taxation system that provide significant benefits to farmers and agricultural estates. BPR is a relief from Inheritance Tax (IHT) that can substantially reduce the value of gifts made during an individual's lifetime or on death. It is applied at either a rate of 50% or 100%, depending on the type of property and how it is owned. BPR applies to relevant business property that has been owned for over two years and is not wholly or mainly an investment or dealing business. Woodlands may also be eligible for BPR.

APR, on the other hand, reduces the taxable value of agricultural land if specific conditions are met. It is available on the agricultural value of the land but not on its non-agricultural value, such as development value. There are ownership and occupation conditions that must be fulfilled for APR to apply.

In order to claim these reliefs, it is crucial to understand the eligibility criteria and the requirements set by the UK tax authorities. It is advisable to seek expert advice from professionals who have in-depth knowledge of the intricacies of these reliefs.

Now, let's consider a hypothetical case to illustrate the application of BPR and APR in the UK tax year 2023-2024.

John is a farmer who owns a large agricultural estate in the UK. He wants to ensure that his estate is protected from excessive Inheritance Tax liabilities so that his family can continue running the business after his passing. John seeks professional advice to explore the availability of BPR and APR.

The tax expert advises John that his farming business may qualify for BPR. To qualify, the business must have been owned by John for at least two years, be carried on for gain, and not mainly deal in land, buildings, or investments. The expert also explains that BPR can be claimed at a rate of 100% for partnership assets or 50% for assets used in a partnership owned by a partner.

In addition to BPR, the expert informs John about the potential eligibility for APR on his agricultural land. To qualify for APR, the land must be used to grow crops or rear animals and be part of a working farm. The buildings on the land must also be appropriate for farming. The expert advises John that APR can reduce the taxable value of his agricultural land, but not the non-agricultural value, such as any potential development value.

Based on this advice, John decides to proceed with the necessary steps to claim BPR and APR for his farming business and agricultural land. He understands that these reliefs are not about avoiding tax, but about preserving the land and ensuring the continuity of his family business for future generations.

In conclusion, BPR and APR are valuable reliefs within the UK taxation system that can significantly reduce the Inheritance Tax liabilities for farmers and agricultural estates. It is important to seek expert advice to understand the eligibility criteria and ensure compliance with the tax rules and regulations. By utilizing these reliefs, individuals like John can protect their assets and enable the smooth transition of their businesses to the next generation.

Exempt transfers refer to specific types of transactions that are not liable to taxation in the UK. These transactions are not restricted by taxation, preventing individuals or organizations from having to handle their tax payments. Examples of these transfers include inheritances and gifts that individuals receive. Detailed rules and thresholds for exempt transfers, such as the annual gift allowance and the inheritance tax threshold, are determined by the UK. Thus, these exemptions allow individuals to move funds or wealth free from tax obligations. It is crucial to carefully examine the UK tax rules for the 2023-2024 tax year to ensure compliance with the law and maximize applicable exemptions.

The liabilities arising on chargeable lifetime transfers and on the death of an individual

Chargeable lifetime transfers have significant tax implications under the UK taxation system. These transfers refer to gifts or transfers of value that are subject to immediate inheritance tax (IHT) at a rate of 20% [1]. This means that if you make a chargeable lifetime transfer, you will be liable to pay 20% of the value of the transfer as IHT.

However, it's important to note that there are certain exemptions and reliefs available for lifetime transfers. Some transfers may be exempt from IHT, such as gifts between UK domiciled spouses, gifts to charities and political parties, gifts for national benefit, gifts up to £3,000 each tax year, and regular gifts out of surplus income [1].

Additionally, there are specific exemptions for lifetime transfers, including gifts up to £3,000 per tax year, gifts to spouses and charities, and regular gifts out of income [1]. These exemptions allow individuals to make transfers without incurring any IHT liability.

For transfers that do not qualify for exemption, the IHT liability will depend on the timing and nature of the transfer. Gifts to individuals will only be subject to IHT if the donor dies within seven years [1]. If the donor survives for more than seven years after making the gift, it will be completely exempt from IHT.

However, if the donor passes away within seven years, the value of the gift will be included in their estate for IHT purposes. The amount of tax payable on these chargeable transfers will depend on the available nil rate band at the time of death. Any chargeable transfers that exceed the available nil rate band may be subject to IHT at a rate of 40% [1].

It's worth noting that transfers of business or agricultural property may qualify for relief at up to 100% if held for two years or more

[1]. This relief aims to support businesses and encourage the preservation of agricultural assets.

In conclusion, chargeable lifetime transfers have tax implications under the UK taxation system. While some transfers may be exempt from IHT, others may be subject to immediate IHT liability at a rate of 20%. It's important to consider the available exemptions, reliefs, and the timing of transfers when planning for tax implications. Seeking advice from a tax professional can help ensure compliance with the UK tax rules and optimize tax planning strategies based on individual circumstances.

Hypothetical Case: Let's consider a hypothetical case of Sarah, a UK resident. In the tax year 2023-2024, Sarah decides to make a chargeable lifetime transfer by gifting her daughter a property worth £500,000. As this transfer falls under the category of a chargeable lifetime transfer, it will be subject to immediate inheritance tax at a rate of 20%. Therefore, Sarah would be liable to pay £100,000 as inheritance tax on this transfer.

However, if Sarah survives for seven years after making this gift, it will become exempt from inheritance tax, and she will not be required to pay any tax on it. On the other hand, if Sarah were to pass away within seven years, the value of the gift would be included in her estate for inheritance tax purposes. If the value of her estate, including the gift, exceeds the available nil rate band, the excess amount would be subject to inheritance tax at a rate of 40%.

It's important to note that the tax rules and rates may change over time, so it's crucial to stay updated with the latest UK tax regulations and seek professional advice for accurate tax planning and compliance.

Transfers made within seven years of death can have tax implications under the UK taxation system. When valuing the estate of a deceased individual, it is important to consider any transfers they made during this period. Inheritance Tax is levied on a person's estate upon their death, with a standard rate of 40% applied to the value above the threshold. However, if at least 10% of the estate is left to charity, a reduced rate of 36% may apply [1].

In addition to transfers made within seven years, Inheritance Tax can also be due on transfers into a trust, on trust anniversaries, on transfers out of a trust, and when a trust is involved in the deceased's estate. The tax is applicable to relevant property such as money, shares, houses, or land [1]. Certain types of trusts, such as bare trusts and interest in possession trusts, may be exempt from Inheritance Tax. For example, if assets are transferred into a bare trust and the transferor survives for seven years, no Inheritance Tax is due. Interest in possession trusts may have different rules depending on when the assets were transferred [1].

Special rules and exemptions apply to trusts for bereaved minors and disabled beneficiaries [1]. To determine if Inheritance Tax is due, all assets involved in the estate, including trusts, must be valued. The tax is paid using form IHT100, which is submitted to HM Revenue and Customs (HMRC) [1]. It is important to note that more detailed guidance on trusts and Inheritance Tax can be obtained from HMRC or through professional tax advice.

In a hypothetical case, let's consider the situation of an individual who passed away in the tax year 2023-2024. The deceased had an estate valued at £1.5 million, which includes a house worth £500,000, shares valued at £600,000, and cash savings of £400,000. Within seven years of their death, the deceased had made a transfer of £200,000 into a trust.

To calculate the potential Inheritance Tax liability, we start by subtracting the tax-free threshold, which is currently £350,000 [1]. This leaves us with an estate value of £1.15 million. As the estate exceeds the threshold, Inheritance Tax will be levied at the standard rate of 40%.

The tax payable on the estate would be £460,000 (40% of £1.15 million). However, if the deceased had left at least 10% of their estate to charity, the rate could be reduced to 36%. In this case, if £150,000 (10% of £1.5 million) was left to charity, the tax payable would be £414,000 (36% of £1.15 million) [1].

In addition to the estate value, the transfer of £200,000 into the trust within seven years of death would also be subject to Inheritance Tax. As the transferor did not survive for seven years, the full value of the transfer would be included in the estate for tax purposes. Therefore, an additional tax of £80,000 (40% of £200,000) would be due.

In conclusion, transfers made within seven years of death can have significant tax implications under the UK taxation system. Inheritance Tax is calculated based on the value of the estate, with a standard rate of 40% applied to the amount exceeding the threshold. Special rules apply to trusts, and exemptions may exist for certain types of trusts and beneficiaries. It is advisable to seek professional tax advice to ensure compliance with the relevant regulations and to understand the specific tax implications based on individual circumstances [1].

When dealing with the tax liability arising on a death estate in the UK, it is important to understand the procedures and requirements set by HM Revenue and Customs (HMRC) for reporting income. The specific information you need to send to HMRC depends on factors such as the value of the estate, the income generated during the administration period, and whether any tax is owed.

For "simple" estates valued at less than £2.5 million, with total tax due below £10,000, and no more than £500,000 worth of assets sold in a single tax year, you can report tax owed by writing a letter to HMRC. However, if the only income received during the administration period was bank account interest less than £500, there is no need to report it [2].

For "complex" estates, you must register the estate online and submit a Self-Assessment tax return. Registration must be done by 5 October after the tax year, and the necessary details must be provided. Once registered, you can manage and update estate information. HMRC will then provide a Unique Taxpayer Reference (UTR) for the estate. To file the return and pay any tax due, you can fill in a Trust and Estate Tax Return or use tax software by the deadline of 31 January [2].

It is important to note that the taxpayer has the primary responsibility of declaring their taxable income or transactions, which is a widely adopted principle in tax law [3]. Therefore, when dealing with a death estate, it is crucial to ensure accurate reporting and compliance with the UK tax rules for the specific tax year, in this case, 2023-2024.

To demonstrate the application of UK tax rules for the tax year 2023-2024, let's consider a hypothetical case. Imagine a death estate with a value of £2 million and total tax due of £8,000. The estate generated £15,000 of income during the administration period, which includes bank account interest exceeding £500. In addition, assets worth £300,000 were sold within the tax year.

Based on these circumstances, this estate would be classified as a "simple" estate, as it meets the criteria of being valued below £2.5 million, with total tax due below £10,000 and assets sold within the allowed limit. Therefore, the tax owed can be reported by writing a letter to HMRC [2].

However, if the estate value exceeded £2.5 million, the total tax due exceeded £10,000, or the assets sold exceeded £500,000, the estate would be considered "complex." In this case, online registration of the estate with HMRC is required, followed by the submission of a Self-Assessment tax return. The return should include all relevant income and sales information, and any tax due must be paid by the deadline of 31 January [2].

In conclusion, when dealing with the tax liability arising on a death estate in the UK, it is crucial to understand the specific requirements set by HMRC. Depending on the complexity of the estate and the applicable thresholds, the reporting process may vary. Accurate reporting and compliance with the UK tax rules for the specific tax year are essential to ensure the proper management of the estate's tax affairs.

Understanding the Tapered Withdrawal of the Residence Nil Rate Band in the UK Taxation System

Introduction:
In the realm of UK taxation, the residence nil rate band (RNRB) plays a significant role in reducing or eliminating inheritance tax liabilities on the estates of homeowners. However, it is essential to comprehend the tapered withdrawal of the RNRB, particularly when the net value of the estate exceeds £2 million. This article aims to provide a clear understanding of the tapered withdrawal,

its implications, and how it affects inheritance tax planning in the UK.

Tapered Withdrawal and its Impact:
The tapered withdrawal of the RNRB comes into play when the net value of the estate exceeds £2 million [2]. For every £2 by which the net estate exceeds this threshold, the available RNRB is reduced by £1. This means that as the net estate value increases, the amount of RNRB that can be claimed diminishes.

For instance, let's consider a hypothetical case where the net value of an estate stands at £2.5 million. In this scenario, the estate exceeds the taper threshold by £500,000 (£2.5 million - £2 million). As per the tapering restriction, for every £2 exceeding the threshold, the available RNRB is reduced by £1. Therefore, the RNRB would be reduced by £250,000 (£500,000/£2 * £1), resulting in a reduced RNRB available for inheritance tax planning.

Impact on Inheritance Tax Planning:
The tapered withdrawal of the RNRB can have significant implications for individuals planning their estates and inheritance tax liabilities. As the net value of the estate increases, the available RNRB decreases, potentially leading to higher inheritance tax liabilities.

To mitigate the impact of the tapered withdrawal, it is crucial for individuals to engage in effective tax planning strategies. Considering the complexity of the legislation surrounding the RNRB, seeking advice from tax professionals or estate planners is highly recommended. These experts can provide valuable guidance on optimizing the available RNRB and minimizing inheritance tax liabilities.

Additionally, spousal transfers can offer some relief in navigating the tapered withdrawal. The estate of the second spouse is entitled to claim double the RNRB available at the time of the second death [2]. This provision ensures that if the first spouse died before the RNRB came into effect and their estate exceeded £2 million, the estate of the second spouse can still benefit from an increased RNRB.

Conclusion:
Understanding and applying the tapered withdrawal of the residence nil rate band is crucial for effective inheritance tax planning in the UK. As the net value of the estate exceeds £2 million, the available RNRB diminishes, potentially leading to higher inheritance tax liabilities. By seeking professional advice and employing effective tax planning strategies, individuals can navigate the tapered withdrawal and optimize the available RNRB to minimize their inheritance tax burdens.

Please note that the information provided in this article is based on the UK tax system as of the 2023-2024 tax year and is subject to change. It is always advisable to consult with a qualified tax professional for personalized advice and up-to-date information on tax regulations and their implications.

Mitigating the Impact of Decreased Lifetime Gifts' Value: Relief Measures in the UK Taxation System

Introduction:
In the ever-evolving landscape of the UK taxation system, individuals often encounter situations where the value of their lifetime gifts decreases. This can occur due to various factors such as market fluctuations or unforeseen circumstances. To address this concern, the UK tax rules for the year 2023-2024 provide relief measures to assist taxpayers in mitigating the impact of a fall in the value of lifetime gifts. In this article, we will explore these relief measures and provide insights into their application through a hypothetical case study.

Understanding Relief Measures:
The UK tax system recognizes that individuals should not be unduly burdened by circumstances beyond their control. Therefore, relief measures are in place to offer respite when the value of lifetime gifts diminishes. These measures aim to ensure fairness and provide taxpayers with an opportunity to manage their tax liabilities more effectively.

Hypothetical Case Study: John's Estate
Let's consider a hypothetical case involving John, a UK resident, who made a substantial lifetime gift to his daughter, Emma, in the tax year 2023-2024. However, due to a significant downturn in the

market, the value of the gifted asset has dramatically decreased. As a result, John is concerned about the potential tax implications and seeks relief under the UK tax rules.

Relief Measures in Action:

Gift Relief:
Under the UK tax rules, if the value of the lifetime gift falls within a specified period, taxpayers can claim relief based on the difference between the original value and the current diminished value. This relief effectively reduces the tax liability associated with the gift, reflecting the decrease in value.

Capital Gains Tax (CGT) Relief:
If the lifetime gift falls within the scope of CGT, relief can be claimed by adjusting the base cost of the asset. By recalculating the base cost to reflect the reduced value, taxpayers can effectively reduce their CGT liability.

Carry-Back Relief:
In some cases, taxpayers may have made substantial gifts in previous tax years that have now decreased in value. The UK tax rules allow for carry-back relief, enabling individuals to revise the value of their previous gifts to account for the decrease and potentially claim a refund or reduce their tax liability for those years.

Conclusion:
The UK taxation system acknowledges that a fall in the value of lifetime gifts can have significant financial implications for individuals. To address this concern, relief measures have been incorporated into the tax rules for the year 2023-2024. These measures aim to alleviate the burden on taxpayers by providing relief in terms of reduced tax liabilities or potential refunds. By understanding and applying these relief measures appropriately, individuals like John can navigate the complexities of the UK tax system more effectively, ensuring fairness and promoting a balanced approach to taxation.

Disclaimer: The information provided in this article is for general guidance purposes only and should not be construed as professional advice. Taxpayers are advised to consult with a qualified tax professional for personalized guidance based on their specific circumstances and the prevailing tax laws and regulations.

Quick Succession Relief: Minimizing Inheritance Tax Through Successive Transfers

Introduction:
In the United Kingdom, inheritance tax (IHT) is levied on the estate of a deceased person at a rate of 40% on the value exceeding the nil-rate band threshold. However, the tax burden can be mitigated through various reliefs and exemptions, one of which is Quick Succession Relief (QSR). QSR allows for the transfer of assets at a reduced or zero rate of IHT when there are successive deaths within a short span. This article explores the operation of QSR, its benefits, and provides a hypothetical case study illustrating its application.

Understanding Quick Succession Relief:
Quick Succession Relief is designed to prevent double taxation on inherited assets when there are quick successions of deaths within a family. It aims to provide relief by reducing the IHT payable on assets that were part of a previous taxable estate. QSR applies when an individual inherits an asset and passes it on to another person within a period of five years. In such cases, the IHT paid by the first heir can be deducted from the IHT payable on the subsequent transfer, thereby minimizing the overall tax liability.

Eligibility and Conditions:
To be eligible for Quick Succession Relief, certain conditions must be met. Firstly, the second transfer must occur within five years of the first death. Secondly, the asset being transferred must form part of the deceased's estate for both transfers. Finally, the relief is limited to the value of the asset at the first death and cannot exceed the IHT paid on the first transfer.

Benefits of Quick Succession Relief:
Quick Succession Relief offers several benefits for individuals and families. By reducing the IHT liability, it allows for the preservation of family wealth and facilitates the smooth transfer of assets between generations. It can be particularly advantageous in cases where the family home or other significant assets are involved. Furthermore, QSR provides an opportunity for

individuals to plan their succession effectively, ensuring the tax burden is minimized and the intended beneficiaries receive the maximum benefit.

Hypothetical Case Study:
To illustrate the application of Quick Succession Relief, let's consider a hypothetical case. Mr. Smith, a UK resident, passed away in March 2023, leaving his estate valued at £1.5 million. His wife, Mrs. Smith, inherited the entire estate. Unfortunately, Mrs. Smith also passed away in November 2023, leaving the same estate to their son, John.

Under normal circumstances, John would face a substantial IHT liability on the inherited estate. However, due to the operation of Quick Succession Relief, the tax paid by Mrs. Smith upon inheriting the estate from Mr. Smith can be deducted from John's IHT liability. Suppose the IHT paid by Mrs. Smith was £200,000. In this case, John's IHT liability would be calculated based on the estate value of £1.5 million minus the tax paid by his mother, resulting in a reduced tax burden.

Conclusion: Quick Succession Relief is a valuable tool within the UK taxation system that allows for the minimization of IHT liability in cases of successive deaths within a family. By taking advantage of this relief, individuals can ensure the preservation of family wealth, facilitate smooth asset transfers, and provide financial security for future generations. It is important to consult with a qualified tax professional to understand the specific eligibility criteria and maximize the benefits of Quick Succession Relief within the context of personal circumstances.

Exploring Double Tax Deduction for Inheritance Tax in the UK

Introduction:
Within the context of UK's taxation framework, the concept of double tax relief proves of great significance, notably relating to inheritance tax. This article provides an in-depth exploration of double tax relief, introducing a tangible instance showcasing its practical uses and benefits. Additionally, it provides a breakdown of the newest regulations and guidelines for the fiscal year 2023-2024, with an aim to guide individuals in efficiently leveraging the

concept of double tax relief in cutting down their inheritance tax burdens.

What is Double Tax Relief?

Designed as a method to avoid having the same assets or income taxed in separate jurisdictions, double tax relief ensures individuals do not face extreme tax pressures when inheriting possessions from various countries.

How Does Double Tax Relief Work in relation to Inheritance Tax?

Generally, when an individual pass away in the UK, their global assets bear the weight of inheritance tax. Nonetheless, double tax relief arrangements are in place to alleviate the effects of double tax factors. The UK has established double tax treaties with a multitude of nations to circumvent the likelihood of double taxing of inherited assets.

In accordance with these agreements, a person who has to pay inheritance tax on overseas assets within the UK can potentially apply for a reduction in the foreign taxable amount. Usually exhibited as a credit adjustment within the UK inheritance tax liability, the overall tax demand is considerably reduced.

Hypothetical Instance:

Take the following hypothetical scenario to grasp the concept of how double tax relief truly works. Assume that, Sarah, a UK resident, inherits real estate based in France from her deceased aunt. After the property is valued at £500,000, according to both French and UK tax law Sarah must pay inheritance tax.

Given the present double tax treaty between France and the UK, Sarah is legally capable of applying for relief from the taxes due in France to offset her inheritance tax obligation in the UK. Therefore, with the French inheritance tax complied at £100,000 on her French asset, this sum can be removed from the conceivable inheritance tax due in the UK.

Given an inheritance tax rate of 40% in the UK, Sarah would originally owe £200,000 (40% of £500,000) in tax over that property. Although, following the application of the double tax relief protocol, after clearing the French tax liability, Sarah's UK inheritance tax considerably shrinks down to a more manageable bill of £100,000.

Conclusion:
In being conversant with the details pertaining to double tax relief and the specific rules for the tax year 2023-2024, individuals maneuvering through the complexity of UK's taxation system may avoid undesirable financial situations and innocuous marauding. Absolutely vital for those inheriting assets from other countries, minimizing potential fiscal obligations is navigated by efficiently tapping into relief when taxes are paid within foreign jurisdictions. Concurrent to fairness and balanced treatment towards inheriting assets, this also lays down the bricks of implication for creating more cooperative reciprocal practices of international taxation.

Estate planning and ensuring the effective transfer of assets after death calls for crucial attention towards inheritance tax. The UK levies a 40% inheritance tax on estates surpassing a value of £325,000 [1]. Nevertheless, certain methods, like varying wills, can help lessen its influence.

A will variation, otherwise known as a deed of variation, empowers beneficiaries to revise their resources from a will post death of the testator [3]. Cutting down the inheritance tax, resonation of inheritance, or catering to situational changes can motivate this step. A will variation can allow beneficiaries to shrink the inheritance tax due on their share of the estate.

An advantage of a will variation is asset redistribution amongst beneficiaries in a manner favourable for tax. If a beneficiary, for example, pays less tax than the other, a part of their inheritance can be assigned to the highly taxed beneficiary—resulting in saving for the entire estate.

Additionally, maximizing certain tax reliefs and exemptions can be realized with will variation. For example, part of one's inheritance assigned for a noble cause can benefit from a reduced 36% inheritance tax [2] through will variation, consequently lightening the estate's overall tax load.

Notably, alterations via a will variation should be done not beyond two years following the testator's death for it to implicated for tax reasons [3]. It's also important to consider total estate effects due to amendments and appropriately consult a tax expert for the UK's compliance norms.

To exemplify a potential inheritance tax influence alongside a will variation's benefits, consider Jan, a UK resident who passed away in the tax year 2023-2024, leaving a £1,000,000 estate. His original will equally divide his whole estate between his children, Sarah and Michael. However, savvy tax planning caused both of them to apply will variation for a more effective inheritance distribution.

Sarah under a higher tax slab compared to Michael agreed to shuffle £150,000 of her inheritance part to Michael with a will variation. Thus, Sarah managed to bring down her inheritance tax due while helping Michael steer clear from a higher inheritance tax on the supplemental £150,000.

The fluctuation left Sarah's inheritance at £425,000 while elevating Michael's inheritance to £725,000. Resultantly, Sarah's inheritance tax due fell from £60,000 (40% of £150,000) to £30,000 (40% of £75,000), and Michael's alike.

Ideally, in this hypothetical situation, a will variation was beneficial for Michael and Sarah to maximize their income tax situations and to utilize their inheritance in the most tax friendly manner. By adhering to UK tax legislation and not excluding professional advice, they succeeded in reducing the estate's overall tax obligation and ensuring distribution according to individual preferences and requirements.

Finally, varying wills can be instrumental in dealing with an estate's inheritance tax. Prudent asset redistribution and leveraging tax proficiencies can aid in downsizing inheritance tax liabilities. Nonetheless, it's vital to conscientiously vary wills, seek expert tax advice, and to confirm compliance with the UK tax legislation.

Maximizing Inheritance: Unlocking the Benefits of Charitable Bequests in the UK Tax System

Introduction:
In the realm of estate planning, one often encounters the complex subject of inheritance tax (IHT). However, navigating the intricacies of this tax need not be a daunting task. In the United Kingdom, individuals have the opportunity to reduce their IHT liability by bequeathing a portion of their estate to charity. This not only helps support noble causes but also enables the benefactor to take advantage of the reduced rate of IHT payable. In this article, we will delve into the benefits, rules, and implications of incorporating charitable bequests within estate planning strategies, painting a vivid picture of how these provisions play out in the UK tax system.

Understanding Inheritance Tax:
Inheritance tax is a tax levied on the estate (property, money, and possessions) of a deceased individual. As per the current UK tax rules for the 2023-2024 tax year, IHT is charged at a standard rate of 40% on the portion of the estate that exceeds the nil-rate band threshold (£325,000). However, certain exemptions and reliefs are available, including the reduced rate for charitable bequests.

The Advantages of Charitable Bequests:
When a person includes a charitable bequest in their will, the value of the gift is deducted from their estate before calculating the IHT liability. This reduction can result in significant tax savings, as the estate falls within a lower IHT bracket. In fact, bequests to charities are exempt from IHT altogether, meaning they are not subject to the 40% tax rate.
For instance, let's consider a hypothetical case to illustrate the potential tax benefits. Mr. Smith, a UK resident, has an estate valued at £1,500,000. Without any charitable bequests, his IHT liability would be calculated as follows:

Estate value: £1,500,000
Nil-rate band threshold: £325,000
Taxable estate: £1,175,000 (£1,500,000 - £325,000)
IHT liability: £470,000 (£1,175,000 × 40%)

However, if Mr. Smith were to leave 10% of his estate (£150,000) to a registered charity, his IHT liability would decrease substantially:

Taxable estate: £1,025,000 (£1,175,000 - £150,000)
IHT liability: £410,000 (£1,025,000 × 40%)

By incorporating a charitable bequest, Mr. Smith saves £60,000 in IHT, which can be directed towards a cause close to his heart.

Conditions and Considerations:
To qualify for the reduced rate of IHT, there are a few key conditions to keep in mind:
The charitable organization must be registered in the UK or within the European Economic Area (EEA).
The bequest must be stated in the will and made outright to the charity.
The bequest can be in the form of money, property, or other assets.
The charitable donation must be at least 10% of the taxable estate. It is essential to consult with a professional tax advisor or solicitor to ensure compliance with the specific rules and regulations surrounding charitable bequests. They can provide tailored guidance based on individual circumstances and help optimize the tax benefits.

Conclusion:
By incorporating charitable bequests into estate planning strategies, individuals in the UK can reduce their IHT liability while making a lasting impact on charitable causes. The reduced rate of IHT payable on bequests to registered charities offers tax advantages that can unlock significant savings. By understanding the rules and conditions surrounding charitable bequests, individuals can make informed decisions that align with their philanthropic goals and contribute to a better future while maximizing the benefits within the UK tax system.

Trust Transfer Liabilities

I) Define a trust:

A trust is a legal arrangement in which one person, known as the settlor, transfers assets or property to another person or entity, known as the trustee, for the benefit of a third person or group of people, known as the beneficiaries. The trustee holds and manages the assets on behalf of the beneficiaries according to the terms and conditions set out in the trust deed. Trusts are commonly used for estate planning, asset protection, charitable purposes, and ensuring the financial well-being of family members. They provide a means of preserving and managing wealth, while allowing for flexible distribution and control over assets.

Trusts can be revocable or irrevocable, meaning they can be modified or terminated by the settlor or are permanent, respectively. They can also be discretionary, where the trustee has the discretion to determine how and when to distribute the assets, or fixed, where the distribution is predetermined. Trusts offer various tax advantages, such as potential reductions in estate taxes, income tax planning opportunities, and protection against creditors.

In the context of the UK taxation system, trusts are subject to specific tax rules and regulations. The tax treatment of a trust depends on its type, purpose, and the nature of the assets held within it. The UK tax year 2023-2024 introduces certain changes and updates to the tax rules governing trusts. It is essential for trustees and beneficiaries to understand these rules to ensure compliance and optimize tax planning strategies.

Hypothetical Case: XYZ Family Trust

To illustrate the application of the UK tax rules for the tax year 2023-2024, let's consider a hypothetical case involving the XYZ Family Trust. The trust was established by Mr. John Smith, the settlor, for the benefit of his children, Emma and James, who are the beneficiaries. The trust holds a portfolio of stocks, rental properties, and a family business.

Under the updated tax rules for the 2023-2024 tax year, income generated by the trust's assets will be subject to income tax at the appropriate rates. The trustee is responsible for preparing and filing the trust's annual tax return, reporting all income, gains, and deductible expenses. The trustee must also consider any changes in the tax thresholds, allowances, and rates applicable to trusts for the given tax year.

Additionally, the trustee must consider the potential inheritance tax implications of the XYZ Family Trust. Inheritance tax is levied on the transfer of assets upon death or certain lifetime transfers. The tax rules specify the thresholds, exemptions, and reliefs available, which may vary depending on the relationship between the deceased and the beneficiaries. Proper estate planning and the use of trusts can help minimize the potential inheritance tax liability for the beneficiaries.

Furthermore, the XYZ Family Trust may also have implications for capital gains tax (CGT). If the trust disposes of any assets and realizes a gain, CGT may be payable. However, specific rules and exemptions apply to trusts, and the tax rates may differ from those for individuals. The trustee must carefully consider the timing and nature of any asset disposals to optimize CGT planning within the trust.

In conclusion, trusts play a crucial role in the UK taxation system, providing individuals with a flexible and efficient means of managing and distributing assets. The tax rules for trusts in the 2023-2024 tax year introduce certain changes and considerations that trustees and beneficiaries must be aware of. By understanding and adhering to these rules, individuals can optimize their tax planning strategies and ensure the effective management of trust assets.

Different Types of Trusts

There are various types of trusts, each with its own unique characteristics and purposes. Here are three common types of trusts:

Revocable Trusts: A revocable trust, also known as a living trust, allows the grantor to retain control over the assets placed in the trust during their lifetime. The grantor can modify or revoke the trust at any time. This type of trust is often used for estate planning purposes, as it allows for the seamless transfer of assets to beneficiaries after the grantor's death, bypassing the probate process.

Irrevocable Trusts: Unlike revocable trusts, irrevocable trusts cannot be modified or revoked without the consent of the beneficiaries. Once assets are transferred into an irrevocable trust, they are considered separate entities and are no longer owned by the grantor. This type of trust offers various benefits, such as asset protection, tax planning, and charitable giving.

Testamentary Trusts: A testamentary trust is created through a will and takes effect upon the grantor's death. It allows the grantor to specify how their assets should be managed and distributed to beneficiaries. Testamentary trusts are commonly used when there are minor or incapacitated beneficiaries who require ongoing financial support or when the grantor wants to delay the distribution of assets until a certain event occurs.

Each type of trust serves a specific purpose and offers distinct advantages and disadvantages. It is essential to consult with a legal professional to understand which type of trust is most suitable for your specific situation and objectives.

(Note: The above information is provided based on general knowledge and understanding of trusts. It is always advisable to consult with a qualified professional for specific legal advice regarding trusts and taxation laws in the UK.)

   In the UK, making property part of a trust can result in consequences concerning inheritance tax. Such tax is due on a person's assets upon their death. Once assets migrate into a trust, they sit outside of the individual's estate, potentially making them immune to Inheritance Tax following the person's death [2]. Nonetheless, these assets still can be targets of Inheritance Tax when they become part of a trust, upon the anniversary of a decade of the trust, or when the trust dies. In these situations, the absence within trust-associated 'relevant property' — money, shares, property, or land [1] — is where the tax hits. Belongings beyond the exemption threshold face a default tax rate of 40%, this drops to 36% if the individual bequeaths more than 10% of their estate to charity through their will [1].

The precise nature of the trust could also alter the application of Inheritance Tax rules. Trusts of some kinds, including bare trusts and interest in possession trusts, come with unique Inheritance Tax guidelines [1]. For trusts intended for grieving minors and disabled beneficiaries, it is important to note that there are exceptional terms [1]. It is critical to understand the tax implications when you want to make transfers of assets into a trust. To navigate the maze of rules and regulations applicable to trust-associated Inheritance Tax, professional advice is strongly suggested [2]. With professional consultation, individuals have a stronger capacity to manage their assets effectively, lower tax loads and offer their beneficiaries an adequate level of asset protection [2].

Let's use a fictional example to study the inheritance-tax-related consequences of moving property into a trust. Imagine that in the 2023-2024 fiscal year, a Mr. Smith moves property worth £500,000 into a discretionary trust. The current limit for Inheritance Tax stands at £325,000 [2]. Considering that the property's worth accurately warrants an immediate application of Inheritance Tax since the worth marches over the bar. The standard tax rate is 40% taxed on the amount over the bar. Yet, if Mr. Smith decides to leave over 10% of his assets to charity in his will, the tax rate goes down to 36% [1].

What must be stated is that this calculation strictly respects the Inheritance Tax rates and ceilings of the 2023-2024 fiscal year alone. Future adjustments to these rates and thresholds, if so they assumed, so individuals are better off consulting the most recent guidelines from HMRC or obtain professional tax advice for precise computation.

Rounding off, inheritance tax consequences present an inherent risk while moving property into a trust. It is key to grasp all the regulatory info around Inheritance Tax and trusts to handle your estate capably while also lowering your tax burdens. Averting complications within the UK's intricate tax landscape is best done by procuring professional advice [2].

Inheritance tax can be confusing and complex for many people, but it's important to understand its role in personal finance and future planning. One way to mitigate the impact of inheritance tax is by setting up a trust. A trust is an effective way to pass assets to family members, significantly minimizing tax complications. It is a legally binding arrangement that involves lending money, property, or investments to others for the benefit of the beneficiaries. Key roles in a trust include the trustee who handles the assets, and the beneficiary who reaps the benefits. An added benefit of a trust is that the assets held within it are not part of your estate, protecting them from inheritance tax when you die.

Since there are many different types of trusts, each with their own rules and regulations, selecting the right one will depend on individual circumstances and requirements. Some trusts, like bare trusts or interest in possession trusts, have specific rules for inheritance tax. Others may have their own individual tax rules.

Trust assets are not subject to inheritance tax during your lifetime, with those assets remaining for beneficiaries. However, inheritance tax may still be due with assets moving in or out of the trust or after 10 years. Therefore, it's crucial to seek professional guidance when setting up a trust, in order to be well-informed about any tax liabilities and obligations.

Consider this scenario: A UK resident, John, recently inherited £500,000. In an effort to pass this on to his children in the most tax-efficient way, he sets up a discretionary trust with the £500,000. The trust is professionally managed and his children are named as the primary beneficiaries. The trust operates independently of John's estate, meaning his assets are not taxed during his lifetime or upon his death. However, various tax implications affect the trust's operation, depending on factors like profit margin, overall revenue, and investment earnings.

Trust tax law can be complicated and can change unexpectedly. That's why professional tax expertise or financial consultancy is key for potential trustees, so they can manage financial outcomes effectively. To conclude, setting up a trust, while a practical financial strategy, is complex. Nevertheless, with proper understanding and careful financial decisions, it can greatly safeguard loved ones and protect your financial legacy. Trusts allow future generations to benefit from secure assets of great sentimental value.

In the UK, trustees may be required to pay inheritance tax on certain occasions. When assets are held in a trust, inheritance tax is payable by trustees in the following scenarios:

When assets are transferred into the trust: If a settlor transfers asset into a trust, inheritance tax may be due. The value of the transfer is considered a gift and is subject to inheritance tax if it exceeds the available exemptions and thresholds.

When certain events occur within the trust: Inheritance tax may be payable by trustees when certain events occur within the trust. For example, if a beneficiary receives a distribution from the trust, or if the trust reaches a certain anniversary, inheritance tax may be due on the value of the assets involved.

When assets are transferred out of the trust: If assets are transferred out of the trust, inheritance tax may be payable by the trustees. The tax liability will depend on the value of the assets transferred and the available exemptions and thresholds.

It is important for trustees to seek professional tax advice or consult HMRC to determine their inheritance tax obligations and ensure compliance with the UK tax rules. Each situation is unique, and the tax implications can vary based on the specific circumstances involved. Therefore, it is advisable to obtain personalized advice to accurately assess the inheritance tax liability for trustees.

Tax exemptions and reliefs

Understanding the UK's complex taxation system, particularly in regard to inheritance tax, can help ensure your heirs receive the maximum value of your estate. Utilising secondary benefits and disregards may further decrease the amount of taxable inheritance. A common detail to note is the marriage or civil partnership exemption, permitting a tax-free transition of complete estate possession to your spouse or civil partner. This exemption doesn't have a monetary limit and can theoretically cover the entire estate. However, only spouses or civil partners permanently residing in the UK are eligible. One can also take advantage of the annual exemption, allowing inheritance tax-free gifts below a certain annual cap, currently set at £3,000 for the 2023-2024 tax year, with additional reductions attainable under specific circumstances.

There are regulations that might provide certain tax benefits to commercial assets, with portions of privately-owned enterprises potentially exempt from taxation if they meet certain criteria, such the business being held for at least two years and actively trading.

By applying a mixture of tax deductions and good estate management, beneficial financial results can be achieved. Expert legal and tax advice can reveal the most suitable strategies. For instance, consider a hypothetical UK domiciled Mr. Smith, who has an estate worth £1.5 million. Assuming his survivors include his spouse, who is UK resident, and two kids, he could utilize the spousal exemption to pass on his entire estate tax-free. Furthermore, his annual gifts of £3,000 to each of his children, totaling £6,000, avoid taxation. If he owns a private business the value, assuming it meets regulations, could be partially sheltered from tax due to relevant business property reliefs.

A better understanding and strategic use of tax exemptions and deductions can provide peace of mind and minimalize your estate's inheritance tax liabilities. Professional guidance should be sought to ensure tax-efficient future inheritance planning.

Inheritance tax administration simplified

In the UK, there are certain occasions on which inheritance tax may be paid by instalments. One such occasion is when an individual inherits a property that qualifies for the Residential Nil Rate Band (RNRB). The RNRB allows for additional tax relief on the main residence, provided certain conditions are met. If the value of the estate exceeds the available RNRB, the excess amount can be paid in equal instalments over a period of up to ten years. This can help ease the financial burden on beneficiaries who may not have sufficient funds to pay the entire tax liability upfront.

Another occasion where instalments may be allowed is when an individual inherits a business or shares in an unlisted company. In such cases, if the assets qualify for Business Relief or Agricultural Relief, the inheritance tax can be paid by instalments over a period of up to ten years. This allows for the preservation of the business or farm, as the tax payment can be spread out over time.

It is important to note that interest will be charged on the outstanding tax balance, and the payment of instalments must be made within the specified timeframes to avoid penalties. Additionally, if the inherited property or business is sold before the full tax liability is paid, the remaining balance becomes due immediately.

In summary, the UK tax system allows for the payment of inheritance tax by instalments in certain circumstances, such as when inheriting a property eligible for the Residential Nil Rate Band or when inheriting a business or shares that qualify for Business Relief or Agricultural Relief. These instalments help alleviate the financial burden on beneficiaries and allow for the preservation of assets. However, it is crucial to adhere to the payment deadlines and be aware of the interest charges and potential penalties associated with late or non-payment.

Inheritance tax in the UK is charged on someone's estate after they've passed away. The times that this tax needs to be paid fluctuates depending on the situation. Generally, if the estate has an inheritance tax imposed, it needs to be declared to HM Revenue and Customs within six months after the person died. The tax would typically be payable within this six-month timeframe. However, special scenarios and tax reliefs may extend the due dates and decrease the tax liability, and in some instances remove it altogether.

Interest charged on late inheritance tax payments stands at 2.6% yearly. If payment is late, interest is charged on what remains unpaid. Penalties might also apply for paying or disclosing the tax past the due date. The penalty is calculated based on the hold-up period and the estate's value.

Let's display the tax rules for the 2023-2024 taxable year in the UK using a hypothetical case. Let's say a man named John dies and leaves an estate worth £2 million — he has a primary residence valued at £1.5 million, investments amounting to £300,000, and personal belongings enriched to £200,000.

The current rules state an inheritance tax exemption — the nil-rate band — is set at £325,000 per person, meaning John's estate above the threshold will be taxed at 40%.

There could be tax reliefs applied to decrease inheritance tax though. John's primary residence, under the residence nil-rate band, could an avail an extra £175,000 exemption per individual for the 2023-2024 tax year — and this may be passed onto a living partner, hence raising the nil-rate band.

Other reliefs like the business property relief or agricultural estate relief can further cut down the taxable assets within the estate.

To calculate what John would owe, one must contemplate the estate's value and the exemptions and tax rates. It's crucial to work with a certified tax advisor or refer to the HM Revenue & Customs regulations to confirm that information is accurate and recent.

In conclusion, inheritance tax is a nuanced British tax field notable for its particular deadlines, interest charges, and penalties. A thorough reading of the regulations and following them properly is quintessential for fulfilling the regulations and controlling your tax repercussions. You should seek tax counsel to effectively guide you through the process.

Overseas corporation tax complexities

The scope of corporation tax

Corporate tax is a form of taxation imposed on the profits earned by corporations. In the United Kingdom, resident companies are subject to tax on their worldwide profits, while non-resident companies are taxed on certain profits related to UK activities. The current general corporation tax rate is 19% but is set to increase to 25% in 2023 [2].

When it comes to companies with investment business, the calculation of corporation tax involves considering the taxable profits generated from these activities. The taxable income is determined by deducting allowable expenses from the revenue earned. Allowable expenses may include costs directly related to the investment business, such as management fees, professional fees, and interest payments on loans used for investment purposes.

To illustrate this with a hypothetical case, let's consider a UK-based company engaged in investment business. In the tax year 2023-2024, the company generates a revenue of £1,000,000 from its investment activities. The allowable expenses incurred for the same period amount to £250,000. Therefore, the taxable profits for the company's investment business would be £750,000 (£1,000,000 - £250,000).

Applying the current corporation tax rate of 19%, the corporation tax liability for the investment business would be £142,500 (£750,000 x 19%). It is important to note that this computation is based on the current tax rules for the UK tax year 2023-2024 and the given information [2].

In conclusion, corporate tax is a crucial component of the UK taxation system. For companies engaged in investment business, the calculation of corporation tax involves determining the taxable profits by subtracting allowable expenses from the revenue generated. By understanding and adhering to the relevant tax rules and rates, companies can ensure compliance with the UK tax authorities while effectively managing their tax liabilities.

Situation 1:
A close company refers to a company that is owned and controlled by a small group of individuals, usually family members or close associates. These individuals have significant influence over the company's decisions and operations. Close companies are subject to specific tax rules in the UK.

A close company, within the realm of UK taxation, embodies an entity that finds its roots in the familial or closely-knit associations of individuals. It is a corporate structure where a limited group of individuals, often bonded by blood or deep bonds of camaraderie, wield substantial sway over the company's affairs. As per the UK tax system, close companies are subject to a distinct set of regulations and obligations.

Situation 2:
Another example of a close company is a business founded by two siblings who hold all the shares and actively participate in the decision-making process. Since the company is controlled by a small group of individuals with family ties, it falls under the category of a close company for taxation purposes in the UK.

Let us envisage a scenario wherein a venture, conceived by two siblings, materializes into a close company. These siblings, being the sole shareholders, intricately engage themselves in the company's strategic determinations. Given the familial bond that unites them, this enterprise assumes the character of a close company in accordance with the UK taxation framework. Thus, it becomes subject to the nuanced tax provisions that govern such entities in the United Kingdom.

Please note that the tax computation and hypothetical case you requested would require specific instructions and details to generate an accurate response. If you can provide the necessary information, I would be happy to assist you further in creating a comprehensive answer based on UK tax rules for the year 2023-2024.

Tax Implications of Close Companies and Close Investment Holding Companies in the UK

Introduction:
In the United Kingdom, the tax implications for companies can vary depending on their classification as a close company or a close investment holding company. Understanding these distinctions is crucial for businesses to effectively manage their tax obligations. This article aims to provide a comprehensive overview of the tax implications associated with these company types, utilizing the UK tax rules for the 2023-2024 tax year.

Close Companies:
A close company refers to a privately-owned company with five or fewer shareholders, who possess a substantial interest in the company's share capital. The tax implications for close companies differ from those of other types of companies.

Corporation Tax:
Close companies are subject to corporation tax on their profits, just like any other company. However, there are specific rules that apply to close companies, such as the treatment of loans to participators and distributions made to shareholders. These rules aim to prevent tax avoidance by closely held companies.

Dividend Tax:
When a close company distributes profits to its shareholders in the form of dividends, the shareholders may be subject to dividend tax. This tax is applicable to individuals receiving dividends above their tax-free dividend allowance, which is £2,000 for the 2023-2024 tax year.

Loans to Participators:
Close companies need to be cautious when providing loans or advances to their directors or shareholders. If such loans are not repaid within nine months of the company's year-end, the company may incur a tax charge known as the "section 455 tax." This charge is refundable once the loan is repaid.

Close Investment Holding Companies:
A close investment holding company (CIHC) is a specific type of close company that mainly holds investments rather than

conducting active trading activities. CIHCs are subject to additional tax implications due to their nature as investment-focused entities.

Investment Income:
CIHCs are subject to corporation tax on their investment income, which includes dividends, interest, and rental income. This tax is levied at the standard corporation tax rate, which for the 2023-2024 tax year is 19%.

Capital Gains Tax (CGT):
Close investment holding companies are also liable for capital gains tax on any gains arising from the disposal of their investments. The rate of CGT depends on the type of asset being disposed of and the overall taxable gains of the company.

Hypothetical Case Study: XYZ Ltd.

To illustrate the tax implications of close companies and CIHCs, let's consider the case of XYZ Ltd., a close company operating as a CIHC. XYZ Ltd. holds a diverse portfolio of investments, including shares and rental properties.

In the 2023-2024 tax year, XYZ Ltd. earns a total investment income of £200,000, consisting of £150,000 in dividends and £50,000 in rental income. The company's capital gains from the sale of shares amount to £100,000.

Based on the UK tax rules for the 2023-2024 tax year, XYZ Ltd. would be subject to corporation tax at a rate of 19% on its investment income of £200,000. This would result in a tax liability of £38,000.

Additionally, XYZ Ltd. would be required to calculate the capital gains tax on the £100,000 gain from the sale of shares. The rate of capital gains tax would depend on the nature of the shares and the company's overall taxable gains.

Conclusion:
Understanding the tax implications of being a close company or a close investment holding company is essential for businesses operating in the United Kingdom. Close companies are subject to

specific rules regarding corporation tax, dividend tax, and loans to participators. Close investment holding companies have additional considerations like investment income taxation and capital gains tax. By adhering to the relevant tax regulations and seeking professional advice when needed, companies can effectively manage their tax obligations and optimize their financial performance in the ever-evolving UK tax landscape.

Accounting periods play a significant role in the administration and winding up of a business. Firstly, accounting periods provide a structured timeframe during which financial transactions are recorded, summarized, and analyzed. This allows for the efficient management of financial data and aids in decision-making processes. By dividing the financial year into specific periods, businesses can monitor their financial performance, identify trends, and make necessary adjustments.

In the context of winding up a business, accounting periods are crucial for tax purposes. When a business is being wound up, its financial affairs need to be settled, and tax liabilities must be determined. The accounting period helps in calculating the taxable income for the relevant period and assessing the tax liability accordingly. The accurate determination of tax obligations during the winding-up process ensures compliance with the UK tax rules and regulations.

Additionally, accounting periods impact the distribution of profits during winding up. In the UK, the distribution of profits is subject to capital gains tax and income tax. The accounting period determines the tax rates and allowances applicable to these distributions. As a result, businesses must carefully consider the timing of winding up to optimize tax planning and minimize tax liabilities for both the company and its shareholders.

Furthermore, accounting periods are crucial for maintaining accurate financial records, which are essential during the winding-up process. By adhering to proper accounting practices and using the relevant accounting standards, businesses can ensure that their financial statements provide a true and fair view of their financial position. This is particularly important when dealing with creditors, shareholders, and other stakeholders during the winding-up procedure.

In summary, accounting periods have significant implications for the administration and winding up of a business. They provide a structured framework for financial reporting and analysis, aid in tax calculations and planning, and ensure the accuracy and transparency of financial records. By understanding and adhering to the UK tax rules and regulations regarding accounting periods, businesses can effectively manage their financial affairs during the winding-up process and fulfill their tax obligations.

In the UK, multiple factors dictate the tax liabilities of shareholder returns after the commencement of a company's winding-up process. In usual circumstances, a company's assets are liquidated to settle debts when it undergoes winding up. Any remaining funds are shared among the shareholders. Tax involved with these distributions could vary based on their interpretation as capital or income.

Capital distributions may attract Capital Gains Tax (CGT). This is a tax imposed on gains made from the sale/disposal of an asset. The tax rate hinges upon the taxpayer's income tax level. A basic rate tax payer must pay the current CGT of 10%, whereas higher and additional tax rate individuals pay 20%, applicable from the 2023-2024 tax year.

Alternatively, when the distributions are perceived as income, they might incur an income tax. This is a tax on individual earnings, including dividends from shareholdings. The income tax rates also rely on your income tax bracket. A basic rate taxpayer needs to pay a 20% income tax, and higher taxpayers must pay either 40% or 45% for the additional taxpayers, as per the current rules in the 2023-2024 tax year.

It must be highlighted that dealing with tax affairs of shareholder returns after a company's winding-up is complex. Therefore, consulting tax experts or accountants for professional help on complying with specific UK tax rules, relative to the wading-up circumstances, is recommended. Since tax regulations and rates may update over time, referring individuals should always adhere to recent information provisions by HM Revenue and Customs (HMRC) or consult tax professionals to learn about latest tax policies and calculations.

In the UK, certain rules and regulations govern the tax consequences of a company buying its own shares. The tax treatment for an enterprise that purchases its own stocks is classified as an "unquoted company purchase of own shares", from a taxation perspective. Depending on whether these shares are held as treasury stocks or cancelled, the taxation approach differs.

When such shares are annulled, a tax known as the "repurchase tax" must be paid by the company. The tax is calculated against the marginal value of the stocks being bought back, and cannot be deducted from corporation tax liabilities.

In cases where the shares are held back as treasury shares for re-selling later, the tax norms differ based on the timing of sale. When these treasury shares are sold off within one year of their purchase, any profits or losses are subject to tax on income. However, selling the shares after one year subjects the profits or losses to the capital gains tax.

Naturally, varying specific situations may lead to a different tax treatment when a company seeds to purchase its own stocks. Thus, companies are always advised to consult with tax professionals to ensure they are adhering to all relevant tax regulations.

The personal service companies (PSCs) are entities that supply services via an individual contractor, who is concurrently the director and owner of the firm. This setup is often utilized by freelancers, consultants, and persons catering to a restricted clientele. In the United Kingdom, the tax regime treats PSCs differently from other business setups, making it crucial to understand the tax implications of functioning as a PSC.

Functioning as a PSC has its benefits, with the main advantage being tax efficiency. This is because the directors and shareholders of PSCs can be paid in dividends, attracting lower tax charges compared to ordinary income. Meanwhile, efforts to curb PSC misuse have led to the introduction of rules like the off-payroll working laws, requiring medium-to-big businesses to determine whether their contractors ought to be accounted for as employees when setting tax assessments.

The provision of services through a PSC requires that the association between the company and its clientele is genuinely self-employed. This prevents potential liabilities if an employment-based relationship is established by the relevant authorities. The PSC would then become susceptible to 'employee taxes' such as National Insurance contributions and PAYE. The IR35 regulation aimed to prevent PSCs from evading employment taxes, covering contracts in which the service provider would essentially be an employee if individually retained by the client.

By analyzing a fictitious case of a freelance graphic designer operating via a PSC, one can better understand these tax implications. Let's say the designer, also the firm's sole director and shareholder, pulls revenue of £100,000 and accrues expenses of £20,000, taking an annual salary of £12,500 and dividends totaling £37,500. As per the 2023-2024 UK tax rules, the firm would have to settle corporation tax from its £67,500 profit. This GB£12,825 charge would be taxed at 19%. The director's £12,500 salary would be subjected to income tax and National Insurance payments, and the £37,500 dividends would come under divisor tax.

Crucially, the director's £15,000 personal allowance is subtracted from his/her salary for tax calculation, resulting in an income tax liability of £1,500. The dividends, in keeping with the 7.5% taxation rate, then register a tax liability of £2,813.

To sum it up, while operating as a PSC can be financially attractive to freelancers and consultants due to tax benefits, one must ensure that this setup is truly reflexive of a self-employed relationship with clients. Considering the complex nature of UK PSC tax laws, and that it is subject to change, advice from a professional is suggested-default to navigate the current regulations.

Taxable total profits

Qualifying research and development (R&D) expenditure for small or medium-sized enterprises (SMEs) includes both capital and revenue costs. SMEs can deduct an additional 86% of their qualifying costs from their yearly profit when claiming R&D tax relief [2]. This relief is designed to support companies engaged in innovative projects in science and technology. Moreover, SMEs can claim a payable tax credit worth up to 10% of the surrender able loss if they meet the standard definition of R&D. To be eligible for the relief, a company must be an SME with fewer than 500 staff, a turnover under 100 million euros, or a balance sheet total under 86 million euros. It is important to note that linked and partner enterprises are also considered when determining SME status [2].

In the UK, qualifying costs that may be claimed for R&D tax relief include consumables, payments to subjects of clinical trials, data and cloud computing costs, and staff costs directly involved in the R&D project [2]. However, there are certain conditions and restrictions to be aware of. For example, the company must not receive excessive state aid or subcontract the R&D work. These regulations help ensure that the relief is targeted towards genuine R&D activities. It is crucial for SMEs to carefully analyze their expenditures and meet the specific criteria outlined by the UK taxation system to qualify for the R&D tax relief [2].

Hypothetically, let's consider a case study for a small technology company based in the UK. ABC Tech Ltd. is an SME with 250 employees and an annual turnover of £80 million for the tax year 2023-2024. The company has been actively involved in developing innovative software solutions for the healthcare industry. During this tax year, ABC Tech Ltd. incurs qualifying R&D costs of £1.5 million, including staff salaries, consumables, and cloud computing expenses.

Based on the UK tax rules for 2023-2024, ABC Tech Ltd. can claim an additional 86% of their qualifying R&D expenditure, which amounts to £1.29 million (£1.5 million x 86%). This deduction will be applied to the company's yearly profit calculation, reducing their taxable profit by this amount. Additionally, if ABC Tech Ltd. incurs a surrender able loss as a result of their R&D activities, they can claim a payable tax credit worth up to 10% of this loss.

In this case, if ABC Tech Ltd. incurs a surrender able loss of £500,000, they can claim a payable tax credit of up to £50,000 (£500,000 x 10%). This payable tax credit can be used to offset the company's tax liabilities or be received as a cash payment if the company has no tax liabilities.

By taking advantage of the R&D tax relief, ABC Tech Ltd. can significantly reduce their tax burden and allocate more resources towards further innovation and growth. It is important for SMEs to consult with tax professionals and ensure they meet all the necessary criteria and documentation requirements to maximize their eligibility for R&D tax relief under the UK taxation system.

In the UK taxation system, the treatment of non-trading deficits on loan relationships depends on whether it is a trade or non-trade loan relationship [3]. Non-trading deficits (NTDs) occur when a company's debits on its non-trading loan relationships and derivative contracts exceed the credits in a given accounting period [2]. To calculate loan relationship debits and credits, companies need to consider the specific tax rules [3].

When it comes to claiming relief for NTDs, companies can utilize them by offsetting them against their current year profits. However, it's important to note that relief for NTDs can only be claimed after offsetting any trading losses brought forward, provided those trading losses arose prior to April 1, 2017 [2].

Let's consider a hypothetical case to better understand the tax treatment of non-trading deficits on loan relationships. Imagine a company, ABC Ltd., with non-trading loan relationship deficits of £100,000 in the tax year 2023-2024. The company also has trading losses brought forward from previous years amounting to £50,000.

According to the UK tax rules for the tax year 2023-2024, ABC Ltd. can claim relief for the non-trading deficits by offsetting them against their current year profits. However, before doing so, they must first offset the trading losses brought forward. In this case, ABC Ltd. would deduct the £50,000 trading losses from the non-trading deficits of £100,000, leaving a remaining non-trading deficit of £50,000.

After offsetting the trading losses, ABC Ltd. can claim relief for the remaining non-trading deficit of £50,000 against their current year profits. This relief will reduce their taxable income, resulting in a lower tax liability for the company.

It's important for companies to accurately calculate and utilize their non-trading deficits on loan relationships to optimize their tax position. Seeking professional advice from tax experts or consulting the HM Revenue and Customs (HMRC) guidelines is recommended to ensure compliance with the UK tax regulations.

The impending UK tax year 2023-2024 is prompting debates among businesses of various sectors and sizes about the diverse treatments of intangible assets - patents, trademarks, copyrights, franchises and goodwill. While crucial to businesses due to the competitive edge they offer in today's information-based marketplace, tax treatments of these assets often pose challenges leading different companies to choose unique approaches according to their strategic needs.

The Corporation Tax Act 2009, part 8 in the UK, provides provisions for intangible asset tax treatment, influencing a company's financial architecture greatly. However, this area, like other tax domains, invites complex situations. We consider two hypothetical companies - TechTrends (technology-oriented) and TradON (traditional business) to understand how different businesses may necessitate unique intangible asset treatments in the forthcoming tax year.

TechTrends, a tech-centered company, predominantly values its intangible assets like technology copyrights, patents, and software codes. They commonly enjoy tax relief on R&D expenditure. Yet, TechTrends need to meet HMRC's strict "new" asset development criteria to claim tax deductions for the asset's amortization or impairment based on the accounting treatment.

Hence, for Tax Year 2023-2024, TechTrends can benefit from capitalizing their R&D costs for new technology or software development, securing its amortization and tax relief over the newly developed asset's lifespan.

Conversely, TradON, a traditional trader, may depend more on intangible assets like goodwill or trademarks. A UK tax law permits companies to deduct goodwill and customer-related intangible asset amortization costs for tax purposes when acquired after 1st April 2019. Thus, TradON could claim major tax deductions if it purchases a trademark or proves its goodwill value in tax year 2023-2024.

In Tax Year 2023-2024, if TradON acquired a business with notable goodwill worth £1,000,000 lasting 10 years, TradON can deduct the £100,000 p.a. amortization accounting from their taxable profits, decreasing their tax liability.

The above cases emphasize how companies can leverage tax rules concerning intangible assets effectively. However, UK tax law complexities demand meticulous study and navigation of pertinent rules and regulations, backed with accurate documentation and professional advice to reap maximum benefits while complying. While TechTrends may prefer capitalizing R&D costs and TradON may consider goodwill and trademark amortization, the best tactic predominantly depends on their respective situations and strategic views, indicating there isn't a standard method for intangible asset tax treatment.

Key Tax Treatments of Intangible Assets:

Intangible assets in the UK generally undergo two primary tax treatments: capital allowances and deductions for revenue expenditure. They differ in how and when intangible asset-associated costs get deducted from taxable profits.

Capital Allowances:

Capital allowances offer tax relief, enabling companies to deduct the cost of purchasing or creating an intangible asset from their taxable profits, spread over the "writing down period". In the tax year 2023-2024, intangible assets usually have a five-year writing down period (may vary for certain types). The deduction amount gets calculated based on the asset cost and writing down period.

Deductions for Revenue Expenditure:

These deductions permit companies to deduct costs related to maintaining or enhancing intangible assets from their taxable profits, incurring in the same year. They include legal fees, advertising expenses, and research and development costs.

Illustrative Case Study:

Let's consider an illustrative case with two UK-based tech sector-companies: Company X and Company Y. Company X recently acquired a patent for innovative software, while Company Y spent heavily on R&D to develop a groundbreaking technology platform.

Company X can apply for capital allowances for the patent acquisition cost. They can deduct a part of the acquisition cost from taxable profits yearly over a five-year writing down period, reducing their taxable profits and tax liability.

On the other hand, Company Y could claim deductions for revenue expenditure due to R&D costs. They can deduct the entire cost amount from taxable profits, immediately enjoying tax relief, offsetting the costs and reducing their tax liability that year.

Best Treatment Selection:

The best treatment for intangible assets banks on the companies' individual cases and objectives. Capital allowances provide Company X with steady and predictable impact on profits and tax liabilities by spreading the patent acquisition cost over five years. For Company Y, deductions for revenue expenditure prove more beneficial as the immediate R&D cost deductions offer timely tax relief, reducing that year's tax liability, leading to potential further growth or investment.

Introduction

When exploring the complex UK tax system, it's hard to ignore two significant components: transfer pricing and thin capitalization rules. These regulations aim to maintain transparency and fairness in companies' transaction pricing and capital management. It's crucial for companies operating in the UK to comprehend the implications of these rules to avoid potential penalties and reputational harm. This article delves into the implications of transfer pricing and thin capitalisation rules in the UK for the tax year 2023-2024.

Transfer Pricing:

Transfer pricing is the system used to price transactions between interrelated entities, such as parent companies and their subsidiaries. The UK adheres to the Organisation for Economic Co-operation and Development (OECD) guidelines in determining transfer prices. Transfer pricing rules endeavor to make sure that intercompany transactions are conducted at arm's length, implying that prices are comparable to those in transactions between independent entities.

For businesses, the impact of these rules is twofold. Firstly, they must confirm that their policies align with the arm's length principle. This necessitates a comprehensive review of comparable transactions and pricing methods to establish the correct transfer pricing. Failure to comply could result in adjustments to taxable profits, leading to extra tax liabilities and potential fines.

Secondly, these rules can affect how profits are allocated among affiliated entities. Careful consideration of the functions, assets and risks associated with each entity within a transaction is necessary to ensure profits are allocated based on individual contributions. Neglecting to comply can result in challenges from tax authorities and possible disputes.

Hypothetical Case Study:

Consider the hypothetical instance of Company X, a UK multinational corporation with global subsidiaries. The company makes electronic devices and sells them to its subsidiaries. The transfer pricing rules necessitate that Company X establishes suitable pricing for these transactions.

In the tax year 2023-2024, Company X must carry out a transfer pricing analysis to confirm compliance with the arm's length principle. This analysis involves identifying comparable transactions between unrelated parties to select a suitable pricing methodology. These pricing methods ensure pricing is consistent with similar, unrelated transactions, complying with the guidelines and reducing the risk of profit adjustment.

Thin Capitalisation:

Thin capitalisation rules are designed to prohibit companies from relying excessively on debt financing. These rules strive to ensure that companies maintain a reasonable balance of debt and equity to reduce tax avoidance via excessive interest deductions.

For companies, the impact of thin capitalisation rules is primarily monetary. Those exceeding the prescribed debt-equity ratio may have limitations on interest expense deductions, leading to increased taxable profits and tax liabilities. To document and demonstrate their debt-equity ratios, companies may face higher compliance costs.

Hypothetical Case Study:

Continuing with the hypothetical example of Company X, the effects of the thin capitalisation rules are clear. In the 2023-2024 tax year, Company X decided to finance its operations through a mix of debt and equity, but it exceeded the UK's thin capitalisation rules' debt-equity ratio.

Consequently, the company faces restrictions on interest expense deductions associated with excessive debt, leading to higher taxable profits and tax liabilities. To alleviate the impact of thin capitalisation rules, Company X may opt to reduce its debt levels or increase its equity.

Exploring the Role of Losses During Ownership Transitions: A Study on the UK Tax System

In the UK, the domestic tax system rules extend beyond static issues, reaching into dynamic areas such as changes in company ownership. Specifically, under these rules, there are applicable restrictions on utilising losses following significant alterations in ownership. For clarity, a 'loss' refers to instances where a company's taxable income dips below zero, affecting its liability for corporation tax. Whereas, a 'change in ownership' is when over 50% of the company's shares are transferred to new owners.

These changes can cause complications, especially concerning the application of losses carried over from past accounting periods. In this article, we will shed light on these complexities, focusing on the UK tax year 2023-2024.

The UK Tax Rules on Ownership Change and Loss Transfer

Primarily, UK tax rules place certain restrictions on companies carrying forward trading losses after an ownership change. These restrictions are in place to avoid companies from acquiring others simply for using their tax losses.

When a company is sold and has losses that it can carry forward, if its trade changes in nature or conduct within the following three years, it will not be able to offset these losses against future profits. This rule plays a significant role in preventing fiscal exploitation, allowing only legitimate businesses to take advantage of the loss relief.

A Theoretical Application

Take a company named "Alpha Ltd." for instance. Ending the UK tax year on 5 April 2024, Alpha Ltd reports a trading loss of £300k. On 1 May, the company undergoes an ownership change. The new management team decides to shift from bespoke furniture to vintage clothing trade while continuing to use the company's losses.

Under the UK tax rules of 2023-2024, there will be a restriction on using preceding losses. Since significant changes were made to the trade within three years after the ownership change, Alpha Ltd would not be able to offset its £300k trade loss from the profits made from its vintage clothing business. The new trade is considered greatly different from the initial furniture business.

Handling Exceptions

However, there are exceptions. If there are no major changes in the nature or conduct of trade, the losses can be transferred as long as there is no more than a three-year gap in trading before reclaiming the losses.

Consider "Beta Ltd", a company that has experienced a change in ownership but continues carrying out its original trade of producing stationery supplies. In this instance, Beta Ltd will be allowed to carry forward their losses and offset them against future profits, since there has been no significant shift in its trade after the change in ownership.

Final Remarks

Understanding the restrictions on utilising losses following company ownership changes is essential, not only for those involved in the transaction, but also for tax professionals advising on the tax consequences. Always recall that individual circumstances must be considered, and the complexity of the UK tax law, particularly the rules from the UK tax year 2023-2024, must be correctly comprehended for appropriate use.

These rules help maintain a balance between aiding businesses to grow and preventing corporations from exploiting tax reliefs. Consequently, it's always wise to seek tax consultancy services or carry out a thorough review when maneuvering these intricate tax laws during business transitions.

Introduction

Under the UK tax system, restrictions exist on the application of carried forward trading losses and capital losses for companies whose profits surpass £5 million. The objective of these restrictions is to prevent larger companies from excessively profiting from loss-relief provisions and to ensure an equitable tax position. For companies with profits exceeding £5 million, understanding these restrictions is essential as they can significantly impact tax planning and financial strategies. This article will outline the specific restrictions on carried forward trading losses and capital losses for such companies in the context of the UK tax system, specifically for the tax year 2023-2024.

Carried Forward Trading Losses Restrictions:

Carried forward trading losses are losses a company accrues across previous accounting cycles that can be used to offset future profits, thereby reducing tax liabilities. However, for companies with profits exceeding £5 million, limitations exist regarding the quantity of these losses that can be applied within a single accounting period.

As outlined by the UK Corporation Tax Act 2010, for companies with profits over £5 million, the proportion of carried forward trading losses that can be offset against profits is capped at 50% of profits exceeding the £5 million limit. Thus, only half of the profits above this threshold can be mitigated using the carried forward trading losses.

To illustrate this, let's consider a hypothetical case of Company X, a UK-based manufacturing company with profits of £7 million in the tax year 2023-2024. Company X has £2 million in carried forward trading losses. According to the restriction, only 50% of profits exceeding £5 million (£2 million) can be offset by carried forward trading losses. Thus, Company X can use £1 million of the carried forward trading losses to decrease its taxable profits to £6 million.

Capital Losses Restrictions:

Capital losses are losses a company incurs from the sale of capital assets, like property, investments, or equipment. Similar to carried forward trading losses, limitations exist on the application of capital losses for companies with profits surpassing £5 million.

For companies with profits over £5 million, capital losses are regulated similar to carried forward trading losses. The volume of capital losses that can be offset against profits is capped at 50% of profits exceeding £5 million.

Using the hypothetical example of Company X, suppose that the company experiences capital losses of £1 million after selling an investment property. Under the restriction, only 50% of profits exceeding £5 million (£2 million) can be offset by capital losses. Therefore, Company X can apply £1 million of its capital losses to decrease its taxable profits to £6 million.

The comprehensive calculation of the corporation tax liability

Introduction:

The OECD Model Tax Convention on Income and on Capital is an international framework that guides the creation of double taxation treaties between nations. These treaties are meant to stop double taxation and delineate how taxing rights are shared amongst nations. In the United Kingdom, the impact of the OECD's model double taxation treaty on corporation tax is considerable, as it paves the way for international trade and investment, mitigates tax obstacles, and advocates for economic collaboration. This analysis will appraise the impact of the OECD model double tax treaty on corporation tax in the UK, factoring in the UK's tax rules for the fiscal year 2023-2024.

Impact of the OECD Model Double Tax Treaty:

Double Taxation Avoidance:

A pivotal aim of the OECD model double tax treaty is the prevention of double taxation on income and capital. Double taxation arises when the same income or capital is taxed in more than one country. The treaty offers mechanisms like tax credit or exemption provision and distribution of tax rights to prevent income and capital from being taxed twice. This removal of barriers to international trade and investment boosts economic activity.

Tax Right Distribution:

The OECD's model double tax treaty offers a guide for tax right allocation amongst nations. It prescribes the rules determining which nation has the right to tax specific kinds of income or capital. For instance, the treaty might grant the taxing right of business profits to the nation in which the business resides. This helps to avert conflicts over income and capital taxation.

Lowering of Withholding Taxes:

Withholding taxes are those deducted at source from certain types of income like dividends, interest, and royalties when paid to non-residents. Often, the OECD model double tax treaty involves terms to reduce or eliminate withholding taxes on international payments. This promotes international commerce and investment by easing the tax burden on non-residents, thereby encouraging the flow of capital globally.

Hypothetical Case Study:

To shed light on the impact of the OECD model double tax treaty on UK corporation tax, we will consider a hypothetical scenario involving Company X, a multinational corporation in the UK with overseas subsidiaries. Company X generates business profits in both the UK and a foreign country that has a double tax treaty with the UK.

Based on the treaty, Company X's profits are divided between the UK and the foreign country following the treaty's provisions. This ensures that each nation can tax the portion of profits within its jurisdiction. It also offers measures to prevent double taxation, such as enabling the deduction of taxes paid in one country from the tax owed in another.

As a result of the treaty, Company X benefits from the avoidance of double taxation and the reduction of withholding taxes. This facilitates cross-border activities, reduces tax barriers, and promotes economic collaboration between the UK and the foreign country.

Decoding the Notion of a Permanent Establishment and its Tax Implications in the UK

The UK tax laws with their ever-evolving and intricate rules can often seem like a complex labyrinth for individuals and corporations to navigate. The quirks and nuances of these taxation rules often present a plethora of challenges, especially when it comes to the intricacies of a "permanent establishment". We aim to dissect this term and its implications within the context of UK tax laws for the fiscal year 2023-2024.

Understanding a Permanent Establishment
A Permanent Establishment (PE) at its core represents a foreign entity's fixed business presence in the UK that brings taxable

profits. It serves as a conduit bridging international business activities and the UK tax net. While seemingly simple, the notion of a 'Permanent Establishment' is layered, each layer playing a crucial role in determining its tax implications. For example, under the UK tax regulations, a PE could range from a branch, office, factory or workshop, to a mine, and could even extend to include agency status.

The UK shapes its regulations on PEs based on the guideline provided by the Organisation for Economic Co-operation and Development (OECD) model tax convention. The UK tweaks this model to align with its unique fiscal environment.

Demystifying the Tax Implications

When a foreign firm establishes a PE in the UK, it is inevitably enmeshed in the UK tax system. It entails that the profits connected to the PE will be subjected to the Corporation Tax in the UK, following the fiscal regulations for the year 2023-2024. However, computing these taxable profits may not be a straightforward task.

The tax regulations spell out two major methods to calculate these profits: the direct and the indirect methods. The former accounts for the actual income and expenses related to the PE, while the latter estimates the profitability of the PE. The choice of method depends upon the PE's specific circumstances.

An Illustrative Scenario: Jack's Construction Ltd

To exemplify the concept and tax implications of a Permanent Establishment, let's navigate through a hypothetical case involving Jack's Construction Ltd. This company, based in the USA, decided to establish an office in London in the year 2023, creating a PE.

Assuming that there are no existing implications from any Double Taxation Agreement (DTA), their UK profits as per the 2023-2024 UK tax rules will be subject to the UK Corporation Tax. Presuming a gross income of £1 million from UK operations and an operational expense of £500,000 for the year, their taxable UK profit stands at £500,000 (£1,000,000 - £500,000), rendering them liable to a Corporation tax of £95,000 at a tax rate of 19% (applicable for the year 2023-2024).

Charting the Course

The complexities of a permanent establishment can often lure a business into a maze full of tax intricacies, which call for prudent navigation. With the dawn of new fiscal landscapes in the tax year 2023-2024, it is vital for businesses to understand thoroughly the tax consequences related to their PEs, thereby enabling them to strategize their business operations optimally. Thus, comprehending the 'Permanent Establishment' concept is about more than just legal compliance with the tax rules; it is about shaping smart and effective business strategies.

Understanding the Tax Impact of Controlled Foreign Companies for UK Businesses

As you traverse the environment of business and finance, you may find yourself sifting through countless tax-related documents. This proves particularly critical for operations with worldwide reach. Today, we'll delve into an exceptional aspect of international commercial enterprise: the tax consequences of Controlled Foreign Companies (CFCs) under the United Kingdom's tax framework.

Defining Controlled Foreign Companies

To expel any confusion, a Controlled Foreign Company (CFC) is a corporate entity established and conducting business outside the UK, yet governed by a UK parent company. 'Control' in this context typically implies authority over strategic decisions or the power to exploit profits, generally exerted by owning over 50% of the company's voting shares.

The UK government has consistently been cautious of profit shifting, a common strategy where UK-based corporations move their legal bases overseas, primarily to evade taxes imposed in the UK, reducing their overall tax bill. To stem this form of 'tax evasion', the CFC regulations were established.

Comprehending CFC and Its Tax Consequences

Introduced by the Finance Act 2012, the UK's CFC framework
emerged from an intent to comply with Organisation for
Economic Co-operation and Development (OECD) guidelines.
This aims to prevent parent companies from manipulating their
tax liabilities by transferring profits into low-tax jurisdictions.
Under these regulations, the UK parent corporations must include
any profits allocated to their CFC in their corporate tax returns
unless certain exclusions or reductions apply.

So, how might your business be impacted? While it may present
an added hurdle, the existence of CFC rules is crucial to securing
tax fairness worldwide, ensuring that the profits generated by the
economic activity of the CFC are effectively taxed.

Case Study: Tax Computation

To elucidate the point, let's consider a hypothetical case. Visualize
'Company A', a UK-based business that owns 'Company B', a
foreign-controlled corporation located in a country with lower
corporate tax rates. For the tax year 2023-2024, Company B
managed to generate profits of £5 million.

From this profit amount, £2 million can be ascribed to finance
income while the remaining £3 million is non-trading income.
According to the UK's CFC regime, Company A must report
these profits in the UK, subject to the prevailing corporate tax
rate which, for the sake of this example, is assumed to be 19% for
the 2023-2024 fiscal year.

However, exceptions apply. The Finance Company Exemption,
for instance, permits 75% of the finance income to be exempted
from UK tax. Therefore, of the £2 million, only £500,000 is
subjected to taxation while £1.5 million is exempted. Therefore,
Company A's total taxable income becomes £3.5 million (£3
million non-trading income and £500,000 from finance income).
The UK tax obligation then amounts to £665,000 (£3.5 million x
19% corporation tax), not considering other reliefs and
deductions available under the UK tax laws.

Navigating the Regulations of the CFC

Keep in mind, this hypothetical scenario is simply illustrative and meant to offer a basic introduction. Real-world tax calculations are far more complicated, taking into consideration several factors such as capital allowances, loss relief, and group relief, among others.

Indeed, finding your way through the UK's CFC regulations can be intimidating, especially given the complex international context it entails. But with a firm understanding of how it operates, potential tax consequences, and the available exemptions, the journey becomes substantially less daunting.

Companies with international operations must reassess their structures in light of the CFC rules. Compliance is not just about avoiding penalties; it pertains to the broader responsibility that companies have to society. An accurate understanding of tax responsibilities related to controlled foreign companies helps align your enterprise with these commitments.

While tax legislation's fine print might occasionally appear distant, financial wisdom obliges us to scrutinize and understand these rules, assisting in distinguishing gains from losses and strides from missteps in your business's journey to success.

UK Tax Implications for Foreign Companies

This article explores the tax implications for foreign companies operating within the United Kingdom (UK), focusing on how these businesses are impacted by the UK's highly organised and regulated tax structure.

As a major global economic powerhouse, the UK draws businesses from all around the world. While they benefit from operating within the UK's vibrant market, these companies also need to navigate the associated tax obligations. Thus, understanding the intricacies of the UK's tax system becomes crucial.

Necessities of Taxation Policies

The UK's tax system is based primarily on residency. Generally, only the profits earned through the UK-based activities or branches of foreign companies are subjected to taxes, not their worldwide income. These companies could face various types of taxes, including Corporation Tax, Value-Added Tax (VAT), and potentially, withholding taxes on certain kinds of income.

Corporation Tax

If a foreign company maintains a 'permanent establishment' in the UK, it typically becomes liable for corporation tax on its profits. A permanent establishment is defined by the UK as a fixed place through which a company conducts its business, either partially or entirely.

For the 2023-2024 tax year in the UK, the corporation tax rate is 25%. However, foreign companies are only taxed on the profits attributable to their UK permanent establishment, not on their worldwide profits.

Take, for instance, XYZ Limited, a company based in Country A but has a branch in the UK. Let's assume it has a global profit of £1 million, with its UK branch accounting for about 40% or £400,000 of this amount. Hence, XYZ Limited will have to pay Corporation Tax on this £400,000 at a rate of 25%, resulting in a tax bill of £100,000.

Value-Added Tax (VAT)

The UK charges a standard VAT rate of 20% for the tax year 2023-2024. Foreign companies offering taxable goods or services in the UK should register for VAT if their VAT taxable turnover exceeds £85,000 over a 12-month span.

Withholding Taxes

The UK levies withholding taxes on yearly interest and royalty payments. The usual rate is 20%, but double tax agreements often reduce this rate, in some cases even to zero.

Double Taxation Relief

Many foreign companies are based in countries that have Double
Taxation Agreements (DTAs) with the UK. These agreements
prevent companies from being taxed twice on the same income.
Consequently, the tax paid in the UK is often credited against the
company's tax liability in the home country.

Conclusion

Understanding the tax implications can be challenging for
companies doing business in foreign lands, particularly when
dealing with complex tax systems like that of the UK. However, a
thorough understanding of the fundamental rules can guide one
confidently through this terrain. Consulting a tax advisor is
recommended to ensure compliance with all UK tax requirements
and to maximize tax efficiencies.

An In-depth Analysis of Double Taxation Relief in the UK for the Fiscal Year 2023-2024

Across the globe, one key element of efficient tax systems is the
provision for double taxation relief. Simply put, this mechanism
ensures that a company or an individual does not pay tax twice on
the same earnings. In our interconnected global sphere, it is not
uncommon for an enterprise or individual to have income from
multiple countries. In such cases, the mechanism of double
taxation relief plays a crucial role in fostering a just and equitable
tax atmosphere. The UK's complex tax system, bolstered by its
economic prowess, thoughtfully includes such systems. With the
introduction of dynamic changes, understanding the double
taxation relief has become crucial for the tax year 2023-2024.

The UK has mutual agreements with various countries to prevent
double taxation. UK taxpayers that have paid tax in a foreign
country can seek relief on the same in the UK, thus ensuring that
the same income is not taxed twice. This relief does not translate
into reduced taxes but prevents over-taxation of the same income.

To better conceptualize this, let us consider a hypothetical scenario:

Assume a company based in the UK "HypothetiCo", also operates in the USA. In the tax year 2023-2024, the company makes a profit of £500,000 in the UK and £300,000 from its US branch. The US charges 20% tax, costing HypothetiCo £60,000. The total income of £800,000 (£500,000 + £300,000) is subject to UK corporation tax at the rate of 25%, resulting in £200,000 UK tax. The double taxation relief that HypothetiCo can claim in the UK is the lower amount of the UK or foreign tax, in this case, £60,000. This will then be subtracted from the original UK tax liability, reducing it to £140,000 (£200,000 - £60,000).

However, the relief does not automatically apply. Taxpayers must declare this in their Self-Assessment tax return, providing details of the foreign tax paid and corresponding income, along with documentary evidence.

Note that the figures used above are entirely illustrative. Calculating and claiming double taxation relief can be highly complex, with several factors such as income's nature and origin, individual's tax residence, and the specific double taxation agreement between the UK and the foreign country playing essential roles in the final calculation. It is always recommended to seek professional advice in this regard.

Understanding the principle of double taxation relief, an integral part of the UK's tax process, helps taxpayers make more informed decisions and effectively manage their tax liabilities with foreign income.

Introductory Note:

Double taxation relief is designed to eliminate the chances of company or individual's earnings being subject to tax twice in different regions. The relief may feature tax credits or exemptions, which prevents undue taxation. Knowing how to compute this relief is essential for those who operate in more than one jurisdiction, helping them arrange their tax payments optimally and avoid double taxation. This guide provides an understanding of calculating double taxation relief in the UK for the fiscal year 2023-2024.

How to Compute Double Taxation Relief:

Hypothetical Case Study:

Let's consider a hypothetical situation involving a UK-based individual, Mr. Smith, who earns income in both the UK and the United States. Between the UK and the US, there is a double tax treaty that provides relief.

In 2023-2024, Mr. Smith earns £50,000 in the UK and $60,000 in the US. The tax rates in the UK and the US are 20% and 25%, respectively.

The first step is to calculate his tax liabilities in both jurisdictions. In the UK, he would owe £10,000, and in the US, he would owe $15,000.

The double tax treaty between the two countries allows for a tax credit from one jurisdiction to the other. In this case, Mr. Smith can claim a $15,000 tax credit against his UK tax liability.

The final step is to calculate the final tax liability, which is £5,000 considering the tax credit from the US.

Essential Advice on Calculating Double Taxation:

Know the Applicable Relief Mechanism:

Familiarize yourself with the provisions of the relevant double tax treaty or unilateral relief provision.

Consult Professionals: To navigate through the complexities of double taxation relief, engage tax professionals who are experts in international taxation.

Maintain Accurate Records: Keep detailed records of your income and paid taxes along with their relevant evidence. These records will be essential during your tax calculations and later tax audits.

Stay Updated with Legislative Amendments:

Regularly check for updates from tax authorities and consult with tax professionals to stay informed about changes in the UK's double taxation relief rules.

The effect of a group structure for corporation tax purposes

Understanding UK Taxation: Allocating Annual Investment Allowance in Group and Related Companies

UK tax laws can be quite complex when it comes to allocating Annual Investment Allowances (AIA) amongst companies in the same group or related entities. Various aspects about the tax year 2023-2024 are to be considered, understood, and properly implemented.

Let's start by understanding AIA. It is a tax relief method which allows companies to deduct the worth of qualifying capital expenditure from their taxable profits up to a maximum limit. For the designated tax year, this limit is set at £1 million. Such allocations and associated tax benefits promote business investments.

Let's now focus on groups or related companies. They are companies that share a common umbrella or are tied together in certain ways. These companies tend to share the AIA, due to the common belief that their finances are intertwined. The complexities emerge here, as the approach chosen is often contingent upon the nature of their relationship.

Key Guidelines for AIA Allocation in Group or Related Companies

There are two principal guidelines when it comes to UK tax rules related to groups or associated businesses. The first one stipulates that if the companies under consideration form a 'group' (under common control), they need to collectively determine the division of the £1 million AIA. This guideline offers flexibility allowing the participating companies to assess their investment plans, and divide the allocation in a way that benefits most, if not all companies.

The second principle concerns 'related' companies (those not part of a group but having common stakeholders), entitling them just to a portion of the whole AIA. The basis for division here is simple - the total AIA (£1 million for 2023-2024) is divided by the number of related companies.

However, a caveat exists that if a related company surpasses their proportionate share of the AIA, they cannot claim the excess investment even if their counterparts haven't used their full share.

Imaginary Case Study

Let's demonstrate these rules with a hypothetical situation. Consider three companies: Alpha Ltd, Bravo Ltd, and Charlie Ltd. These companies are grouped under common control. In the tax year 2023-2024, Alpha anticipates significant capital expenditures and propounds using the majority of the AIA. Bravo and Charlie, with lesser capital expenditure, give their nod but under the condition that they get an equal share of the remaining allowance.

Post discussions, they concur on Alpha claiming £800,000 and Bravo and Charlie receiving £100,000 each. This arrangement adheres to the AIA allocation rules for grouped companies under UK tax law, provided the total claimed does not exceed £1 million.

On the contrary, if these companies were merely related with shared stakeholders, the AIA would have been equally shared. Alpha, Bravo, and Charlie each would have received £333,333 (£1 million/3) of the AIA.

UK Tax Implications of Intangible Assets Transfers

Under the UK tax system, the transfer of intangible assets, such as brand recognition, patents, trademarks, copyrights, and goodwill, may result in significant tax repercussions, particularly for businesses. Given the substantial contribution these assets often make to a company's total worth, it's crucial to understand these tax implications and devise strategies for their effective management.

In UK tax law, it's not the intangible asset transfer itself that incurs tax charges but the resulting gain or profit. This is particularly true when assets are sold or shifted for a consideration, either between affiliated entities or with external parties.

Calculating Taxable Gains: A Hypothetical Example

We'll illustrate this with a hypothetical scenario where TechCo Ltd, a UK-based tech company, decides to sell a critical patent to MedCo Ltd, a UK-based medical company. TechCo bought the patent for £500,000 ten years ago and now sells it to MedCo for £2,000,000. In this case, TechCo's taxable gain will be £1,500,000 (£2,000,000 minus £500,000), which will be the basis for tax computation.

Corporation Tax and the Goodwill System

The relevant tax here would be the Corporation Tax, which is imposed on companies' profits. The Corporation Tax rate for the tax year 2023-2024 is 25%. Therefore, TechCo will owe £375,000 (25% of £1,500,000) in Corporation Tax.

The UK's Goodwill and other intangibles tax rules further complicate the situation. A different set of rules under the Corporation Tax Act 2009 apply to most intangible assets, including goodwill. These "Corporate Intangibles" rules could be more advantageous to businesses regarding the taxing of gains from intangible asset transfers.

Reliefs and Amortisation

Under the Corporate Intangibles Regime, TechCo may be entitled to relief or 'amortisation'. This mechanism spreads the tax liability over the asset's useful economic life (up to 20 years), as opposed to being levied on the full gain in the transfer year.

However, these rules are complex, and the tax implications vary based on factors like when the assets were acquired or created and the specificities of the transferring and receiving parties. Thus, detailed tax planning and professional advice are highly recommended for transactions involving intangible assets.

Introduction

In the UK, trade and assets transfers under common control come with substantial tax implications. Common control implies that the entities engaged in the transfer are either under identical or related management or ownership. The tax consequences of such transactions are vitally important to all involved parties, as they may significantly influence their tax obligations and potential liabilities. This article will delve into these tax consequences under the UK's taxation laws for the 2023-2024 tax year.

Tax Implications Following the Transfer of Trade and Assets:

Capital Gains Tax:

The sale of trade and assets might invoke capital gains tax (CGT) for the transacting party. CGT is a levy applied to the profits resulting from the disposal of assets. The taxable amount is the difference between the selling price and the original purchase price of the assets.

Conforming to Transfer Pricing Regulations:

Transactions involving the exchange of trade and assets among related entities adhere to transfer pricing rules. These regulations ascertain fair trading practices by ensuring the transfer is made at an arm's length price, i.e., a price agreed between independent, unrelated parties. Avoiding changes in the tax treatment of the transfer necessitates that both transferor and transferee comply with these guidelines.

The Possibility of Deducting Acquisition Costs:

The acquiring entity may deduct the costs related to the procurement of the trade and assets, such as legal fees and valuation charges. However, the deductibility of these costs hinges on the specific situation and the stipulations of the UK tax rules.

Hypothetical Case Example:

Let's examine a hypothetical case to understand the tax implications of a trade and assets transfer under common control better. Suppose this involves Company X and Company Y, both under common control and based in the UK. Company X decides to transfer its trade and assets to Company Y.

For tax year 2023-2024, Company X could encounter a CGT liability on the transfer of the trade and assets. This liability would be the result of the disparity between the transfer proceeds and the initial cost of obtaining the assets. The applied CGT rate depends on the specific circumstances, along with the relevant tax rules for 2023-2024.

The transfer pricing regulations would apply to Company Y in respect of the trade and assets transfer. The transfer's cost must be determined using the arm's length principle, creating a parity with the transaction rates between unrelated parties. To avoid potential deviations in the tax treatment of the transfer, Company Y must adhere to these guidelines.

Furthermore, Company Y could potentially deduct the acquisition costs of the trade and assets. Such costs, acknowledged as part of the overall asset procurement cost, might be deductible over time, subject to UK tax laws.

Guidance on Trade and Assets Transfer Tax Implications:

When dealing with trade and assets transfer tax implications under common control, it is essential to:

Understand the tax rules:

Be well-versed with the UK tax guidelines and HMRC's advice on trade and assets transfer to grasp the tax implications and uphold compliance.

Seek expert advice:
Engage with tax experts or consultants specializing in transfer pricing and related-party operations to handle the intricacies of the transfer, ensuring conformity with UK tax regulations.

Maintain thorough records:
Keep detailed records of all transfer-related documentation, contracts, and asset valuation reports. This will help validate the tax treatment of your transfer and meet tax authorities' requirements.

Consider possible deductions:

Examine the deductibility of costs associated with acquiring the trade and assets. Seek guidance from tax professionals to understand specific deductibility rules and potential limitations or restrictions.

Introduction

The concepts of consortium owned companies and consortium members within the UK's tax system pertain to specific organizational structures involving multiple entities. Understanding these terms is key in navigating a company's tax responsibilities and positions. This article aims to illuminate these concepts within the context of UK tax practices, as per the tax laws for the fiscal year 2023-2024.

Understanding Consortium Owned Company:

A consortium owned company is a business co-owned and jointly controlled by several other businesses. Under this structure, the consortium members hold collective ownership and authority over the consortium owned company, which is recognized as a standalone legal entity. Its control and ownership, however, are spread across the consortium members.

Companies often organize into consortiums for specific projects requiring a blend of specialized knowledge, resources, and collaboration. These projects can range from research and development endeavors to large-scale infrastructure initiatives and allow the consortium members to pool their abilities, risks, and resources towards a shared objective.

Definition of a Consortium Member:
A consortium member is a company participating in a consortium arrangement. It is part of a group of companies that jointly own and administer a consortium owned company. Each consortium

member possesses a stake in the company and participates in its operations and strategic decisions.

The roles and responsibilities can differ across consortium members, with some providing financial resources and others contributing specialist knowledge or market access. For the consortium owned company to realise its goals, the consortium members work together and coordinate their efforts.

Case Study:

The concept of consortium owned companies and consortium members is illustrated by a hypothetical scenario of a consortium established to launch a renewable energy project consisting of three members: Company X, Company Y, and Company Z.

In this context, the consortium owned company is a separate legal unit formed to manage the renewable energy initiative. The three consortium members, Company X, Company Y, and Company Z, share equal ownership and control of this company.

Companies X, Y, and Z collectively steer the consortium owned company, each having a certain ownership stake and contributing their assets and expertise. Let's say Company X provides financial resources, Company Y supplies technological know-how, and Company Z offers market access. The consortium members collaborate and jointly decide on matters to ensure the renewable energy project's success.

Recommendations for Consortium Owned Companies and Consortium Members:

For businesses engaged in consortium arrangements, it's essential to:

Be aware of legal and tax implications: Understand the related UK tax laws and legal requirements for consortium owned companies and consortium members to comply with regulations and optimize tax advantages.
Create clear contracts: Prepare precise agreements outlining each consortium member's accountability, roles, and ownership stakes.

These should encompass issues such as the decision-making process, division of profits, and resolution of disputes.

Maintain meticulous records: Retain comprehensive documentation of the consortium arrangement, including details of ownership stakes, contributions, and decision-making protocols. This helps validate the tax treatment and satisfy tax authorities' conditions.

Seek expert advice: Consult with tax professionals or advisors knowledgeable about consortium arrangements. They can provide guidance on tax planning, compliance, and maximizing the consortium's tax position.

Understanding Consortium Relief in the UK Tax System

The operation of consortium relief is crucial to navigating the complexities of the UK tax system, offering various types of relief available to businesses and individuals. It proves especially beneficial to companies in a consortium. This guide aims to give a comprehensive understanding of how consortium relief works within the UK taxation system for the 2023-2024 tax year.

Decoding Consortium Relief

A consortium typically consists of two or more individuals, companies, organisations, or governments that engage in a particular activity or pool resources to achieve a common goal. Consortium Relief in tax terms is a tax relief applicable to consortium-member companies to help distribute any losses between member companies based on their stake or share in the consortium.

In layman terms, if one company within the consortium has a financially challenging year but the others are successful, profits from flourishing companies can offset losses from the struggling company. This reduces the total corporation tax liability of the consortium significantly.

Eligibility Criteria for Consortium Relief
To avail Consortium Relief in the UK, a company must fulfil several necessary conditions, which include being UK or EU-

based and being a member of a consortium with at least 75% ownership of the ordinary share capital in the loss-making company. Also, each consortium member must have at least a 5% interest.

It should be noted that the ownership structure and consortium relief group tests are unique. Even completely owned subsidiaries may not qualify, while companies that are not subsidiaries can qualify if they meet the criteria.

Hypothetical Case for a Practical Understanding of Consortium Relief

Consider a hypothetical case to understand how Consortium Relief operates. If Companies A, B, and C form a consortium with equal shares in a losing Company D, the loss incurred by D for the tax year 2023-2024 (£600,000) can offset the profits of Companies A, B, and C within the same financial year. This reduces their overall taxable profits.

The computation for Consortium Relief would involve:

25% corporation tax rate for the 2023-2024 tax year
Each company can claim the losses equal to their shares, which is 1/3 in this case due to equal shares
Company D's loss: £600,000 — Company A's share of the loss: £200,000 (1/3 of £600,000)
Company B's share of the loss: £200,000 (1/3 of £600,000)
Company C's share of the loss: £200,000 (1/3 of £600,000)
The tax reduction for each company would be 25% of £200,000 = £50,000.

As such, with Consortium Relief, each company saves £50,000 in corporation tax due to Company D's losses.

Pre-entry losses and their tax treatment in the UK explained

Navigating the complex arena of taxation can be difficult, particularly when contemplating your company's annual financial gains and losses. Within the UK's taxation system, special measures are in place for managing different types of losses, one of which is referred to as pre-entry losses.

Definition of Pre-Entry Losses

Pre-entry losses pertain to capital losses experienced before a company joins a group. These losses chiefly occur when a company's 'chargeable asset', which is subject to Capital Gains Tax if sold at a profit, goes through a loss before the company joins a group. The term 'group' denotes a collection of companies that have a particular connection, for example, common ownership.

Tax Aspects of Pre-Entry Losses

UK tax regulations regarding pre-entry losses have undergone numerous revisions. Previously, these losses were ring fenced and only available for utilization by the loss-incurred company. However, a 2002 amendment allowed for pre-entry losses to be relocated to another company within the same group. The revised policy is beneficial for businesses as it aids in efficient tax planning.

With respect to the 2023-2024 tax year, according to current legislation, pre-entry losses can be handed over to another group member under certain restrictions. For instance, only that part of the loss corresponding to the value decline of the asset during the transferee company's ownership can be moved. Additional intricate rules are also in place, particularly concerning assets that are at a loss immediately before joining a group.

Theoretical Situation of Pre-Entry Loss

Consider a hypothetical example for a better comprehension of these rules and restrictions. Let's say a company 'Pegasus Ltd.' joins the 'Alpha Group' on April 1, 2023. Before this, Pegasus

Ltd, an independent entity, suffers a loss of £100,000 on a chargeable asset.

In the tax year 2023-2024, Alpha Group decides to counterbalance the pre-entry loss of Pegasus Ltd with the capital gains of another 'Alpha Group' company. However, since the asset was not part of Alpha Group's ownership at the loss time, the tax authorities would curtail the surrender of this pre-entry loss under the UK tax regulations for the respective tax year.

Consequently, understanding pre-entry losses and their tax treatment provides businesses and individuals with a depth of taxation law knowledge and assists in tax planning.

These laws can be intricate to operate, so it's advisable to consult a professional. This ensures that the legalities are adhered to, and the tax situation is optimized within the law's parameters.

"Degrouping Charge" is the term used for the cost imposed on companies when they exit a group within six years of earning an asset through a no gain/no loss transaction, as outlined under UK tax legislation and is a segment of the capital gains tax network. A no gain/no loss transfer happens when an asset is moved within the group, typically among parent and child companies, without incurring a capital increase or decrease at the moment of transfer.

To demonstrate this concept, we will use a didactic example reflecting the UK tax rules for the fiscal year 2023-2024. Let's scrutinize a scenario with Apex Tors Ltd, a UK-based parent firm. The firm transferred an asset valued at £1,000,000 on a no gain/no loss basis to a subsidiary company, Bevy Link Ltd, during the 2023-2024 tax period. However, Bevy Link Ltd departed the group after two years, and it is now necessary to calculate the degrouping charge for Bevy Link Ltd.

To perform this, the first step involves determining the deemed disposal value of the asset after Bevy Link's group exit. Assuming the asset's open market value stood at £1,300,000 post-departure, that would be the deemed disposal value.

The subsequent step entails calculating the gain from the deemed disposal by subtracting the original transfer value from the deemed disposal value. Therefore, we get £1,300,000 - £1,000,000, leading to a £300,000 output.

The degrouping charge is then figured out by multiplying the declared gain by the Corporation Tax rate for the year Bevy Link exited. With the Corporation Tax rate for 2023-2024 as 25%, Bevy Link's degrouping charge equals 25% of £300,000, summing up to £75,000.

In conclusion, Bevy Link Ltd.'s degrouping charge post-departure from the Apex Tors Ltd group for the 2023-2024 fiscal year would be £75,000.

Through this scenario, we attempt to elucidate the tax implications that come with asset transfers within business groups. It specifically uncovers the sudden tax obligation the asset-receiving firm might struggle with upon leaving the group, represented by the degrouping charge. It also highlights the essentiality of both corporate groups and individual members to consider possible tax expenses in their asset and company management tactics.

Calculating the degrouping charge may seem like a taxing and intricate task filled with tax lingo, convoluted calculations, and strict timelines. Yet, with a thorough understanding of the fundamental principles, careful tracking of asset moves, and timely action upon corporate restructuring, companies can proficiently handle these charges, stave off tax shocks, and uphold seamless financial procedures. It's vital to remember that effective tax management doesn't only involve grasping current tax norms but also predicting future changes and proactively adjusting to them.

Anti-Avoidance Measures and Their Impact on Companies Leaving a Group in the UK Tax System

The UK tax legislation incorporates several anti-avoidance mechanisms intended to uphold tax compliance and foil attempts by companies to deceptively alter financial transactions to minimize their tax obligations. These provisions include guidelines impacting the financial activities of firms when they decide to depart from a group structure. By closely inspecting these regulations, we can gain a deeper appreciation of their implications for businesses.

There can be varied reasons a company might decide to exit a group. It could be a strategic move towards better opportunities, merger or acquisition, or possibly a crisis. Here, we explore how such re-arrangements are handled within the UK tax context.

Tax Consequences

Let's look at a hypothetical situation to better comprehend the implications. Assume a Company 'Building Blocks Ltd' is part of a bigger group 'Property Pioneers PLC'. 'Building Blocks Ltd' decides to break away from the group - this act might activate certain tax consequences as per the Corporation Tax Act 2010.

The company's decision to depart might lead to an asset exchange between the involved parties. Any taxable gains or losses as per TCGA 1992 would be retained. As per the de-grouping charge regulations of the Corporation Tax Act 2010, outlined in section 179, these taxable gains or losses would be treated as if they accrued to 'Building Blocks Ltd' when it exited the group. As a result, taxable gains or losses become liable for corporation tax.

Furthermore, the anti-avoidance provisions stipulate that if the company that is exiting the group artificially deflated its value by eliminating profits or surpluses before the exit, HMRC would deploy transfer pricing rules. This would correct the consideration for tax aims to display an arm's length sum, potentially enlarging the amount of taxable income or gains under tax.

Recouping Previously Denied Relief

To further clarify, let's expand our hypothetical case. If 'Property Pioneers PLC' had provided a loan to 'Building Blocks Ltd' that is waived off when it leaves the group, the latter company might benefit from a tax reduction under typical circumstances. But, as per section 362 of the Corporation Tax Act 2009, this relief can be withheld to prevent any tax evasion intention behind such group financial transactions. With this provision, the UK tax system ensures fair taxation processes, discouraging companies from participating in any tax evasion strategies during their exit from a group.

If the company that left re-enters the group within six years, sections 179(3) and 179(4) of the Corporation Tax Act 2010 dictates that the deferred de-grouping charge is recouped, and the previously denied relief becomes available again. This re-grouping can effectively negate the tax consequences of de-grouping, provided the company rejoins the same group.

The 'Five-Year Rule'

The Corporation tax legislation also enacts a five-year rule for intra-group asset transfers. If a company exits a group within five years after acquiring an asset from another group corporation, a de-grouping charge could be imposed. This rule is in place to dissuade companies from evading corporation tax by temporarily shifting assets within a group.

Tax Implications for UK Companies With Foreign Branches

The UK tax system has unique guidelines for foreign branches of UK companies. It's important to note that the UK government doesn't view foreign branches as separate entities. Instead, these branches are viewed as extensions of the UK parent company, and their profits are subject to UK corporation tax.

Understanding Corporation Tax

UK companies are required to pay taxes on their global earnings, which includes profits generated by foreign branches. For the tax rule year 2023-2024, the established rate for corporation tax is 19%. Therefore, any profits obtained from a foreign branch activity will be subjected to this rate of corporation tax.

Nevertheless, there are rules to prevent companies from facing double taxation on the same income. These rules are known as Double Taxation Agreements (DTAs) and often offer tax credits to companies that have paid taxes in both the UK and the foreign jurisdiction.

Example Case

Take, for instance, a hypothetical UK-based company 'XYZ Ltd' that operates a branch in Germany and made £1,000,000 profit for the tax year 2023-2024.

The German tax authority imposes a tax rate of 15%, amounting to £150,000. Simultaneously, the UK tax authority also imposes a tax of 19% (£190,000) on these profits. However, due to the double taxation treaty between the UK and Germany, XYZ Ltd can minimize their UK tax bill by the amount of tax already paid in Germany (i.e., £150,000). As a result, the UK corporation tax due will be £40,000 (£190,000 - £150,000).

Branch vs. Subsidiary

Companies planning to expand overseas need to decide whether to establish the foreign operation as a branch or a subsidiary. A branch is seen as part of the parent company, while a subsidiary is a separate legal entity. The tax implications can vary significantly between branches and subsidiaries, and often, a subsidiary can offer greater tax efficiency, especially if it incurs losses in its early years. Please consult your tax advisor to fully comprehend the specifics of your situation.

An Overview:

The tax treatment of foreign branches is a key factor in the UK's taxation system. Foreign branches are business facilities located outside the UK but run by a UK resident company. It's crucial for UK companies with international operations to understand the tax implications of a foreign branch, impacting their tax positions and possible tax liabilities. The advice provided in this article is based on the UK tax rules for the year 2023-2024.

Tax Treatment of a Foreign Branch:

Residence for Tax Determination:

The UK company's residence status determines the tax treatment of a foreign branch. If the UK company is recognized as a UK taxpayer, it has to pay UK corporation tax on its global earnings, inclusive of the earnings made by the foreign branch.

Taxation on Branch Earnings:

The earnings generated by a foreign branch are generally subjected to UK corporation tax. The UK tax regulations require the UK company to consider the foreign branch's profits in their tax calculations similarly to its UK operations. The profits are assessed as per the applicable tax regulations and rates.

3. Thread of Double Taxation Relief:

To prevent double taxation where the foreign branch profits are taxed in both the foreign country and the UK, double tax relief may be offered. This relief can be given through double tax treaties or through one-sided relief mechanisms. These mechanisms ensure the same income isn't taxed twice, providing relief as tax credits or exceptions.

Hypothetical Case Review:

Let's examine a hypothetical case regarding Company A, a UK-based manufacturing company with a branch in Country B, making £500,000 during the tax year 2023-2024.

As a UK resident company, Company A needs to pay UK corporation tax on all its profits globally, including the profits of its foreign subsidiary. The tax liability will be calculated based on the applicable tax regulations and rates.

Double tax relief might be applicable if the foreign branch's profits are also taxed in Country B. This relief could be executed through a double tax treaty between the UK and Country B or via unilateral relief mechanisms in the UK tax laws. The relief ensures those profits aren't taxed twice, offering tax credits or exceptions to prevent double taxation.

Advice on the Tax Treatment of a Foreign Branch:

When considering the tax treatment of a foreign branch, it's essential to:

Understand the taxation regulations:
Acquaint yourself with the UK's tax regulations and HMRC's advice on foreign branches to abide by the rules and comprehend the tax implications.

Evaluate the residence status:

Establish the UK company's residence status for taxation purposes. This will determine the scope of its tax duties and plausible exposure to UK taxes on the foreign branch's earnings.

Seek expert advice:

Consult with tax experts or advisors specializing in international taxation to guide you in the complexity of foreign branch taxation, ensuring compliance with the UK tax laws.

Follow changes in legislation:

Stay updated with any amendments in the UK tax regulations regarding the foreign branches' treatment. Regularly review HMRC guidance and consult with tax experts to remain compliant with current laws.

The use of exemptions and reliefs in deferring and minimising corporation tax liabilities

Understanding the Use of the Substantial Shareholdings Exemption in the United Kingdom's Tax System

Tax systems can present a labyrinth of complexity, but there are specific provisions, like the 'Substantial Shareholdings Exemption' (SSE), designed to alleviate the pressured journey. Specifically targeting corporate groups, the SSE can provide relief from Capital Gains Tax (CGT) on gains made from selling substantial shareholdings, under particular conditions.

The SSE, a vital element of the UK tax law, is predominantly put into practice to help corporations in their tax planning processes. Corporations in-depth understanding of its requirements and strict adherence to those stipulations allows this application.

For the fiscal year of 2023-2024, there are essential requirements within the UK tax law to be eligible for this exemption: The company must hold a significant share of at least 10% in the company being sold for a continuous stretch of a minimum of 12 months two years prior to the sale; the company being sold must be a trading company or the core company of a trading group for that 12-month period up to the disposal date.

Take for example Company X, which has held a 15% stake in Company Y for the past 18 months. If Company X decides to sell its entire stake in Company Y, the subsequent profit would generally be subject to CGT. However, the SSE could nullify the CGT on this gain, provided all conditions are fulfilled.

It's essential to strategically plan and undertake such transactions to ensure the SSE can be employed to achieve substantial CGT savings. A careful analysis of all relevant factors, such as the company's trading status, the holding period and shareholding extent, is crucial during this process. Sometimes, a review of subsidiary companies may also be required.

The SSE has undoubtedly been a significant contributor to the wider corporate tax planning environment within the UK. It has facilitated unrestricted transfers and reorganizations between companies, offering enormous benefits and potential tax savings for qualifying UK firms.

Continuous monitoring of the changing and evolving UK tax laws is critical to fully reap the benefits of the SSE. As the saying goes - 'Knowledge is Power.' The more companies know, the better they can use the resources available to them.

Though tax intricacies can be overwhelming, with the right know-how and application, the journey can be made significantly smoother. The SSE is a valuable tool in the UK tax system that, when used correctly, can lead to substantial tax savings for corporate groups.

It is important to understand the context and rules surrounding the substantial shareholdings exemption in the UK taxation system to utilise it effectively. This exemption is a clause in the

UK tax law that allows certain gains on share sales to be free from CGT.

According to UK tax rules for 2023-2024, the substantial shareholdings exemption applies to gains from share sales in a trading company or a member of a trading group. To be eligible, the company or group must have been trading for at least one year before the shares were sold. The seller must also own at least 10% of the company for a continuous year before the disposal.

The substantial shareholdings exemption exists to incentivize investment and business growth by providing tax breaks for companies and individuals owning significant stakes in trading companies. By making gains from share sales in these companies tax-free, the UK tax system aims to encourage long-term business investments and stability.

Consider a hypothetical case of Company X, a UK trading company that manufactures and distributes electronic devices. Mr. A, a shareholder for the past three years, owns a 15% stake in Company X. In the 2023-2024 tax year, he decides to sell his shares.

Under 2023-2024 UK tax regulations, Mr. A may apply the substantial shareholdings exemption if certain conditions are met. Company X must be a trading company, which means it's engaged in trade or business. Additionally, Company X must have been trading for a minimum of one year before disposing of the shares.

Lastly, Mr. A must own at least a 10% stake in Company X continuously for a year before the disposal. Mr. A meets this criterion as he has been a shareholder for three years.

Provided all conditions are adhered to, Mr. A can apply the substantial shareholdings exemption to the gain from sale of his shares in Company X. This implies that the proceeds from this sale would be free from capital gains tax, leading to some tax relief for Mr. A.

Stamp taxes

The scope of stamp taxes

In the UK's taxation framework, specific taxes such as stamp duties are imposed on particular categories of properties. These encompass stamp duty, stamp duty land tax (SDLT), and stamp duty reserve tax (SDRT), each having its own set of regulations and applicability to diverse property deals.

Stamp duty is a tax on the transfer of shares or securities and its calculation is based on the asset's worth. During the UK tax year 2023-2024, fluctuations in stamp duty rates and thresholds are probable, making it crucial to examine the specific tax specifications for that year. If an individual trades company shares in this tax year, the value of the shares may determine the stamp duty they need to pay.

SDLT is levied on the purchase of land or property within the UK and it's computed based on the value of the property. Changes to the rates and thresholds for stamp duty land tax may occur according to the circumstances and the relevant tax year. Should an individual buy a residential property during the 2023-2024 tax year, SDLT may be applied, but the specific rates and thresholds for that year will determine this.

SDRT, similar to the others, is a tax applied to selected electronic share and security transactions. Although akin to stamp duty, SDRT particularly targets electronically finalized transactions. In the event that a person purchases electronic shares during the 2023-2024 UK tax year, they may be obligated to pay SDRT, considering the specific rules and rates for that year.

To give an example of how stamp taxes operate, let's examine the case of Mr. B, a UK resident, who purchases a London residential property in the 2023-2024 tax year. The house costs £500,000. Mr. B would be required to pay SDLT proportional to the property's price, relative to the SDLT rates and thresholds of the year.

If the SDLT rate for residential properties priced between £500,000 and £925,000 stands at 5%, Mr. B would need to compute 5% of his £500,000 property, resulting in a total of £25,000. This would be the sum Mr. B needs to pay as SDLT for his property purchase.

Identify and advise on the liabilities arising on transfers

The Intricate Network of UK Stamp Taxes on Share and Security Transfers

Stamp taxes remain an invaluable yet frequently disregarded facet of transaction planning, and their wide-ranging applicability extends to shares and securities transfers. The UK taxation system incorporates this critical component. The myriad of complexities reflected in their evaluation mirror the metaphor in the Ancient Mariner's saying: 'water, water everywhere, but not a drop to drink'. In this case, however, we are surrounded by a flood of stamp tax rules.

The first point of discussion is defining Stamp Duty. This is a tax imposed on legal documents, particularly those regarding asset or property transfers. The HM Revenue and Customs (HMRC) necessitates the payment of any outstanding Stamp Duty within a certain period following the transaction. Importantly, there exist different classifications of stamp duties, namely Stamp Duty Reserve Tax (SDRT) and Stamp Duty, with unique regulations for each category.

Upon purchasing shares, notwithstanding whether they are paperless, they remain subject to either stamp duty or Stamp Duty Reserve Tax (SDRT) in the UK. The rate generally stands at 0.5% of the acquisition price for shares and securities.

Navigating the Labyrinth of Numbers

To make these concepts more tangible, let's illustrate with a hypothetical example. Imagine James, a fervent player in the UK stock market, purchases 1000 shares at a unit price of £5 in ABC Ltd. during the 2023-2024 UK tax year. Here, the comprehensive value of these shares would be £5,000. Subsequently, the stamp duty charged on this transaction, presuming the standard rate of 0.5%, would be calculated as follows:

£5,000 (share value) x 0.5% (stamp duty rate) = £25

James would, therefore, owe a stamp duty of £25 for this transaction. This charge must be paid within 30 days of the transaction, or James may incur penalties or interest.

However, transactions involving the transfer of stocks and shares on a recognized stock exchange are typically duty-free.

Further Observations and Exceptions

Although the standard 0.5% rate is most commonly used, it is crucial to underscore certain exceptions. For one, transactions up to £1000 are exempt from stamp duty. Moreover, a situation may arise in the course of investment activities where a company circulates shares in another company to its shareholders. This is regarded as a 'dividend in specie,' where stamp duty or stamp duty reserve tax liabilities do not apply.

In the digital age where electronic transactions are commonplace, SDRT gains significant relevance. Specifically, when shares are obtained electronically (without a physical document), an SDRT at the standard 0.5% rate is charged on the transaction value.

Additionally, certain conditions may warrant the application of 'relief.' This reflects the importance of understanding the intricacies of the taxation system. For example, when shares are gifted, and no money or value is received in return, no SDRT is required.

A Glimpse into the Future

Given the ever-changing nature of the UK's taxation scene, it's critical to remain abreast of the latest regulations. As we enter the UK Tax Year 2023-2024, we can expect modifications to the rules concerning stamp duties. A thorough understanding of the marketplace, cohesive strategies, and regular updates will act as the guiding lights towards effective financial planning.

Therefore, stay informed about new developments and don't shy away from seeking professional advice in this intricate area of taxation. Consulting an accountant or tax professional who can render accurate and tailored advice based on your personal predicament is recommended.

A word of caution: Tax laws are subject to alterations and differ from person to person. Accordingly, this article should not be the sole source of personal tax advice. Always consult a professional for tailor-made guidance.

An In-Depth Guide to Understanding Stamp Taxes on UK Land Transfers

Financial transactions, especially those involving large assets like land, can end in an unpleasant surprise due to unexpected taxes. An often-misunderstood tax within the UK's taxation system is the Stamp Duty Land Tax (SDLT), informally known as the "stamp tax". This comprehensive guide delves into the essence of this tax, its consequences and different aspects influencing it.

Mastering the Stamp Taxes Notion

The SDLT, a tax primarily imposed on paperwork, is applicable in the UK. The "stamp duty" tax is paid to the government when a person is purchasing land or property either freehold or leasehold, surpassing a specific price limit. It applies to both residential and commercial properties and it is dependent on the purchase price. So, how does it relate to land transfers? SDLT basic principle is applicable to land ownership transfers regardless of whether an actual property sale is involved.

SDLT Rates Overview

Stamp taxes do not have a fixed rate. Instead, they apply on a tiered basis, much like an income tax, so various portions of the property price get taxed at uneven rates. For the tax year 2023-2024, SDLT rates for residential properties oscillate based on the property's cost, commencing from 0% for properties below £125,000 to 12% for those exceeding £1.5 million. For non-residential properties or mixed-use land, £150,000 is the minimum threshold and the maximum is 5% for properties beyond £250,000.

These tiers play a vital role in the calculation of stamp taxes.

Here's how you can figure them out.

Unravelling the SDLT Calculation

A Case Hypothesis

Suppose you're buying a residential land piece worth £300,000. The SDLT calculation would proceed as follows:

The initial £125,000 of the property would prompt 0%, hence no tax.

The subsequent £125,000 (from £125,001 to £250,000) would draw a 2% tax, which would sum up to a tax of £2,500.

The last £50,000 (from £250,001 to £300,000) would draw a 5% tax, resulting in a tax of £2,500.

Consequently, the total stamp tax on this property would be £5,000.

However, there might be certain cases where the tax might be alleviated or entirely removed.

Tax Discounts and Exceptions

Certain SDLT reprieves and exceptions could apply, depending on your case's specifics. For instance, first-time homebuyers pay no stamp duties on the initial £300,000 of the property if its overall cost is under £500,000. Additionally, there are special cases such as properties in disadvantaged areas, zero-carbon homes or multiple dwellings where stamp duty reliefs can be requested.

Though navigating the complex maze of stamp taxes and thoroughly utilizing any accessible reliefs or exceptions can be challenging. Professional help and utilizing tools like the SDLT calculator available on the UK government site or consultation from an expert adviser can simplify this task. Regardless, understanding stamp taxes fundamentals on land transfers is an important step in avoiding any unexpected financial shock during these transactions.

Comprehension of stamp taxes on land transfers is crucial in the UK's taxation system. This article explores these taxes for the tax year 2023-2024 when tied to such transactions. Both the value and specific circumstances determine the payable Stamp Duty Land Tax (SDLT). In a hypothetical example of Mr. D buying a residential property for £400,000 during that tax year, SDLT payable would be 5% equivalent to £20,000 falling within the third threshold. Other considerations during land transfers, such as capital gains tax (CGT) or inheritance tax (IHT), could also play a part. It is essential to refer to the specific tax laws for the relevant tax year.

The use of exemptions and reliefs in deferring and minimizing stamp taxes

In the complex system of UK taxation, the concept of transfers involving no consideration holds a significant place. These transfers, simply speaking, are processes where no goods, services, or payments are exchanged from one party to another. Understanding these transactions is crucial in grasping taxation practices in the UK due to their substantial impact on related tax liabilities.

For instance, imagine a man called Mr. Woods, a thriving entrepreneur from Birmingham, decides to gift his daughter a piece of land in scenic Scotland. Mr. Woods doesn't ask for any sort of exchange from his daughter, qualifying this as a transfer involving no consideration.

At first glance, you may think, where does tax come into play here? There's no money changing hands. However, this is where the complexity – or for some, the puzzlement - of UK Tax Legislation unfolds.

Interestingly, the UK Tax Legislation within the Finance Act 2023-2024 stipulates that transfers involving no consideration, such as gifts, can trigger Capital Gains Tax (CGT) when sold.

This tax is levied on the gain between the market value at the time of gifting and the original acquisition cost. This gain constitutes the taxable base.

For clarity, let's delve into some figures. Assume Mr. Woods bought this land in 2010 for £250,000. By 2023, the buoyant Scottish property market turns the odds in his favor, hiking up the value of the land to £500,000. As Mr. Woods gifts this land to his daughter, she effectively 'inherits' a potential CGT obligation.

This tax is only activated if and when she decides to dispose of this land. Let's assume that she sells it in the same tax year 2023-24 for £600,000. The CGT base will be the gain, which is £600,000 (sale price) minus £500,000 (value at gifting time), equaling £100,000. After considering the annual tax-free allowance for 2023-24, assumed to be £12,300, her chargeable gain will be £87,700.

Although official tax rates for CGT for the tax year 2023-24 aren't disclosed at the time of writing, if we take it to be 20% for basic tax payers and 40% for those at the higher rate. If we assume Miss Wood is a higher-rate taxpayer, her tax owed will amount to £35,080 (£87,700 × 40%).

To summaries, while 'gifts' like transfers involving no consideration might seem initially profitable, it's always wise to be aware of potential tax implications hidden within. Each part of the UK Tax landscape comes with its own unique narrative; it's all about understanding and maneuvering through it.

Understanding Group Transactions within the UK Taxation Structure

Group transactions, a key element in the realm of corporate and commercial finance, represents financial exchanges between companies under the same ownership or parent corporation. A comprehensive understanding of the nature of these transactions, along with their potential impacts and the corresponding tax behaviour according to the UK Taxation System, is imperative. This article will explore the specifics of group transactions within the UK tax environment for the 2023-2024 tax year.

The Nature of Group Transactions in the UK

Group transactions entail the financial operations happening within a consortium of companies. Within the UK environment, these transactions typically involve entities with the same parent ownership, ranging from intercompany asset transfers and loans to mutual service agreements and sharing use of resources.
In terms of benefits, consolidated reporting, efficient tax planning strategies, and centralized cash management are offered through in-group trading. However, the trading is also prone to several tax consequences according to UK law, especially relating to VAT and corporation tax obligations.

UK Corporation Tax and Group Transactions

In the UK, company profits are generally subject to corporate tax. The government, acknowledging the reality of group transactions, has instituted rules to prevent double taxation. For the tax year 2023-2024, profits from intra-group transactions are not likely to be doubly taxed.

This essentially means that if a company within the group sells products or services to another within the same entity, the selling company will have to include any profits gained in its corporation tax calculation. However, the purchasing company can deduct the expense of the goods or services from its taxable profits, which can potentially result in a tax-neutral situation for the group.

Treatment of VAT on Group Transactions

The handling of VAT on group transactions is a different matter. VAT is usually applied to the supply of goods or services, but if services are shared within a VAT group (a group of companies recognised as a single VAT entity), VAT charges will not be applied to these internal supplies.

The tax year 2023-2024's UK VAT rules will allow a group to apply to HMRC to be considered as one VAT entity. This provision would usually disregard intra-group transactions for VAT purposes, potentially leading to significant VAT saving for the group.

Example: Peerex Group

We should consider a hypothetical situation involving Peerex Group, a UK-based group of companies. Assume Peerex Properties used a £1 million intercompany loan from Peerex Finance, another member of the group, for property development.

In this case, Peerex Finance would have to consider Corporation Tax on the interest income it earned. For the tax year 2023-2024, the Corporation Tax rate will be 25%. Hence, Peerex Finance would be liable for £25,000 (25% of the £100,000 interest income) in Corporation Tax.

Yet, Peerex Properties could deduct the interest expenditure from its taxable profits, thereby reducing its Corporation Tax obligation. It, however, would not get to enjoy this advantage if it does not make a profit in the same tax year.

Concluding Insights

It is clear from the above that group transactions can require navigating a complex set of tax implications. Grasping tax requirements and planning these transactions efficiently require a deep understanding of the relevant tax laws, which come with unique guidelines for each tax year. Although this article offers a general understanding of group transactions concerning the UK taxation system, it is recommended to consult a tax professional for specific scenarios.

Effective management of group transactions can lead to significant benefits concerning tax efficiency and capital utilisation within the group. Therefore, it is crucial for business leaders and managers to fully comprehend the implications of these transactions and ensure that they comply with the relevant tax rules. Tax authorities like HMRC in the UK provide resources and guidance, assisting businesses to comprehend and comply with these regulations.

VAT, Tax Admin, UK Tax

This article offers an easily comprehensible in-depth explanation of what VAT is and the registration requirements for it in the United Kingdom for the tax year 2023-2024.

VAT, or Value Added Tax, is essentially a consumption tax that is applied to goods and services in the UK. It is calculated using the economic value added during each supply chain stage. Generally, a standard 20% VAT applies to most goods and services, with some exceptions that are given a reduced rate or are exempt from VAT entirely.

Registration for VAT is primarily based on the taxable turnover of a business. Taxable turnover refers to the total value of everything a business sells that is not VAT exempt in a year's time. According to UK tax rules for the tax year 2023-2024, businesses with a VAT taxable turnover exceeding £85,000 within a 12-month period must register for VAT. Businesses who do not meet this threshold may, however, voluntarily register. Such an option can bring benefits, such as allowing businesses to recover VAT on purchases, or improving their corporate image by proving tax compliance to potential clients or investors.

Businesses can quickly register for VAT online through HM Revenue and Customs' (HMRC) website. During this process, the business will have to provide some basic information like the nature of its business, the business bank account information, and the projected turnover of the business.

After successfully registering, HMRC will issue a VAT registration certificate in approximately 14 working days. This certificate includes the VAT number and crucial dates like when the first VAT return is to be made and the deadline for payment.

The article also provides a hypothetical example to better understand how VAT registration implications for businesses with a specific case study of a tech-based company, Techie Solutions. Based on their taxable turnover and deductible VAT, the process of calculating VAT payable is shown.

Overall, understanding the VAT registration requirements is a crucial aspect of running a business in the UK. Despite this guide's depth, however, it is equally significant to be aware of other intricacies related to VAT like keeping correct records, handling VAT returns, and creating suitable invoices to avoid any hassles later on. The more one knows about VAT regulations, the better equipped they will be to manage the UK taxation universe, whether they're an established business owner or a budding entrepreneur.

An Exploration of VAT Liabilities in the UK Taxation Landscape

Taxation is how governments fund their spending and can be a deeply complex topic to fully understand. A key part of the UK tax framework, and often a source of confusion, is the Value Added Tax or VAT. This financial mechanism involves a detailed calculation aimed at determining the tax due on products and services at each production or distribution stage.

Examining the workings of VAT liability calculation, it's crucial to shed light on the underlying rules that govern the process. According to the UK tax laws for 2023-2024, VAT is levied on most business transactions and services. This generally means that if a firm's total sales exceed the VAT registration threshold set by HM Revenue and Customs, it must add VAT to the sale price of the goods or services it offers.

The Complexities of VAT Calculation

Working out VAT isn't a simple task. The calculation involves finding the difference between the VAT charged to customers and the VAT a company owes its suppliers. To simplify, VAT liabilities are the total VAT payable in a specific period. Yet, getting the hang of the concept of VAT rates is critical to comprehending VAT calculation.

UK tax laws for 2023-2024 include standard, reduced, and zero-rated VAT. The standard VAT is charged at 20%, the reduced rate at 5%, and zero-rated, as the name suggests, means no VAT is charged. The rate applied largely depends on the type of goods or services provided.

A Hypothetical Case Study

Consider a hypothetical scenario to unpack the complexities of VAT calculation. Let's take a company 'Y' that sells both standard-rated and reduced-rated goods. In the 2023-2024 tax year, company 'Y' sold standard-rated goods amounting to £200,000 and reduced-rated products worth £50,000. The company also had costs of £60,000 on standard-rated goods and £10,000 on reduced-rated ones.

The computation begins by adding VAT to sales. For standard-rated goods, the total VAT is £200,000 × 20% = £40,000, and for reduced-rated goods, it's £50,000 × 5% = £2,500, totaling £42,500 in VAT charged to customers.

Next, we subtract the VAT owed to suppliers. The VAT on standard-rated costs would be £60,000 × 20% = £12,000, and for reduced-rated, it's £10,000 × 5% = £500. The total VAT owed to suppliers amounts to £12,500.

Finally, to calculate VAT liabilities, we subtract VAT owed to suppliers from VAT charged to customers: £42,500 - £12,500 = £30,000. As a result, company 'Y' has a VAT liability of £30,000 for the 2023-2024 tax year.

Conclusion

In conclusion, comprehending and calculating VAT liabilities is crucial for responsibly managing tax duties in the UK. This allows companies to comply with tax laws, maintain their credibility and avert penalties. While tax calculations may seem intimidating, they form the financial bedrock of every society, enabling governments to finance public services, construct infrastructure, and propel economic growth.

Comprehending VAT liabilities in the UK taxation system requires an understanding of rules and guidelines set by HMRC. VAT is a consumption tax applied to sales of goods and services. Companies registered for VAT must compute and report their VAT liabilities.

The VATable turnover, which includes total sales and other taxable activities, forms the basis for calculations. Importantly, specific supplies may be exempt or have differing VAT rates, hence companies must understand applicable rules.

Once turnover is determined, VAT due on supplies is calculated. Standard, reduced and zero rates of 5%, 20% and 0% respectively apply to different goods and services. Businesses apply these rates to their supplies to derive VAT amounts.

Besides output VAT, input VAT, or the VAT on firm's purchases and costs, must be considered. Businesses typically reclaim input VAT, subject to specific rules.

To compute VAT liability, firms subtract input VAT from output VAT. If input VAT is greater, firms may claim a refund. If output VAT is higher, they pay the difference.

Maintaining comprehensive records of sales, purchases, and VAT computations is imperative for completing VAT returns and audits by HMRC.

To illustrate, consider a UK-based clothing retailer, company Z. In 2023-2024, it had a VATable turnover of £500,000. At 20% standard VAT rate, VAT due on the firm's supplies is £100,000. If the firm paid £80,000 input VAT, its VAT liability would be £20,000.

Therefore, company Z must pay £20,000 to HMRC for the tax year. It must ensure availability of sufficient funds for timely payments.

In sum, computation of VAT liabilities in the UK involves calculating output VAT, and subtracting the input VAT. Businesses must understand VAT rates, keep accurate records, follow HMRC rules, stay updated on latest VAT regulations, and seek professional advice to ensure compliance with UK tax laws.

Value Added Tax, or VAT as it's commonly known, is a key source of revenue for the UK government. It's a consumption tax applied to the sale of goods and services. Nevertheless, the impact of VAT can be influenced by the specific circumstances of businesses. Acknowledging this, the HM Revenue and Customs (HMRC) has presented a series of special schemes to provide businesses with alternative ways to compute and report their VAT obligations.

The Flat Rate Scheme (FRS) is one such special scheme. Tailored to ease VAT calculations for small businesses, they pay a fixed percentage of their revenue as VAT under this scheme, eliminating the need to compute the VAT due on each separate sale or purchase. They just apply a preset flat rate percentage to their total revenue, which includes VAT. This scheme not only simplifies the VAT computation process but also lightens administrative load for eligible businesses.

Consider a hypothetical example for this scheme, featuring Company Y, a small consultancy firm. They yielded, in the 2023-2024 tax year, £100,000 as a turnover, inclusive of VAT. Their business sector designates a flat rate percentage as per tax regulations, which is 12%. The company uses this flat rate percentage to compute the VAT on the total turnover instead of every individual invoice.

In the given scenario, Company Y's VAT liability would be £12,000 (£100,000 multiplied by 12%). Therefore, for the tax year 2023-2024, the company would owe £12,000 as VAT to the HMRC. Note that under the FRS, companies can't reclaim input VAT on purchases, except on particular capital assets over £2,000.

In addition to FRS, another crucial scheme by HMRC is the Cash Accounting Scheme. This scheme allows qualifying businesses to account for VAT on the actual payments received and disbursed, rather than the invoice dates. This can be particularly beneficial for businesses facing cash flow issues, since they are only obligated to account for VAT when they receive payments from customers.

For instance, suppose we have Company Z, a small retailer. In the 2023-2024 tax year, the company made £80,000 in sales, inclusive of VAT. Under the Cash Accounting Scheme, the company only needs to account for VAT when its customers make payments. If they received £60,000 during the tax year, their VAT liability would be calculated based on this sum, not the total turnover. Assuming a standard VAT rate of 20%, the VAT liability would come to £12,000 (£60,000 times 20%).

The Cash Accounting Scheme can improve cash flow management for companies, as they no longer have to pay VAT on outstanding invoices. However, it's vital to understand that companies using this scheme can't reclaim input VAT until they've paid suppliers in full.

In conclusion, the HMRC's special schemes like the FRS and Cash Accounting Scheme shape the way businesses calculate and report VAT liabilities in the UK tax system. The overall aim of these schemes is to simplify VAT calculations, lessen administrative duties, and offer more flexibility for eligible businesses. By remaining updated on these rules and conditions, companies can opt for the most appropriate scheme for managing their VAT obligations. Businesses must continue to remain informed about VAT regulations and seek expert advice to ensure they meet all UK tax system requirements.

In the UK's expansive tax system, Value Added Tax (VAT) is a crucial component. This consumption tax can have varying implications on different sectors of the economy. This discussion focuses on how VAT impacts the provision of land and buildings within the UK.

Typically, the standard VAT rate under the UK tax system is 20%, but most categories of land and buildings are usually exempt from VAT. Standardly, a building and associated land meant for residential use are exempted from VAT whether it's being sold or leased.

However, there isn't a blanket exemption on this. Certain circumstances may permit VAT to be charged at a standard, reduced, or zero-rate. For example, when a new residential building is being sold or leased under a long-term contract, the transaction can be subject to a zero-rate VAT. In contrast, a 5% reduced VAT rate may apply if a non-residential building is converted into a residential property.

What does this mean for the supplier? Exempt supplies do not allow the supplier to reclaim any incurred VAT related to the pricing structure. On the other hand, a zero-rate supply allows for VAT cost reclaims.

To further understand these VAT nuances, let's examine a hypothetical case. Suppose a property development company, referred to as "Company A", converted an old factory into residential flats in the 2023-2024 tax year. The total project cost amounted to £1,200,000, including £200,000 VAT. The company intends to sell these units.

According to current UK tax regulations, selling these residential flats will warrant a 5% reduced VAT rate. Therefore, the VAT that the company charges on the sale should equate to 5% of the sales price. For instance, if the selling price amounts to £2,000,000, the VAT will be £100,000 (£2,000,000 × 5%).

As selling residential flats invites a reduced VAT rate instead of an exemption, Company A can reclaim the VAT paid on its expenses. This allows the company to reclaim the £200,000 it spent on VAT during the property conversion. Therefore, the net VAT that "Company A" must pay to the HMRC equals the sale's VAT (£100,000) minus the reclaimable cost VAT (£200,000), resulting in -£100,000. Essentially, the HMRC owes "Company A" £100,000!

Navigating the intricacies of VAT implications on land and building supply in the UK can be complex. Each decision can influence a different financial outcome, either protecting against superfluous taxes or retrieving tax credit. Therefore, it's essential to possess robust knowledge of the UK tax system for the 2023-2024 year, as illustrated in this discussion. This knowledge will be valuable when maneuvering through these VAT complexities.

An In-depth Look at VAT and the Consequences of Partial Exemption in the UK Tax Year 2023-2024

Value Added Tax (VAT), a recognised aspect of the fiscal terminology, is inherently intricate and heavy with layers of regulation. These complexities become particularly noticeable when delving into 'partial exemption', a concept that may hold considerable consequences for individuals and businesses alike navigating through the mazes of the UK Tax System. This piece aims to offer a detailed exploration into the VAT consequences of partial exemption, specifically for the UK tax year 2023-2024.

VAT in its simplest form is a consumption tax applied to a product whenever value is added, from production to sale point. However, not all services and goods are viewed equally under VAT legislation. Some receive exemption, whilst others get partial exemption. This split exemption status often generates complex tax scenarios, necessitating thorough understanding and careful navigation.

Getting to Grips with Partial Exemption

To truly grasp the significance of partial exemption, the concept needs to be clearly defined. Partial exemption arises when a business engages in both taxable and exempt sales. In this situation, a business may not be able to reclaim all the VAT they've paid on purchases, as the exempt sales don't afford the same rights to reclaim VAT compared to taxable sales.

Under regular VAT rules, businesses can recoup VAT on purchases linked directly to taxable supplies. However, when a business deals in both taxable and exempt supplies, complications emerge where reclaiming VAT on purchases is only connected to taxable supplies.

Delving into the Consequences

More broadly, the impact of partial exemptions concerns the intricate system by which it's computed, potentially leading to over or under recovery of VAT. This is typically calculated using the standard method, apportioning residual input tax (that is, VAT on expenditure connected to both taxable and exempt supplies) based on taxable supplies to total supplies ratio.

However, this standard method may not always be a fair representation for specific businesses, hence the need for the approval of an apportionment special method.

This can be illustrated with a hypothetical company, "Tech Haven", dealing in taxable technology equipment sales and exempt technology consultation services. Over the tax year 2023-2024, £500,000 was made through taxable goods and £200,000 through exempt services, with a VAT of £70,000 on their purchases.

Given Tech Haven's taxable and exempt supplies mix, they come under partial exemption rules. Using the standard method, their recoverable VAT would be determined as follows:

(£500,000 / £700,000) * £70,000 = £50,000

Tech Haven can, therefore, reclaim £50,000 of the £70,000 VAT they've paid. But does this fairly reflect their professional activities or would a special method give a more precise outcome? These are the complex issues to resolve when looking at partial exemption implications.

Due to this complexity and potential fiscal fallout, it's vital to understand the VAT implications of partial exemptions. Prudent management and an in-depth evaluation can assist in managing any potential risks and in reaping all the potential benefits.

As taxation rules and regulations continue to evolve, keeping up to date with the legislation relevant for the forthcoming tax year is essential. As we approach the 2023-2024 tax year, individuals and corporations must become acquainted with the most recent laws, guaranteeing they effectively navigate the world of VAT and the complexity of partial exemptions.

An In-Depth Look at Implementing the
Capital Goods Scheme in VAT

The Value-Added Tax (VAT) procedures within the UK can be intricate and confusing to navigate. One critical component requiring a nuanced understanding is the application of the Capital Goods Scheme (CGS). In this thorough discussion, we'll delve into this aspect of VAT within the 2023-2024 UK tax year framework.

The CGS is integral to VAT in the UK since it lets businesses adjust the VAT recovered on specific capital assets over time according to the asset's use. It's primarily applicable to assets with a lifespan of at least five years or ten years for land-related items, and that cost more than £50,000 (excluding VAT).

A Brief Look at the Capital Goods Scheme

CGS was designed to reconcile VAT recovery with the actual usage of an asset. This is due to the potential for a capital asset's usage in producing taxable or exempt supplies to change, thus impacting the portion of input tax recoverable. Essentially, CGS acts like a balancing mechanism that reflects the accurate amount of VAT paid relative to the asset's usage.

If the extent of taxable usage for assets under the CGS changes, it means the original VAT recovered must be adjusted accordingly. Consider this as a 'correction mechanism' to align the amount of VAT you reclaim with the use of your capital asset.

Circumstances When CGS is Necessary

If you have spent over £50,000 (excluding VAT) on:
Purchasing land, a building, or civil engineering work.
Constructing a building or civil engineering work.
Refurbishing, altering, or expanding buildings or civil engineering works.
You're obligated to use the CGS.
To provide clarity on these principles, let's consider an example.

Illustrative Exemple : XYZ Construction Ltd.

Let's imagine a company, XYZ Construction Ltd, which spent £120,000 (excluding VAT) constructing an office space (a capital item) in the 2023-2024 tax year. As they intended to use the space for fully taxable purposes, they claimed a full VAT recovery. However, two years into the adjustment period, they found they had to use 25% of the office space for exempt supplies. This switch triggers a CGS adjustment. UK tax rules would require XYZ Construction Ltd. to repay the relevant portion of the VAT over the remaining lifespan of the asset.

Under CGS, such adjustments happen annually for the length of the asset's life (next five years for standard capital items, or ten years for land and buildings), meaning any changes in use will necessitate an adjustment to the starting VAT reclaimed.

In Conclusion

The often complex and shifting world of taxation, including CGS under UK VAT, necessitates the hiring of skilled professionals or CPAs knowledgeable in UK tax law for compliance.

Remember that CGS ensures the VAT recovered on important capital expenditure accurately reflects any business use changes of the asset over time. Thus, comprehending and correctly implementing the scheme is crucial for any company dealing regularly with significant capital assets.

Ensure to review your CGS calculations annually, keep adequate CGS items and calculations records, as they may be required for inspection by HM Revenue & Customs (HMRC).

Professional help is always available when needed - you don't have to navigate the VAT labyrinth on your own. Armed with the right tools and advice, you can manage compliant financial operations.

In closing, always stay informed with the fluctuating tax regulations, particularly in the light of Brexit and the global pandemic. Taxes are one of life's few constants and understanding them is critical for personal and business financial wellbeing.

Tax Impact and Interaction

Comprehending the UK Tax Framework: Major Taxes and Their Effects

There are several kinds of taxes within the UK's tax system, each pertinent to diverse situations. Whether you're considering starting a business, investing in property or planning for your retirement, being aware of possible tax implications is crucial.

Personal Taxation

For many people in the UK, income tax takes precedence. It is applicable to personal earnings, with corresponding tax bands for the 2023-2024 tax year proportionate to income amounts. There is a tax-free allowance of £12,570 meaning no tax is payable on earnings up to this limit. A 20% basic tax rate is applicable for earnings between £12,570 and £50,270. Earnings ranging from £50,270 to £150,000 are taxed at 40%, and a 45% tax rate is applied to income exceeding £150,000.

Capital Gains Tax may also impact your personal tax situation. It applies to the profit you make when you sell assets that have increased in value over time. The rate will depend on the type of asset and your income tax rate and typically ranges from 10% to 20% for most assets, and 18% to 28% for non-primary residence properties.

Business Taxation

As far as businesses are concerned, Corporation Tax is a primary focus. This tax applies to the profits made by a company. The corporation tax rate for the 2023-2024 tax year is 19% in the UK.

Hypothetical Scenario: Calculating Corporation Tax

Consider a theoretical UK company that made an annual profit of £500,000 in the 2023-2024 tax year. The corporation tax would be worked out like this:

Profit: £500,000

Corporation Tax rate: 19%

Tax amount = Profit x Corporation Tax rate

Tax amount = £500,000 × 0.19

Tax amount = £95,000

Given these conditions, the company is required to pay £95,000 in corporation tax.

Indirect Taxation

On top of these direct taxes, you also have to factor in indirect taxes. Value-Added Tax (VAT), a tax on consumer expenditure, is the most well-known of these. The general VAT rate in the UK is 20% although some goods and services attract a lower 5% rate or are exempt.

Additional Taxation

You also need to consider other taxes like Inheritance Tax, applying to the estate of a deceased individual and Stamp Duty Land Tax, applied to property or land transactions.

Appraising the Influence

The main concern is not just comprehending these taxes, but also understanding their fundamental effects. These impacts financial planning, business strategies, retirement planning and investment actions. Therefore, being adept at navigating the UK tax system is crucial both for personal and business finances.

In essence, the UK tax system is complex, and understanding it is crucial not only for compliance but also for optimizing use of finances, whether on a personal or business level. Taxes are undeniably part of wider financial planning which includes setting goals and allocating a budget.

Whenever planning any action in the UK, it's vital to understand the broad range of relevant taxes and their potential impacts. The UK tax system includes taxes such as income tax, corporation tax, Value Added Tax (VAT), capital gains tax (CGT) and others, each potentially applicable depending on the specific context.

In order to demonstrate tax impacts, let's consider a theoretical Company X who intends to grow its manufacturing business by procuring a new facility. The funding could comprise a combination of bank loans and issuing new shares.

In evaluating this scenario, corporation tax, a tax on profits, is an important factor. The firm also need to consider potential deductions or allowances like capital allowances for assets.

If the company finances the expansion by issuing new shares, the stamp duty tax, a tax on certain transactions including share sales, becomes relevant. The company needs to work out the stamp duty liability based on the value of the issued shares.

Acquiring the new facility might also have implications for VAT. If the purchase is subject to VAT, the company needs to figure out the VAT liability.

Company X must also consider the impact of income tax and CGT for its shareholders or directors. Any assets sold to fund the expansion could trigger a CGT liability based on the capital gains calculation, if dividends are distributed, then shareholders will be liable for income tax on those dividends.

It's paramount for Company X to seek professional tax advice and adhere to all relevant tax laws and guidelines in order to stay within the UK tax norms. The impact of taxes can vary depending on different situations, hence every scenario and current tax rules need to be individually reviewed.

In conclusion, taxes undeniably play a major role in steering financial decisions in the UK and should be considered in all actions. By understanding the specifics of each tax, companies can make informed strategic decisions and better manage their tax liabilities. Regular updates on tax regulations and seeking expert advice is crucial for businesses to remain compliant with the UK tax system.

Impacts of UK Taxation on Personal and Business Financial Results

Understanding the ramifications of taxation on personal or business financial management is critical. Different financial strategies can lead to various tax scenarios. This document offers an in-depth analysis of these different tax implications, based on different ways of pursuing personal or business financial goals within the UK tax system for 2023-2024.

The Significance of Tax Considerations

Tax plays a crucial role in every financial decision, whether it is for personal or business purposes. Often, the effect of taxes on the ultimate financial result is overlooked. Haphazardly making financial choices without considering tax liabilities might result in decreased returns and unexpected costs. Therefore, evaluating the tax implications of every possible financial strategy in advance is essential.

Implications of Personal Tax

Gaining insight into personal tax implications starts essentially with understanding the tax bands and allowances in place for the tax year 2023-2024. Our tax bands, income types, and personal exemptions significantly shape the tax we owe. For example, as per the UK's tax system for 2023-2024, the tax-free Personal Allowance is £12,570. Individuals earning up to £50,270 are in the basic rate bracket, liable for 20% tax, whereas those making more than £50,271 are taxed at a higher rate of 40%.

Implications of Business Tax

Businesses also face a complex tax environment. The kind of business, its legal status, and its outcomes notably influence the size and type of the tax liability.

As an instance, consider the Corporation Tax that a company needs to pay. For the year 2023-2024, the Corporation Tax rate is

19%. If a company makes a profit of £100,000 that year, it would owe £19,000 in Corporation Tax. If the company opted to reinvest some of its profit into purchasing new machinery (say £20,000), this capital expenditure would qualify for the Annual Investment Allowance, effectively lowering its taxable profit to £80,000, thus reducing its Corporation Tax liability to £15,200.

Exploring Different Results

How might different ways of achieving personal or business financial results lead to differing tax implications?

Consider small business owner Elaine, who chooses to take her business earnings as dividends rather than a salary. This is because the tax rate on dividends for the fiscal year 2023-2024 is significantly less than the National Insurance contributions she would have to pay on a comparable salary.

Suppose Elaine ran a successful business in 2023-2024 that declared profits of £60,000 after paying Corporation Tax. Elaine could choose to pay herself dividends up to her remaining basic-rate band limit of, say, £37,700 (£50,270 less the personal allowance of £12,570). On dividends between her Personal Allowance and £37,700, Elaine would have to pay a 7.5% tax rate, considerably less than the roughly 25.8% total National Insurance Contributions (employees and employers) she would have paid on the same amount if drawn as a salary.

Each varying way of attaining financial goals presents a chance to decrease tax liabilities. Consequently, it's crucial to familiarize oneself with the tax implications to truly enjoy the financial rewards. But because tax laws are complex and frequently change, the most effective route is often to seek out professional tax advice.

Assessing Tax Efficacy in Various Transaction Scenarios

Understanding the intricate world of finance requires recognizing tax as a significant repercussion of every action. Scrutinizing taxes involved in a financial transaction and understanding their impact is crucial for informed business decisions. This assessment aims to examine a hypothetical transaction thoroughly, shedding light on tax implications within the UK tax framework for the financial year 2023-2024. This will allow us to evaluate different scenarios and suggest the easiest tax-effective path.

A Short Review of UK Taxation: Fiscal Year 2023-2024

An understanding of UK tax norms for the financial year 2023-2024 is vital for a tax efficiency analysis. The personal income tax rate is 20% for earnings up to £50,270, followed by 40% for incomes ranging between £50,271 and £150,000, and a 45% rate for earnings above £150,000. Furthermore, the Capital Gains Tax rate is pegged at 10% for basic-rate taxpayers, rising to 20% for higher and additional-rate taxpayers.

A Hypothetical Case Study: A Straightforward Transaction

An example helps clarify: hypothetically, John, a higher-rate taxpayer, makes a transaction netting him a profit of £100,000. An assessment of the net profit after deducting the pertinent taxes is as follows. If considered as income, the profit attracts a 40% tax, leaving John with £60,000. Conversely, the profit is charged at 20% if considered as a capital gain, resulting in £80,000 post-tax proceeds for John.

Comparing Possible Outcomes

The comparison of these two potential outcomes shows how profit classification affects the payable tax amount and the surplus. If John's profit is labelled as capital gain instead of income, he saves £20,000 in taxes, retaining a larger sum. This highlights the benefits of strategic tax planning and illustrates how the categorization of a transaction's earnings can cause substantial differences in net profits.

Recommendation for Tax Efficient Action

John can save on taxes by structuring the transaction to be tagged as a capital gain rather than income. This may require selling an owned asset, like company stocks or property, rather than deriving the income via labour (income from employment, for instance). This, of course, must always be done legally and transparently.

Underscoring the importance of understanding tax implications to allow for informed planning, a carefully structured transaction can result in significant tax savings, leading to a higher net retention of transaction proceeds. However, one must bear in mind the variations in personal circumstances and regulations. It is advisable to consult a certified tax advisor to make significant financial decisions to ensure an optimally tax-efficient and legal solution.

To approximate the net receipts from a transaction after taxes and evaluate alternate scenarios, one needs to understand UK's relevant tax laws and rules for the tax year 2023-2024. We will use a hypothetical case to illuminate this process.

Scenario: John works as a freelancer, offering services to clients. He has received a proposal for a contract worth £10,000. John must calculate his net income from the transaction after considering relevant taxes.

Income Tax: As a self-employed individual, he is liable to pay income tax on business profits. For the tax year 2023-2024, the applicable income tax rates are as follows: 20% for income up to £50,270 and 40% for income above the threshold. Here, John's total income from the contract is £10,000. Assuming his income remains below the higher threshold for the year, his tax liability will be £2,000 (£10,000 × 20%).

National Insurance Contributions (NICs): John is also liable for NICs in addition to income tax. The NIC rates applicable for the tax year 2023-2024 are 9% on profits between £9,568 and £50,270, and 2% on profits exceeding this limit. His NIC liability would be £855.12 considering his total profits for the year are below the upper threshold.

VAT: John's services, based on their nature and his VAT registration status, might attract VAT. The standard VAT rate for the mentioned tax year is 20%. If VAT registered, John would charge VAT on top of his fees, equaling £2,000 (£10,000 × 20%). VAT will not be charged if John is not VAT registered, or his services VAT exempt.

Based on these calculations, John's net receipts from the transaction would be as follows:

If VAT registered John would retain £6,145.12 (£10,000 - £2,000 income tax - £855.12 NICs - £2,000 VAT)

If not, VAT registered or services are exempt from VAT, John retains £8,145.12 (£10,000 - £2,000 income tax - £855.12 NICs)

Comparisons of alternative scenarios are essential to understand which will be most tax-efficient, considering each scenario's specific conditions and tax implications. For example, incorporating a limited company could provide John with lower corporate tax rates and more tax-efficient ways of generating income, like a combination of salaries and dividends.

However, the most tax-efficient decision depends on factors like profit levels, future growth plans, administrative requirements, and legal considerations. Professional advice is crucial, as regulations vary, and it's essential to follow the appropriate tax laws while making any decision.

In conclusion, underlying UK tax rules and regulations need to be understood to calculate transaction proceeds net of tax and compare alternate scenarios. By considering income tax, NICs, and VAT impacts, individuals can evaluate the tax efficiency of various actions. Regularly updating oneself with the current tax laws and seeking professional advice can help individuals make informed decisions optimizing tax results.

The Impact of Taxation on Financial Choices in the UK: An In-Depth Look at the UK Taxation System

The substantial complexity and intricacy of the UK taxation system, as with any taxation system, brings about heavy repercussions on financial decision-making, affecting both businesses and individuals. Decision-making on corporate structure, investment, personal expenditure, saving, and even charity donations is often subtly influenced by the taxation system. The following delves into details to give a comprehensive understanding of how different aspects of the UK taxation system influence a range of financial decisions as they'd be in the 2023-2024 tax year.

Unwrapping the Corporate World

Corporations, being as enigmatic and changing as they are, have financial decisions that are multifaceted, tied up with many factors and constantly evolving. A key element of this tricky combination is the Corporation Tax, required by UK law, and calculated based on yearly profit for UK companies. The Corporation Tax rate is expected to be 19% for the 2023-2024 tax year. It's important for businesses to consider that this tax does not depend on the distribution of dividends.

For example, let's consider Zeta Corporation, a fictional UK business, which shows a yearly pre-tax profit of £2 million for the 2023-2024 tax year. With a Corporation Tax rate of 19%, it should ideally set aside £380,000 (£2,000,000 × 19%) for this tax. This significant amount greatly impacts its financial choices concerning profit retention, reinvestment, and the distribution of dividends.

Taxation also plays a role in investment choices for corporations. Businesses often look into tax allowances or relief like the Annual Investment Allowance (AIA), that offers full tax relief for qualifying capital equipment purchases made within the tax year. The limit for 2023-2024 is £1 million each year. Using AIA can greatly cut down a corporation's taxable profit, often encouraging them to invest in qualifying assets, regardless of their capital outlay.

The Scenario for Sole Traders and Partnerships

Unincorporated businesses such as sole traders and companies operating as partnerships follow different tax rules. Rather than Corporation Tax, they are subject to Income Tax. The way they approach tax decisions revolves around understanding the progressive structure of UK income tax bands. For the 2023-2024 tax year, an income higher than £50,270 and up to £150,000 is taxed at 40%—known as the higher rate.

Consider Mr. Brighton, a hypothetical sole trader who has a yearly profit of £70,000. After factoring in his personal allowance (assumed to be £12,570 for 2023-2024), he will fall into two tax bands—the basic rate band (20% on £12,571-£50,270 profit) and the higher rate band (40% on profits between £50,271 and £70,000). His tax duty would therefore be £15,960 (£7,740 from the basic rate and £8,220 from the higher rate). These tax rates significantly impact his decisions regarding business growth and personal withdrawals.

The Personal Finance Puzzle

Taxation affects different aspects of individual financial decision-making, such as spending patterns, savings, and investments. For instance, tax on savings and investments has considerable influence. Though there's a limit up to which savings income is tax-free (£1,000 for basic rate taxpayers and £500 for higher rate taxpayers for 2023-2024), tax must be paid on income that goes over these limits. This means people need to carefully consider where and how much they invest, keeping in mind the potential tax consequences.

Consumption and spending are also heavily influenced by indirect taxes such as Value Added Tax (VAT) which is currently 20%. Individuals may limit their expenditure on goods and services subject to high indirect taxes, which ends up affecting their lifestyle choices.

In summary, the UK taxation system, with all its complexity, represents a chess game of strategic moves. Understanding its intricacies can help businesses and individuals to make the best possible financial decisions. It is key to optimize tax obligations without letting them infringe upon financial decision-making liberties. Remember, effective tax planning can serve as a powerful compass, guiding businesses and individuals towards their financial goals.

The UK Tax System: A Look at Financial and Investment Products

When dealing with personal finances and wealth, taxes are inevitably a crucial aspect that dictates how an individual manages or invests their money. In the UK, the tax procedures for various finance sources and investment products that individuals have access to are distinctly different, thus making it a complex and substantial field for citizens to negotiate. This article seeks to unpack these differences, provide a contrastive viewpoint, and delve into a hypothetical situation providing further illumination on the matter. So, let's decode this fiscal journey together.

Exploring Finance and its Associated Tax Procedures

In the sphere of finance, a myriad of sources and forms present themselves, ranging from a salary, a loan, dividends from investments to capital gains from asset sales. The UK law has its distinct tax procedures for each of these.

The Tax System and Salaries

Starting with the most standard source of finance, salaries are charged as Income Tax and National Insurance contributions. For the 2023 - 2024 tax year, the thresholds are as follows: National Insurance is payable on earnings above £184 per week and Income tax applies to earnings that exceed your Personal Allowance (often £12,570). Bear in mind that the tax rate fluctuates based on income levels, with a peak tax rate of 45% for additional rate taxpayers.

Treatment of Taxes on Investments

Dividends from shares or investments have unique tax procedures. Dividends that individuals receive are taxed at three distinct rates—7.5% (basic rate), 32.5% (higher rate), and 38.1% (additional rate) for the 2023-2024 tax year. However, everyone is entitled to a tax-free dividend allowance (£2,000 for 2023-24), with any amounts exceeding this liable for taxation.

Similarly, capital gains from asset sales are liable for Capital Gains Tax (CGT). Different tax rates apply here as well, depending on individual circumstances and the kind of assets. The current tax-free allowance for CGT is set at £12,300.

Tax Implications of Various Investment Products

Moving on from finance sources, different investment products also have varying tax implications. These investment products include savings accounts, individual savings accounts (ISAs), pensions, and property.

Savings Account Taxation

Interest earned from a savings account may also be taxable. Nonetheless, a sizable portion of this interest can be tax-free, thanks to the Personal Savings Allowance (PSA). This allowance permits a tax-free interest income of up to £1,000 for basic rate taxpayers, and £500 for higher rate taxpayers. Additional rate taxpayers are, unfortunately, not eligible for this allowance.

Taxation of Individual Savings Accounts (ISAs)

ISAs are particularly attractive investment products, primarily due to their favorable tax implications. All income or gains accumulated from ISA investments are completely tax-free, presenting significant saving or investment incentives.

Taxation of Pensions

Pensions also come with tax benefits. Individuals receive tax relief on their contributions, with the rate of relief being equal to their highest rate of Income Tax, up to a certain annual limit.

Property Taxation

However, property investment in forms such as buy-to-let properties can attract Income Tax on the rental revenue after deducting permissible expenses, and Capital Gains Tax payable on any generated gain from selling the property.

Navigating a Tax Scenario
To better understand how these tax laws, apply in real-world scenarios, let's consider a hypothetical case. Assume Mr. Smith is

a higher-rate taxpayer who earned £60,000 in the 2023-2024 tax year. Additionally, he received dividends worth £10,000 from his investments and made a capital gain of £20,000 from his sale of shares.

Subtracting the tax-free allowance of £2,000 leaves £8,000 of the dividends to be taxed at the rate of 32.5%, yielding a tax total of £2600.

Similarly, for capital gains, the first £12,300 is tax exempt, and the remaining £7,700 is subject to Capital Gains Tax at the rate of 20% for higher-rate taxpayers. This would result in additional tax fees of £1,540.

Hence, Mr. Smith is obligated to pay £4,140 in taxes to Her Majesty's Revenue & Customs (HMRC) for his investments, in addition to his income tax dues. This example provides a straightforward illustration of how diverse income sources and investments operate under different tax laws and how even relatively simple financial scenarios can escalate into complex situations.

In conclusion, the tax implications of finance and investment products present a layered landscape that necessitates careful navigation. As the intricacies of taxation increase with financial advancements, understanding and capitalizing on various tax treatments become essential for optimal fiscal planning. Tax-savvy individuals must pay careful attention to the unique thresholds and rates presented in the 2023-2024 tax year. Remember, in the world of taxation, knowledge equates to power and wealth.

Throwing Light on Tax Implications: Elevating Equity and Streamlining Loan Finance in the UK

Comprehending the tax ramifications is pivotal to fundraising via equity and loan finance. In this write-up, we will dive into these implications in line with the UK taxation framework for the fiscal year 2023-2024.
Equity Financing and its Tax-Related Implications
Equity financing, in simpler words, is obtaining funds by trading off a part of the company's shares or equity to investors. It predominantly includes two sorts: common and preferred equity.

From the taxation standpoint, funds acquired through equity financing are not taxable as they are seen as capital not income. That's what makes this financing type attractive. However, such financing doesn't directly impact the company's tax liability, but it holds tax consequences for investors purchasing the shares.

Investors in the UK who acquire equity as a part of an equity financing deal are taxed on their dividends and capital gains. As per the tax norms for the year 2023-2024, the dividend tax is layered according to personal income tax brackets. Specifically, basic rate taxpayers give away 7.5%, higher rate taxpayers surrender 32.5%, while additional rate taxpayers surrender 38.1% on dividend income. In contrast, the Capital Gains Tax (CGT) for share disposal is either 10% or 20% depending on an individual's income tax rate.

Loan Financing and its Tax-Related Implications

Conversely, loan financing pertains to borrowing money that necessitates repayment over a specified period with interest. Loans can be obtained from diverse sources such as banks, credit unions, or even acquaintances and family.

As per the UK taxation rules in force for 2023-2024, the interest expense on the loan is tax-deductible. This implies that businesses can deduct interest payments from their profit, thereby reducing taxable income. However, an increase in debt could heighten financial risk owing to the mandatory nature of interest and principal payments.

For instance, consider a company called ABC Ltd., situated in the UK, that secures a bank loan of £1 million with an annual interest rate of 5%. This leads to an annual interest expense of £50,000. According to UK tax norms, this interest is tax-deductible, hence reducing ABC Ltd.'s taxable income by that amount. Ultimately, if the corporation tax rate stands at 24% for the financial year 2023-2024, the company would be able to save £12,000 in taxes (£50,000 × 24%).

Striking a Balance between Benefits and Implications:

In a nutshell, choosing between equity and loan finance is a tricky decision that entails numerous factors like tax implications. Despite being non-taxable and non-mandatory, equity financing may pose a risk to the company's control due to high equity dilution. Conversely, even though debt heightens financial risk, it offers a tax shield, which may potentially boost the company's value.

Companies must judiciously gauge their respective situations and future plans to ensure the chosen financing source aligns with their aims and financial capacity and optimizes their tax position. UK tax guidelines for the year 2023-2024 do incorporate some relief measures, but their complexity necessitates professional guidance. In any case, a clear comprehension and application of tax rules can significantly augment fundraising efficiency and the overall well-being of the company.

Examining the Tax Variations in Lease, Hire Purchase, and Direct Purchase Decisions

There are countless methods that businesses may utilize to finance the assets needed for their operations. In the UK, leasing, hire purchasing, and direct purchasing are among the most prevalent options. These conventional methods of asset acquisition each have their own unique tax implications, just like most financial choices. This article focuses on analyzing the tax variations amongst these three alternatives, referencing the UK taxation system for the 2023-2024 tax year.

Leasing in the UK

Leasing is tantamount to asset renting. Corporations pay a pre-determined rental fee for the duration of the contract, without owning the asset. For taxation purposes in the UK, these lease payments are classified as operational expenses and are, therefore, tax-deductible.

For instance, suppose ABC Ltd. opts to lease machinery for £10,000 annually in the 2023-24 tax year. Over a 5-year tenor, the company may deduct £50,000 from its pre-tax profits, resulting in savings on corporation tax.

Hire Purchase
On the other hand, in a hire purchase agreement, a company agrees to pay for an asset in instalments over a set timeframe,

eventually obtaining outright ownership. Even though the corporation only technically owns the asset after the final payment, immediate tax benefits apply.

According to UK tax regulations, a company in a hire purchase agreement is allowed to claim capital allowances, effectively lowering its tax liability. Suppose, for example, company XYZ Ltd. enters into a hire purchase agreement for equipment worth £100,000 over 10 years. They could claim an Annual Investment Allowance (AIA) worth 100% on the first £1 million spent on plant and machinery (excluding cars), saving £19,000 in corporation tax in that year, given a 19% corporation tax rate.

However, the interest portion of the instalments paid by the company is treated as an expense and also permitted as a tax deduction.

Outright Purchase

In the case of direct purchase, a firm procures the asset by paying the full amount upfront. The asset subsequently features on the company's balance sheet and is depreciated over its economically useful life.

However, the depreciation isn't tax-deductible. Instead, similar to hire purchase, the company can claim capital allowances on the cost of the assets to reduce its tax liability. Therefore, if company PQR Ltd. buys machinery for £500,000, it can claim the Annual Investment Allowance, which is tax-deductible, thus saving on its tax liability.

Conclusion

The choice between leasing, hire purchase, and direct purchase can dramatically affect a company's tax situation. It's crucial to choose an option that resonates with the business's financial objectives and operational requirements. Additionally, other considerations such as the nature of the asset, its economic life, potential technological changes, and the cash flow implications of each option must be contemplated beforehand.
Though each option has its own advantages, it is advisable to seek professional guidance from a tax consultant or chartered

accountant. Such professionals can present a detailed overview of tax liabilities under different choices, tailored to a business's unique financial situation.

Given the ever-changing nature of tax rules, it pays to stay current with the most recent tax allowances and reliefs under UK tax law. This way, your business can maximize tax benefits from lease agreements, hire purchases, or direct purchases, thereby optimizing its tax efficiency.

Examining the Effect of Taxation and Cash Flows on UK Businesses

In the intricate environment of UK business operations, the profound role of the UK taxation system and its substantial effect on cash flows cannot be overstated. Taxes, an inescapable expenditure in business, often impose a significant impact on the flow of finances in a company. Essentially, a business's cash flow reflects the net movement of cash and its equivalents going to and from a corporation, providing an overview of a company's fiscal wellness, a sector that tax influences directly. This passage intends to shed light on the consequential influence of tax on the cash flows of businesses in the UK.

Delving into Taxation

Taxes come in different forms ranging from business rates, corporation tax, Value Added Tax (VAT), to National Insurance contributions. As per the revised UK tax regulations for 2023-2024, UK corporations are necessitated to pay corporation tax at 19% on all profits earned, which significantly reduces the post-tax cash flow of the company.

Understanding the compound taxation system based on various factors is crucial for businesses to sustain a healthy cash flow. They need to comprehend how their income from operations, be it recurring or earned through interest, discounts, or dividends, are impacted by tax obligations.

Effect of Taxation on Cash Flows
The available cash of businesses is directly decreased through taxation, thereby limiting their ability to reinvest or pay dividends

to owners or shareholders. Since taxes entail an outflow, they unavoidably reduce the overall cash flow.

For small to medium-sized businesses with modest earnings, the expense of taxes can have a massive impact. Extreme taxation can suffocate them by limiting their ability to invest, expand, or even carry out daily operations owing to restricted cash availability.

Beyond immediate impacts, taxation can also produce long-term effects on corporations. Retained earnings, which are profits reserved within the business after paying taxes and dividends, would also decrease due to higher tax expenses, thereby reducing the amount available for reinvestment and potentially obstructing future business growth.

Additionally, the timing of tax payment, which is regulated by UK tax policy requiring businesses to pay their taxes at particular intervals, can also influence cash flows. If a business struggles with cash management, this obligation could increase the pressure on its cash flows.

Navigating Tax Challenges: A Hypothetical Case Study

To illustrate the impact of taxation on businesses, let's consider a hypothetical case of a small manufacturing firm - WidgetCo, situated in Manchester, UK. For the tax year 2023-2024, WidgetCo expects pre-tax profits of £500,000.

In line with UK tax requirements, WidgetCo is subject to corporation tax at 19%, which equates to £95,000 (£500,000 × 0.19). This tax is paid from the company's cash reserves, reducing the total cash available for reinvestment and daily operations.

As a result, WidgetCo's post-tax net income or cash flow would be £405,000 (£500,000 - £95,000). Therefore, the company would have £405,000 left to distribute as dividends to shareholders, repay debts, reinvest, or retain within the company. This example brings to light how the cash flow of a business can be affected due to the UK's tax policies.

Final Thoughts

In sum, the reach of taxation is pervasive and unavoidable. Being a significant part of conducting business in the UK, tax can considerably influence a business's cash flow. It is imperative for businesses to have a proactive tax approach and comply with tax obligations to maintain their operation. The hypothetical case of WidgetCo offers practical insight into the effects tax could have on a company's cash positioning, underlining the importance of sound financial and tax planning for sustainable business operation.

Taxation can have a considerable impact on a business's finances in the UK in various ways, including tax payment, tax liabilities' timing, and the availability of tax allowances and reliefs.

A key aspect of taxation's impact on cash flows is the payment of taxes. Companies are required to pay income or corporation tax on their profits depending on the legal structure, reducing the available cash for reinvestment or shareholder distribution. Additionally, tax payment timings are crucial as companies need to manage their finances to fulfil tax obligations.

Moreover, tax allowances and reliefs can also impact a business's finances. These, such as capital allowances or R&D tax credits, can lower taxable profits and hence, tax liabilities, leading to increased cash flow by retaining more earnings. It is crucial for businesses to understand and utilize the available tax allowances and reliefs to enhance their cash flow.

Furthermore, changes in tax rates or legislation can affect a business's cash flow. A tax rate increase could lead to higher tax liabilities and reduced finances, while a decrease could lead to lower liabilities and increased finances. Keeping abreast with the latest tax laws and regulations is thus critical for businesses in order to anticipate and prepare for potential changes in their cash flows.

To understand better, let's consider an example with a manufacturing company, Company X, which shows an annual profit of £100,000. Assuming a corporation tax rate of 19% for 2023-2024, the company would have a tax liability of £19,000, reducing its cash availability and impacting its cash flow.

However, if Company X is eligible for capital allowances worth £10,000, its taxable profits would reduce to £90,000, leading to a reduced tax liability of £17,100. The availability of capital allowances enhances the cash flow of the company by reducing tax liabilities.

Managing cash flows carefully in view of tax obligations is crucial for businesses. This includes tax payment planning, leveraging available tax reliefs and allowances, and staying updated on changes in tax rates or legislation. Businesses can make well-informed financial decisions, ensuring efficient financial management by understanding taxation's impact on cash flows.

In conclusion, taxation greatly impacts a business's cash flow in the UK. Tax liabilities deplete the available finance for a business, while tax reliefs and allowances increase cash flows. Tax rates or legislation changes can also affect cash flows. Businesses must understand and plan for their tax obligations to optimize their cash flow and ensure financial stability. Staying current with the latest tax laws and seeking professional advice can help businesses navigate the complex UK tax system and make sound financial decisions.

Grasping the Pros and Cons of Diverse Tax Options in the UK's Tax System

The UK tax system is an extensive framework that calls for a detailed approach, bolstered by the complexity of implementing effective tax methods for UK citizens. Careful and tactful planning can yield a host of benefits on tax-related matters. However, it's also true that certain tax routes can be a double-edged sword, coming with both pros and cons. It's, therefore, of utmost importance to comprehend the tax consequences of different options before taking the plunge. This article will clarify and evaluate the possible tax advantages and disadvantages of engaging in different actions in the UK, based on the tax rules effective for the fiscal year 2023-2024.

Let's kick off by identifying some common tax options and strategies, like tax-efficient investments, exploiting tax allowances, and pension contributions. Each strategy undoubtedly has its own tax benefits, but they come with associated drawbacks, necessitating a balanced approach.

Tax-efficient investments, like venture capital trusts (VCTs), the Enterprise Investment Scheme (EIS), and Seed Enterprise Investment Scheme (SEIS), provide appealing tax exemptions to investors, concurrently infusing essential capital into UK small businesses or start-ups. They may offer income tax relief, Capital Gains Tax (CGT) deferral, or CGT exemption to investors. Under the EIS, for instance, an individual can invest up to £1m in eligible companies in a tax year and secure a reduction in their income tax bill equivalent to 30% of the value of shares purchased.

While these investments seem profitable, there is a downside: these investments generally carry high risk due to the nature of the funded companies. These businesses are frequently in their nascent stages, leading to a high uncertainty of success and profitability. This could endanger the investment and make the benefits of tax relief pale in comparison to the potential losses.

Another approach is to make the most of tax-free allowances. In the tax year 2023-2024, every UK citizen is entitled to specified levels of income and gains they can earn before they are subjected to tax, known as their personal allowance and annual exempt amount, respectively. The personal allowance, for example, is £13,500. Therefore, individuals can earn up to this amount without incurring any income tax.

However, these allowances are reduced or even cancelled for those with high income levels. If your income is over £100,000, your personal allowance is trimmed by £1 for every £2 of income over the £100,000 threshold. Hence, this tax reduction strategy may prove disadvantageous for high earners.

Making payments into a pension scheme can also offer a significant tax advantage. This allows for income tax relief on contributions made up to specified limits and tax-free growth of the pension investment. For instance, a basic rate taxpayer investing £800 into their pension scheme will receive a government addition of £200.

A significant drawback, however, is that access to these funds is restricted. Pension funds typically cannot be accessed before the age of 55 - an age that is set to increase to 57 by 2028. This requires a long-term commitment which may not be feasible for everyone.

Consider a hypothetical example featuring Mr. Smith, a high-earning freelancer. Mr. Smith's taxable income for the tax year 2023-2024 amounts to £150,000, which exceeds the £100,000 income limit for the full personal allowance. His personal allowance would be reduced by £1 for every £2 above the limit, leading to a reduction of £25,000. Therefore, his personal allowance would be £13,500 - £25,000 = -£11,500. However, the personal allowance cannot be negative, which results in Mr. Smith receiving no personal allowance for the tax year.

If Mr. Smith considered making pension contributions, this could lower his taxable income while investing in a retirement fund. Suppose he redirects £40,000 into a pension scheme (the maximum tax-free contribution for the tax year). This reduces his taxable income to £110,000, allowing him to reclaim some of his personal allowance.

It is vital for UK individuals and businesses to weigh the tax pros and cons of different strategies. The tax consequences of various alternatives can significantly influence financial outcomes and should be carefully considered. Let's inspect the tax pros and cons of different strategies through a hypothetical scenario.

Case: Sarah is a freelance consultant contemplating two options for acquiring a new computer for her enterprise. Option A involves buying the computer outright, while Option B entails leasing the computer for a set term.

Option A: Direct Purchase

Advantages:

Ownership: Sarah would immediately own the asset upon purchasing the computer outright, giving her full control over its usage and potential future value.

Capital Allowances: Sarah can claim capital allowances on the computer's price, enabling her to subtract part of the expense from her taxable profits over time.

VAT Reclaim: If Sarah is VAT registered, she may be eligible to reclaim the VAT paid on the purchase, reducing the overall cost.

Disadvantages:

Upfront Cost: Buying the computer outright necessitates a substantial upfront payment which could affect Sarah's cash flow and funds available for other business needs.

Capital Gains Tax: If Sarah decides to sell the computer at a later date, any capital gains she realizes may be taxable.

Option B: Lease

Advantages:

Cash Flow: Leasing the computer allows Sarah to split the cost over regular lease payments, aiding cash flow and offering flexibility.

Tax Deductibility: Lease payments are usually tax-deductible as business expenses, reducing Sarah's taxable profits and total tax liability.

Upgrades: By leasing, Sarah may get the opportunity to upgrade to newer technology at the end of the lease term, ensuring access to the latest equipment.

Disadvantages:

No Ownership: Sarah doesn't own the computer when leasing and therefore doesn't benefit from any potential appreciation in its value.

Long-term Cost: Even though lease payments are spread over time, the total cost of leasing may be higher than an outright purchase.

VAT: Depending on the lease deal, VAT may be applied to lease payments, increasing the overall cost.

Recognizing and adhering to the requirements of the UK tax system is vital for everyone, including individuals and businesses. These obligations involve correctly and promptly paying taxes.

Lack of compliance can lead to severe impact, including fines and accruing interests. It is vital to understand these obligations to avoid any repercussions.

Often, these legal obligations pertaining to the UK tax system are enshrined in law. For instance, all profitable businesses are required to pay a corporate tax, whilst individuals earning more than the basic tax-free Personal Allowance are liable to pay Income Tax. Accompanying these obligations are certain responsibilities, including the accurate reporting of income and expenses and prompt tax payments.

Additionally, these legal obligations also encompass reporting requirements, each of which has its set time limit. Businesses are required to file their tax returns within a year of their accounting period's end. For individuals, if they have been self-employed as a 'sole trader' and earned more than £1,000 in the previous tax year, they must send a tax return. Usually, the deadline for this is 31st January following the end of the tax year.

Through a hypothetical scenario, let's delve into these responsibilities in greater detail. Let's assume John is a self-employed software consultant earning £60,000 from his consulting services in the tax year 2023-2024. Additionally, his income includes savings income of £2000 and dividend of £3000 from his investments.

John's total earned income is £60,000. As it exceeds the Personal Allowance threshold of £12,500, he's liable to pay Income Tax. The next £37,500 is taxable at the basic rate of 20%, and any amount over this is subjected to a higher tax rate of 40%.

His savings income of £2,000 includes a tax-free allowance of £1,000, given his status as a basic rate taxpayer. The remaining sum is taxed at a 20% rate.

Correspondingly, his dividend income qualifies for a tax-free allowance of £2,000, leaving the remaining £1,000 taxable at the basic rate of 7.5%.
If John fails to fully disclose his income or fails to pay his taxes on time, he could incur penalties, interest charges, and even face possible criminal prosecution.

It is essential to comprehend the legal obligations and responsibilities to comply with the UK tax rules and prevent any ramifications. These obligations include accurately completing tax returns, paying taxes on time, and providing full and accurate information to HMRC. Consulting with professionals and staying updated on tax rules can help maintain compliance and avoid any disappointing surprises.

If these requirements are not met, consequences like late filing penalties, interest charges on outstanding tax amounts, loss of certain tax benefits, increased scrutiny from HMRC, and potential damage to reputation could occur. Therefore, it is in every individual's and business's best interest to understand and adhere to these statutory obligations to avoid any unfavorable outcomes.

Tax Minimization Strategies

Tax Liability Reduction: An In-Depth Look at the UK's Taxation System's Impact on Investments and Expenditures (2023-2024)

The volatility of financial market trends leaves the future unpredictable. However, there's one universal fact that remains unaltered: the universal desire to reduce tax payment. How can strategic measures be applied to capitalize on the UK's taxation system for the purpose of reducing taxpayers' duties? Let's explore further.

Our financial strength as individuals or businesses is often juxtaposed with the amount of tax paid. Yet, if navigated wisely, the UK tax system can be beneficial. The oversight of many is not recognizing that certain types of investments and expenses can serve to decrease tax obligations.

Personal Investment Strategies

The clever use of allowances and proper investments are key. As an individual, contributions to a personal or stakeholder pension scheme are beneficial. Consider the scenario of John, a top-tier taxpayer in the UK, who deposits £40,000 into his pension scheme. According to the tax rules for 2023-2024, this reduces his taxable income and allows him to claim a tax relief of £20,000.

This considerable amount has been converted from potential tax into John's pension fund.

Also, injecting funds into Individual Savings Accounts (ISAs) enables tax-free interest earnings on savings and dividends, plus capital gains. Fully utilizing the maximum annual allowance of £20,000 for ISA investments is recommended. All returns from the ISA, whether interest or capital gains, are completely exempt from tax.

For those with higher risk tolerance, venture capital trusts or investments in companies under the Enterprise Investment Scheme or the Seed Enterprise Investment Scheme could be appealing. Despite the increased risk, the tax relief offered can be significant. Furthermore, qualifying investments under these schemes could result in income tax relief ranging from 30% to 50% of the amount invested.

Business Expenditure Strategies

Businesses have the opportunity to reduce tax liabilities through capital allowances. These allowances can be claimed when they purchase assets for business use such as machinery, business vehicles, or equipment. Businesses can deduct the value of these items from their profits before paying tax.

Consider the company XYZ Ltd. which spent £50,000 on machinery for their production line. By claiming the Annual Investments Allowance (AIA) for this expenditure, the full cost can be deducted from their profits before tax, thereby decreasing their tax liabilities. As of April 2023, the maximum AIA relief is £200,000 per annum.

Then there are research and development incentives which provide significant benefits. Companies involved in qualifying R&D activities can claim R&D tax credits. Smaller companies could secure a tax credit of 230% on their eligible R&D expenses, potentially recovering up to 33.35% of the costs.

Businesses registered for VAT can simplify their tax obligations or lower their tax bills through flat rate schemes. This strategy is especially useful for service businesses with minimal VAT expenses.

Pointing out investment and expenditure types that can lead to tax liability reduction is a crucial aspect of tax planning for both individuals and businesses in the UK. By adopting various tax planning methods, tax payers can legally reduce their tax obligations and enhance their financial performance. Some common approaches to achieve this objective include pension contributions, capital allowances, R&D tax credits, Entrepreneur's Relief, and charitable donations.

However, it is pivotal to execute these tax planning strategies within the law's perimeters and in alignment with HMRC's specific regulations. It is essential to seek professional advice and keep abreast of the latest tax rules and regulations to ensure compliance and maximize available tax benefits.

To exemplify the influence of tax planning strategies, consider Company X. This manufacturing business invests in new machinery worth £100,000. By claiming capital allowances on this machinery, a portion of the cost can be deducted from the taxable profits. If the capital allowances rate is 18%, the company can claim capital allowances of £18,000, reducing its taxable profits and overall tax obligations.

UK Tax Planning Strategies

Figuring out taxes can be a demanding task, due to the complexities of tax laws and regulations. However, a well-planned tax strategy doesn't only aid in adhering to tax regulations but also helps in limiting liabilities. Especially in the UK, where tax regulations can be incredibly complex, organizing for tax can be a considerable endeavor. Below, you'll find a variety of legal and conventional tax planning methods that are used by UK individuals and businesses for the tax year 2023-2024.

Optimizing Personal Allowance

In the UK, each individual is given a specific "personal allowance" for each tax year. This is the income amount that one can earn before the tax is applied. For the tax year 2023-2024, this personal allowance is set at £12,570. If you fall into the higher or additional tax rate bands, you can potentially benefit by transferring part of your personal allowance to a spouse or civil partner who pays tax at the standard rate.

Contributing to Pension Funds

Investing in your pension fund is another efficient method for tax planning. Any amount that is invested in a personal pension fund can attract tax relief at your highest rate. For instance, the government generally adds £20 for every £80 you invest. If you are a higher-rate taxpayer, you can claim further relief through the self-assessment tax return.

Claiming Business Expenses

If you own a business, certain expenses can be subtracted from your total income to alleviate tax liability. Office supplies, phone bills, business travel, staff salaries, and business insurance amongst other expenses are claimable.

Utilising Capital Gains Tax Allowances

In the tax year 2023-2024, every individual has a capital gains tax-free allowance of £12,300. Strategically selling assets and effectively utilizing this allowance can save a significant amount on tax payments.

Investing Efficiently

Investments in schemes such as the Enterprise Investment Scheme (EIS), Seed Enterprise Investment Scheme (SEIS), and Venture Capital Trusts (VCTs) can also offer substantial relief from your tax bill. These investments provide various tax reliefs, including income tax and capital gains.

Case Study:

Let's use Mr. Smith, a UK resident making £60,000 in the tax year 2023-2024, as an example.

Out of this amount, £12,570 is his tax-free personal allowance. The next £37,700 is taxed at the basic rate (20%), and the remaining £9,730 is taxed at the higher rate (40%).

Without any tax planning, Mr. Smith's tax bill would look like this:

£37,700 × 20% = £7,540 (basic rate tax)
£9,730 × 40% = £3,892 (higher rate tax)
Total Tax: £7,540 + £3,892 = £11,432

However, by contributing of £10,000 to his pension fund, Mr. Smith's taxable income is reduced, eliminating the higher-rate tax and reducing the basic rate tax to £36,430.

This new calculation would look as follows:

£36,430 × 20% = £7,286 (basic rate tax)
Total Tax: £7,286

With a saving of £4,146 (£11,432 - £7,286) in the tax year after the pension contributions, it's clear how important effective tax planning can be with regard to UK taxation rules. Tax laws and limits are prone to changes, so it's always wise to consult a tax expert or financial advisor for guidance. After all, each penny saved is a penny earned.

Remember these legal tax planning strategies to avoid paying more tax than needed. Keep up-to-date with changes in tax rules, seek expert advice when needed and ensure to utilize your allowances and explore the exemptions and reliefs available. This way, you can devise an effective tax strategy, ensuring your hard-earned finances grow while your tax liabilities are limited.

There are several legitimate tax planning measures that individuals and businesses in the UK can use in order to mitigate tax liabilities resulting from specific situations or actions. These measures aim to optimize tax outcomes legally. Let's explore some associated tax planning measures.

Taking advantage of Tax-Advantaged Accounts: Individuals can utilize tax-advantaged accounts like Individual Savings Accounts (ISAs) and pensions. ISAs are funded from post-tax income and any income or capital gains from the ISA are tax-free. Pension contributions earn relief, reducing taxable income and overall tax liabilities.

Maximizing Capital Allowances: Businesses can increase capital allowances by identifying and claiming allowances on eligible assets. Capital allowances let businesses deduct a portion of an asset's cost from the taxable profits, reducing the overall tax liability. Clarification of specific rules and rates for different types of assets is needed to optimize the allowances.

Research and Development (R&D) Tax Credits: Businesses involved in qualifying R&D activities might be eligible for R&D tax credits. These credits provide tax relief by letting businesses deduct a percentage of their R&D spending from taxable profits. The R&D Expenditure Credit (RDEC) scheme for larger companies and SME R&D Relief scheme for small and medium-sized businesses are available.

Entrepreneur's Relief: Individuals who sell all or part of their business may be eligible for Entrepreneur's Relief which allows for reduced rate capital gains tax (10%) on qualifying gains, up to a lifetime limit.

Making Charitable Donations: Making donations to charity can provide tax benefits for both individuals and businesses. Individuals can claim tax relief on donations made to registered charities and businesses on donations made to qualifying charitable organisations, effectively reducing taxable income (individuals) and taxable profits (business).

Tax planning measures should be performed legally and in line with specific rules and regulations set by HMRC. Obtaining expert advice and staying updated regarding tax rules and regulations are crucial in ensuring compliance and making the most out of the available tax benefits.

To describe the impact of tax planning, consider this case study. Company X, a manufacturing business, plans to invest in new machinery costing £100,000. By claiming capital allowances on the machinery, the company can deduct some of the cost from taxable profits. Assuming an 18% capital allowances rate, the company can claim £18,000 in capital allowances, reducing taxable profits and tax liabilities.

Understanding the Relevance of Potential Investments, Expenditures or Measures in the UK Tax System: A Hypothetical Case Study

Deciphering the complex maze of taxes is not easy, primarily when you try to understand if a specific investment, expenditure or measure is apt for an individual's particular circumstance. The UK taxation system's complexity demands a comprehensive understanding and in-depth consideration of personal financial conditions, future goals and strategic planning.

Consider an imaginary instance of a homeowner named John in the UK, who is also a property development entrepreneur. For the tax year 2023-2024, John invested in a considerable property outside London intending to renovate and sell it profitably. John needs to understand the tax consequences of his investment decisions under the UK tax laws for the given tax year.

In this case, John could be subject to Capital Gains Tax (CGT) on his property investment in the 2023-2024 tax year. CGT applies when a capital asset, such as property or shares, is sold for more than its purchase price. The UK taxation system provides a tax-free allowance, known as the Annual Exempt Amount. Profits exceeding this allowance will be subject to CGT rates for 2023-2024. John's total taxable income in that tax year will determine the CGT rate that he'll be charged.

Let's assume the Annual Exempt Amount for 2023-2024 is fixed at £12,300. John would need to pay CGT if his gains exceed this amount. If his total taxable income, inclusive of gains, does not surpass his personal allowance plus the basic rate limit, he will have to pay CGT at a rate of 10%. This rate increases to 20% if his gains exceed the specified limit.

Further, John also needs to understand Value Added Tax (VAT) regulations related to his property development operations. The UK tax laws for 2023-2024 impose a standard rate of VAT (presumed at 20%) on most goods and services, including property development. Certain products and services attract a reduced VAT rate, so it's critical for John to comprehend VAT rules relevant to his operations to avoid unnecessary expenses.

Additionally, John can claim business expense deductions related to his property development work, such as costs for renovation materials, labor wages, and professional services fees, as well as mortgage interest incurred on property purchase.

In conclusion, intelligent tax planning involves careful consideration of multiple factors. It's crucial for taxpayers like John to comprehend the UK tax system to make informed investment choices. Therefore, taxpayers should continuously keep themselves updated about tax regulation changes or seek tax professionals' help to guarantee the proper and beneficial management of their finances.

When evaluating the suitability of investment, expenditure, or tax strategies for specific taxpayers in the UK, it's crucial to consider their unique circumstances and goals. What may work for one may not be right for others. Let's demonstrate this through a hypothetical case study.

Case: Sarah is a high-income self-employed consultant who wants to minimize her taxes while maximizing her financial results. She's expressed her aim of saving for her retirement and optimizing her tax efficacy.

Several tax strategies could be suitable for Sarah, given her circumstances and goals:

Pension Contributions: Suggesting to Sarah that she contribute to a pension scheme would allow her to attain her retirement savings goal and enjoy tax relief. Pension contributions are eligible for tax relief based on the contributor's income tax rate and can help Sarah decrease her taxable income, reduce her overall tax liability, and build a tax-efficient retirement fund.

Capital Allowance and R&D tax credits: If she invests in eligible assets or carries out eligible R&D activities, Sarah can benefit from capital allowance and R&D tax credits. By claiming capital allowances on her business assets and possibly utilizing R&D tax credits, she can reduce taxable profits, lighten her tax liabilities, support business growth and encourage innovation while optimizing her tax efficiency.

Charitable Donations: Encouraging Sarah to make tax-deductible donations would help her optimize tax efficiency and contribute to causes she supports. The tax relief she can claim on donations would effectively reduce her taxable income, offer tax benefits and align with her declared objectives.

Entrepreneur's Relief: If Sarah plans to sell her business or shares, advising her on the eligibility and advantages of Entrepreneur's Relief could be suitable. This relief allows for a lower capital gains tax rate on qualifying gains, up to a lifetime limit. By using this relief, Sarah can minimize her tax liabilities when realizing her business' value.

It's important to assess these measures' suitability for Sarah depending on her income level, risk tolerance, long-term financial goals, and personal circumstances. Staying updated on tax rules and regulations is crucial, and seeking professional advice can ensure compliance and maximize tax benefits.

Examining Mitigation Strategies for the UK Tax System: An In-Depth Look

The management of finances often crucially depends on tax planning, an aspect that can greatly influence overall financial health. A myriad of tax regulations and systems exist in the UK to establish an equitable and harmonious fiscal architecture. Recognizing top-notch strategies for tax mitigation is vital for both individuals and organizations in this intricate financial environment.

A crucial step towards successful tax mitigation is familiarizing with the different kinds of taxes and understanding their association with one's financial status. Generally, UK tax can be divided into direct and indirect taxes. Direct taxes are those that are explicitly imposed on the taxpayer, namely income tax, corporation tax, capital gains tax, inheritance tax and so forth. On the other hand, indirect taxes are those levied on goods and services, like value-added tax, insurance premium tax, fuel duty, among others. All these direct and indirect taxes add value to the UK Government's fiscal policy, with income tax and VAT being the primary sources of revenue.

Demonstration of Income Tax Calculation – A Hypothetical Scenario

For example, consider Mr. X, a UK resident for the tax year 2023-2024. His annual income from multiple sources amounts to £54,000, and he is entitled to a personal allowance of £12,570. Be aware that the tax rates for the year 2023-2024 are 20% (basic), 40% (higher), and 45% (additional) for income slabs of £0 to £50,270, £50,271 to £150,000, and above £150,000 respectively.

Broadly, the income tax due could be assessed as follows:

Income up to the personal allowance (£12,570): No tax
Income within the basic rate band (£50,270 - £12,570 = £37,700): 20% tax (£7,540)
Income in the higher rate band (£54,000 - £50,270 = £3730): 40% tax (£1,492)
So, the aggregate tax payable by Mr. X would be £7,540 (basic rate tax) + £1,492 (higher rate tax) = £9,032.

Approaches for Tax Mitigation

Every tax mitigation approach is very much dependent on the specific circumstances and fiscal goals of the taxpayer. To illustrate, investing in tax-efficient schemes such as Individual Savings Account (ISA), making pension contributions, taking part in enterprise investment schemes or venture capital trusts that offer tax reliefs, might help mitigate someone like Mr. X's tax.

Moreover, in case if he has a spouse with income less than the personal allowance, he could benefit from the Marriage Allowance, which allows him to transfer nearly 10% of his personal allowance to his spouse.

Another beneficial method would be donating to charities through Gift Aid, reducing taxable income as HM Revenue and Customs (HMRC) adds 25% to the donation made. High-rate taxpayers can further claim to get the difference between their rate and the basic rate on their donation amount.

To guide these mitigation methods, it is important to follow some common principles: make use of all available tax allowances; ensure income sources are increasingly effectively taxed; and remain updated on tax rules and regulations for the specific year.

It's important to stress that tax planning should be incorporated within the broader framework of financial goals and must not be considered as a separate activity. Effective tax mitigation strategies not only ensure law compliance but also facilitate efficient management of personal and corporate finances. It is also advisable to seek expert consultation to effectively maneuver the elaborate maze of UK tax laws and schemes.

Mitigating tax liabilities through numerical analysis and intelligent argument considers the specific circumstances of a taxpayer and offers suggestions based on tax rules and regulations. A hypothetical case is used to demonstrate how this can be accomplished.

Hypothetical Case: Company X, a manufacturing business with high taxable profits, is seeking to cut back its tax liabilities while remaining compliant with the UK tax system. Using numerical analysis and logical argument, we can suggest tax mitigation methods.

Capital Allowances: A thorough analysis of the company's assets will identify opportunities to maximize capital allowances by claiming suitable allowances and reducing taxable profits.

R&D Tax Credits: The company's R&D activities can qualify for R&D tax credits, significantly reducing tax liabilities.

Group Structures and Transfer Pricing: Analysis of the company's group structure and transfer pricing arrangements optimizes tax efficiency.

Tax Planning Measures: Further tax planning measures can be identified by conducting an extensive review of the company's operations and financials.

By employing appropriate tax planning measures, the company can optimize its tax efficiency and reduce its tax liabilities.

Examining the Ethical and Professional Intricacies of Tax Counselling

Tax planning constitutes a convoluted process and marks a crucial component of everyone's financial blueprint. A well-structured tax scheme is integral in reducing liabilities whilst boosting returns. As practitioners in this arena, tax advisors bear a significant accountability load. Still, it's relatively convenient to neglect moral and career-related matters tied to tax planning counsel. This writing seeks to dissect these involved aspects, particularly concerning the UK's tax system.

The laws defining our tax duties are perpetually shifting. A profound comprehension of these elaborate blueprints is compulsory when proffering tax planning solutions. For tax counsellors in Britain, the 2023-2024 fiscal year ushered in appealing changes and hurdles. Therefore, re-examining the career-related duties and morals of tax planning during this specific term carries paramount importance.

Proficient tax guidance encompasses not merely cognizance of regulations and doctrines but also discretion, discernment, and, paramountcy, moral behaviour. As tax consultants, we're governed by a career-related conduct code that directs our everyday operations. We must uphold secrecy, honesty, requisite expertise, attention, and meticulousness whilst aiding our clientele.

Let's ponder over an assumed scenario to further underline this. Imagine our client is a landlord who rents out an apartment for domestic uses. In the fiscal year 2023-2024, they've borne multiple costs, such as loan interest, fixes, and agency fees. Assuming the rental earnings for the apartment are £20,000, and the total costs are £5,000, we can devise an income tax calculation.

In this instance, the net relevant profits would be £15,000 (£20,000 rental earnings - £5,000 costs), which becomes the client's income tax liability. The tax computation will follow the 2023-2024 UK income tax rates. However, a moral predicament might transpire if the client insists on declaring certain non-deductible costs to employ relief measures, not necessarily applicable to them.
As tax consultants, it's critical to note our function includes adherence to exactness and honesty. Encouraging tax evasion or offering guidance based on misleading data not only discredits our career integrity but also brings about potential legal repercussions.

The UK government's endeavors to terminate tax loopholes and curb aggressive tax dodging has incited an even higher demand for moral conduct in tax planning. Ethical tax practices include encouraging transparency, preserving public trust, and championing equity within the setup. Functioning within these confines leads to not only high professional standards maintenance but also public respect for the tax system upholding.

Advisors must remain acquainted with tax legislation changes, interpret these rules accurately, foresee their influence, and guide taxpayers along their tax compliance trajectory, all whilst maintaining an ethical standpoint. In a similar sense, taxpayers' merit clear, correct, and exhaustive advice, empowering them to make informed choices and meet their tax duties without unnecessary stress or perplexity.

The delivery of tax planning advice incorporates ethical and career-related deliberations that tax experts must cognize. Providing tax planning counsel involves aiding clients in legally reducing their tax obligations whilst ensuring the UK tax system's compliance. Let's delve into the ethical and professional questions that stem from delivering tax planning advice.

Confidentiality: Tax experts have a responsibility to uphold client secrecy. They must guarantee that client data remains confidential and not shared with unauthorized entities. This includes delicate financial and tax-focused information likely to be disclosed during the tax planning process. Upholding client secrecy is vital to sustain trust and enforce professional norms.

Professional Competence: Tax experts must have the necessary knowledge, skillset, and proficiency to deliver precise and trustworthy tax planning advice. Keeping abreast with up-to-date tax rules and regulations, participating in career development programs, and seeking suitable counsel when necessary are vital to ensuring professional competence. Providing counsel beyond one's expertise or without proper research can result in inaccurate advice and prospective legal and ethical difficulties.

Conflict of Interest: Tax experts should be cognizant of potential interest conflicts that might emerge when delivering tax planning counsel. They should evade situations where their personal or financial interests might undercut their objectivity or independence. Revealing any potential interest conflicts to clients and acting to their best benefit is critical to sustaining professional incorruptibility.

Compliance with Tax Laws: Tax experts bear a duty to ensure their tax planning advice complies with the UK's tax laws and regulations. They should not engage in or facilitate any illicit or unethical tax practices, such as tax evasion or aggressive tax evasion schemes. Upholding the tax system's integrity and promoting compliance is an essential moral obligation.

Professional Standards and Ethics Codes: Tax experts should adhere to the professional norms and ethics codes set out by entities such as the Chartered Institute of Taxation (CIOT). These standards offer guidance on professional conduct, honesty, and moral behaviour. Abiding by these standards helps sustain the tax profession's reputation and ensures clients receive reliable and moral tax planning advice.

Professional skills
Communication

Understanding the 2023-2024 UK Tax System

The UK taxation system is complex and full-bodied, bolstered by numerous rules and regulations. Each fiscal year sees the introduction of new modifications which mold the nation's economic climate. This piece will explore the intricacies of the UK taxation system for the 2023-2024 fiscal year, demystifying upcoming changes, modifications, and impacts.

UK's tax system encompasses several elements - Income Tax, National Insurance, Corporation Tax, Value Added Tax (VAT), Capital Gains Tax, among others. Each component has its own functions, principles, rates, and exceptions, creating a complex network. Various elements will undergo adjustments reflecting the nation's financial tactics and economic targets for the fiscal year 2023-2024.

Case Study: Illustrative Scenario

Consider this hypothetical scenario to enhance understanding. Let's assume Mr. X, living in London, earns an annual salary of £48,000 apart from £12,000 income from his rent-collecting property, after cutting down permitted expenses.

The tax-free personal allowance as per the income tax slabs for 2023-2024 stands at £12,570. The income exceeding this up to £50,270 is taxed at 20% (basic rate), while additional income up to £150,000 is taxed at 40% (higher rate).

On these terms, Mr. X's income tax calculation would be as follows:

£12,570 from his salary is tax-free, £35,430 (£48,000-£12,570) is subject to a 20% tax while the £12,000 rental income is taxed at 40%. Therefore, Mr. X's tax owed for the fiscal year 2023-2024 would be £14,172 which includes £7,086 from income tax (£12,000×0.40) + (£35,430×0.20).

This indicates just the Income tax part of his payments to the government. Each profit and expense element could be liable to different tax calculations, reliant on existing tax laws and the execution of regulations.

Conclusion

The UK's tax system, recognized for its progressive nature and varied tax bands and percentages dependent on individual incomes, is structured to fairly distribute the tax load across earnings' brackets. Regular changes in rules, rates, and regulations require taxpayers to stay abreast with these modifications. The guiding philosophy of the UK tax system and indeed any democratically capitalistic taxation model is the fair and progressive financial contribution to state functions. Knowledge of the tax system is important to prevent surprises and penalties. Keeping track of new taxation rules in the financial year should help with this.

Tax planning tactics can prove useful to lower tax liabilities for both individuals and businesses in the UK. By using strategies like tax-favored accounts, maximizing capital allowances, claiming R&D tax credits, and making charitable donations, taxpayers can enhance their tax efficiency and lessen total tax liabilities. For example, individuals can make pension contributions to avail income tax rate-based tax relief while businesses may claim capital allowances on qualifying assets to lower taxable profits. Companies with R&D investments may qualify for R&D tax credits, enabling them to deduct a percentage of R&D expense from taxable profits. Charitable donations also offer tax advantages for both businesses and individuals.

The goal here is to illustrate an article on the taxation system of the United Kingdom, explicitly spotlighting tax computations and codes relevant to the fiscal year 2023-2024. While touching upon technical aspects and tax calculations are required, facilitating comprehension through simple, imaginative yet formal language is paramount. Ample, current information that seamlessly aligns with the latest tax reforms is necessary to meet this specification thoroughly.

In order to enhance understanding of tax calculation, let's postulate a fictitious scenario where a taxpayer named Mr. X is a self-employed freelancer based in the UK. His annual income amounts to £100,000 for the financial year 2023-2024.

According to the UK tax regulations, a self-employed individual is exempted from tax on their initial earnings of £12,570, referred to as the personal allowance. The consequent £87,430 (deducting £12,570 from £100,000), places Mr. X in the basic rate tax bracket (20%) for the initial £37,700, and the higher-rate tax bracket (40%) for the remaining £49,730.

The tax that Mr. X is obliged to pay is calculated as follows:
Basic rate tax: £37,700 × 20% = £7,540
Higher rate tax: £49,730 × 40% = £19,892
The cumulative tax that Mr. X is liable to pay equates to £7,540 (basic rate tax) + £19,892 (higher rate tax) = £27,432
These computations reflect the tax bands and classifications for the year 2023-2024 as per the UK's progressive tax mechanism. It's worth highlighting that tax situations can vary greatly on an individual basis and seeking professional guidance is always advised.

The Role of Tax Planning in Enhancing Financial Results

Argument 1: Enhancing Tax Efficiency

Tax planning empowers individuals and corporations to enhance their tax efficiency. Use of tax relief, allowances, and incentives can legally decrease tax liabilities, allowing them to hold onto a greater portion of their income or profits. This gives them more resources for investment, savings, or business expansion. Detractors may argue that it's a way to evade taxes, but it's crucial to differentiate between lawful tax planning and unlawful tax evasion.

Argument 2: Promoting Economic Progress and Innovation

Tax planning strategies like Research and Development (R&D) tax credits inspire corporations to invest in innovation and bolster economic growth. These credits can reduce tax liabilities for eligible R&D activities. This motivates businesses to invest in research, development, and technological advancements, thereby stimulating innovation and competitiveness.

Argument 3: Facilitating Charitable Contributions

Tax planning can also encourage charity, benefiting both donors and society at large. By donating to charity, individuals and corporations can claim tax relief, thus reducing their taxable income or profits. This boosts philanthropy and aids charitable institutions to address societal needs. Although some may argue that this is a form of government subsidy, it's essential to acknowledge the positive societal contributions made by charitable organizations.

Analysis and evaluation

Dissecting the UK Taxation System: A Hypothetical Case Study for 2023-2024

Understanding the intricacies of the UK taxation system can seem like cracking a complex code. Therefore, we have aimed to simplify this complex matter, making it more digestible for you. We will delve into a hypothetical case from 2023-24, detailing calculations based on realistic expectations. Let's start!

UK Taxation System Overview

Before we delve into our case study, let's quickly go over the basics of the UK taxation system. The system is designed in a progressive manner, which stipulates the tax rate increases with the increase in taxable income. This system assures fairness, as those who earn more, contribute more. You might pay your tax in various forms, such as Income Tax, Value Added Tax (VAT), Capital Gains Tax, etc. Today's point of focus will be Income Tax.

Hypothetical Situation:

We will use John, a 35-year old living and working full-time in London, as our case study. John earned £85,000 in the 2023-24 tax year. Let us calculate his income tax based on this earning.

For the tax year 2023-24, we'll presume the tax rates and bands are as follows:

Personal Allowance: Earnings up to £12,570 are tax-free.
Basic rate: 20% tax is levied on income between £12,571 - £50,270.
Higher rate: 40% tax is charged on income between £50,271 - £150,000.
Additional rate: 45% tax is imposed on income exceeding £150,000.

This puts John in the higher rate category, as his earnings exceed the basic rate threshold, but do not reach the additional rate threshold.

Income Tax Calculation

Here is how John's income tax would be calculated based on the prior bands:

In the first step, subtract the personal allowance from the annual salary. So, £85,000 - £12,570 = £72,430.

Next, tax the remaining income at different rates. The initial £37,700 (£50,270 - £12,570) falls within the basic rate band and is taxed at 20%, giving £7,540.

The rest £36,230 (£72,430 - £37,700) falls within the higher rate band and is taxed at 40%, which gives £14,492.

Adding the two tax components, we get the total income tax for the year, £7,540 + £14,492 = £22,032.

Hence, John would pay an income tax of £22,032 in the tax year 2023-24, assuming an annual salary of £85,000. Please note that these figures are purely hypothetical and meant for illustration purposes. Actual computations and figures rely on regulations and guidelines of HM Revenue & Customs (HMRC).

Informed Decision-Making: Reflecting on Tax Implications and Advocating Interests within the UK Taxation System

Introduction:

The UK tax system contains numerous complexities. This necessitates a strategic approach in making decisions that will support the financial interests of individuals, businesses, and larger organisations. This article will explain how a careful analysis of tax-related information can aid taxpayers in navigating this intricate system and improve their financial outcomes.

Collecting Relevant Data:

Gathering and understanding essential information from a variety of sources is crucial for informed decision-making. This information may include items like financial records and tax returns, advice on tax planning strategies, trends in the market and economy, as well as legal and regulatory parameters. The analysis of this data can provide taxpayers with a clearer view of their tax responsibilities, their current standings, and opportunities for securing their finances.

Contemplating Implications:

Deliberating on the potential consequences of various options is another vital step. It involves anticipating possible results and evaluating each strategy's pros and cons. For instance, understanding the outcomes of certain tax planning strategies can help taxpayers gauge their inherent risks and rewards. Reflection on these implications allows taxpayers to make informed decisions that align with their financial interests.

Advancing Interests:

A well-thought-out assimilation of information and its calculated implications help taxpayers effectively advocate for their interests. For individuals, potential benefits could include maximizing returns from tax-efficient investments, reducing personal tax burdens, or planning for retirement. Business entities may find advantages in enhancing tax efficiency, managing cash flow, or keeping pace with legal obligations. Through intelligent decision-making, taxpayers can reliably protect their interests and achieve their financial ambitions.

Professional Advice is Key:

For complicated tax issues, it is crucial to consult with a tax professional. These experts have the technical knowledge necessary to interpret intricate data and advise accordingly. They can offer customized guidance, which takes into consideration the taxpayer's unique circumstances and aspirations. By leveraging expert advice, taxpayers can make informed, interest-aligned decisions, reinforced by professional opinions.

Professional, Ethical, and Technical Aspects in the UK Tax System

Introduction:

Interpreting and applying sound judgement in the light of professional, ethical, and technical factors is essential within the UK tax system. Tax practitioners are required to make recommendations or decisions that bear in mind the effects their actions may have on the affected parties or individuals. This discussion delves into the role of ethics in the UK tax system, underlining the importance of a delicate balance between professional competence and the repercussions of decisions.

Adherence to Ethical and Professional Standards:

Tax practitioners navigate their roles based on the ethical and professional standards defined by authoritative bodies such as the Chartered Institute of Taxation (CIOT). These benchmarks emphasize aspects like integrity, professionalism, privacy, and professional competence. In formulating decisions or recommendations, tax practitioners should consider the ethical implications of their actions and confirm compliance with these set standards.

Recognizing Stakeholder Interests:

When dealing with ethical matters, tax professionals must have regard for the interests of all relevant stakeholders. This includes not only the affected individuals or organizations, but also the broader society and community. The ability to reconcile different stakeholder interests is crucial to uphold fairness and transparency, as well as to protect the overall credibility of the tax system.

Understanding Decision Impacts:

Tax practitioners must put into careful thought the potential effects of their decisions on the affected parties or individuals. This involves estimating the possible outcomes, both positive and negative, and balancing them against the ethical and professional standards. For instance, a tax practitioner might suggest a tax planning strategy that decreases tax liabilities for their client; however, they must also contemplate on the possible effects this might have on the wider tax system and the public's perception.

Abiding by Tax Legislation:

Ethical decision-making within the UK tax system requires adherence to tax laws and regulations. Tax professionals must make sure that their conclusions or recommendations are in line with the legal framework set by legislation, including the Income Tax Act 2007, the Corporation Tax Act 2010, the Value Added Tax Act 1994, and the Capital Gains Tax Act 1992. It is crucial to comply with tax laws to preserve the stability of the tax system and to prevent potential legal and ethical issues.

Balancing Professional Ethics and Decision Consequences:

Tax professionals are tasked with the challenge of harmonizing professional ethics with the impacts of their decisions. They must apply professional judgement, in light of the ethical consequences, stakeholder interests, and adherence to tax laws. This necessitates a mindful and cautious approach, considering the prospective impact on the affected parties or individuals and the broader tax system.

Objective Assessment and Decision-Making in the UK Taxation System: A Comprehensive Guide to Prioritizing Issues and Seeking Alternatives

Introduction:

Making calculated decisions in the UK taxation system involves critically analyzing information, pinpointing key issues, and exploring feasible alternatives. Detailed evaluation of available data, identification of missing pieces of information, and consideration of alternative tactics allow for informed decision-making, effective strategizing, and accurate conclusions or recommendations. This article delves into the methodology of information assessment and alternative exploration within the framework of the UK taxation system.

Objective Analysis of Information:

Conducting an objective analysis is imperative for accurate decision-making. This involves scrutinizing the reliability, relevancy, and truthfulness of the procured information. Resources such as government publications and websites, tax consultants, economic news outlets and publications, industry-specific resources and associations, as well as academic research, offer invaluable data. Objective assessment can be ensured by evaluating various sources and cross-verifying information.

Prioritization of Issues:

To tackle the most pressing matters efficiently, prioritizing issues becomes essential. Considering the potential impact, precedence, and relevancy of each issue enables individuals and businesses to allocate resources and attention appropriately. For instance, in the event of an impending tax due date, prioritizing this concern would be more critical than matters of lesser urgency. Prioritization fosters efficient decision-making and ensures timely resolution of critical issues.

Identification of Missing Information:

While assessing information, recognizing any gaps in data or available information is crucial for comprehensively informed decisions. This could involve identifying data omissions, incomplete documents or uncertainties associated with the existing data. Recognizing missing data prompts individuals and businesses to gather necessary additional information or seek professional guidance to bridge the gaps.

Exploring Feasible Alternatives:

Exploring appropriate alternatives is integral to effective decision-making. This might entail examination of diverse tax planning strategies, compliance options, or fiscal management practices. Considering alternatives enables individuals and businesses to evaluate the potential benefits, risks and outcomes of each option. This comprehensive evaluation allows for the selection of the most beneficial strategy.

A Detailed Analysis of the UK Taxation System for Fiscal Year 2023-2024

The United Kingdom boasts one of the most intricate tax systems in the world. Despite its complexity, the fundamental ethos of the system - fairness, the promotion of economic growth, and resource allocation for public spending - remain constant. In this review, we delve into the UK's taxation system for the fiscal year 2023-2024, with our main focus on Income tax and how it applies to the various categories of taxpayers.

Beginning with the aspect of total income, it forms a critical starting point in analyzing the UK tax schemes. Income streams could emanate from several sources such as wages, self-employment, pensions, rental income, savings interest, dividends from shares, and international income. For fiscal 2023-2024, it's estimated that the personal allowance - the income threshold at which one starts to pay income tax - will be £13,000; this is an increase from prior years fueled by the formulation of each new budget.

Take, for example, Mr. Smith, who in the tax year 2023-2024 earns an income of £60,000. His applicable income tax will be determined after subtracting the personal allowance from his overall income, equaling to £60,000 - £13,000 = £47,000.

The UK employs a tiered tax system whereby tax rates ascend as income levels rise. Assuming for the tax year 2023-2024 that the basic rate is 20% for income over the personal allowance up to £37,500; the higher rate is 40% for income between £37,501 and £150,000; and the additional rate is 45% for any income above £150,000.

Hence, the tax is computed as follows:
20% on initial £37,500 (after the personal allowance) equates to £7,500,
40% on the remaining £9,500 equals £3,800,
Thus Mr. Smith's total tax will amount to £11,300, leaving him with a net income after tax of £60,000 - £11,300 = £48,700 for the tax year 2023-2024.
There are additional factors to consider such as national insurance, tax relief, special provisions, capital gains tax, inheritance tax, and corporate tax complexities. Beyond income tax, the broader tax environment comprises a tangled mesh of laws, incentives, regulatory framework, and guidelines that greatly influence economic decisions.

Nevertheless, this provides a solid foundation for understanding the basics of the UK tax system for 2023-2024. Thorough understanding of tax is vital for everyone since it impacts everyone directly or indirectly. As the renowned Oliver Wendell Holmes put it, "Taxes are the price we pay for a civilized society." Understanding it is the first stride towards secure equitable taxation for all.

Demystifying UK Tax Laws: In-depth Illustrations of calculations and lucid statements.

Computational Proof:

Computations are instrumental in elucidating conclusions in the UK taxation system. They involve the tabulation of tax liabilities, allowances, deductions, or any other associated numbers. By delivering accurate and extensive computations, taxpayers can validate their conclusions and uphold transparency in their tax assessments.

Transparent Explanations:

Along with computations, clear explanations are vital in effectively communicating conclusions. Transparent explanations entail a step-by-step clarification of computations, a synopsis of the applicable tax policies and guidelines, and focusing on any presumptions or considerations made during the process. By providing information coherently and succinctly, taxpayers can assure that their conclusions are easily understood.

Hypothetical Example:

Let's look at Company X, a hypothetical small manufacturing business. In alignment with tax rules for the 2023-2024 UK tax year, Company X computed its taxable profits as £200,000. Implementing the corporation tax rate of 19%, the calculated corporation tax liability is £38,000. These computations are supported by citing relevant sections of the Corporation Tax Act 2010.

Furthermore, clear explanations are furnished to sketch the steps taken to reach these conclusions. The explanations include a breakdown of the taxable profit computations, the application of the corporation tax rate, and any applicable adjustments or allowances considered. This ensures the conclusions are easily understood and transparent for all stakeholders.

Scepticism

Delving into the UK's Tax System: Unraveling Potential Problems

The taxation system plays an integral role in a country's economic progression, making it crucial to understand the elements that guide this system, especially in the UK context. Elements such as tax rates, benefits, and who shoulders the tax load clearly impact the system's effectiveness in reaching its intended objectives.

Yet, merely touching on the easily perceivable facets of the system would not provide a full understanding of the complexity embedded in the taxation framework. Therefore, it is vital to apply a degree of critical scrutiny to reveal the concealed internal mechanisms guiding the UK's taxation landscape.

Uncovering the Root Problems

Scrutinizing the UK's taxation system brings to light several fundamental problems. First, the issue of tax evasion and avoidance poses significant challenges. Although tax avoidance is legal and evasion is illegal, these two terms are often inaccurately used interchangeably, hindering tax collection efforts. Focused investigation could fortify legislation against such misuses.

Secondly, the regressive nature of indirect taxes remains a hotly debated issue. These taxes, not tied to a person's income, invariably impact lower-income earners more, undermining the progressive character of direct taxation.

Thirdly, the lack of clarity surrounding the tax policy-making process is concerning. Greater involvement and contribution from diverse groups are required to formulate fair policies that exhibit widespread agreement. This ultimately leads to a need for a more transparent, inclusive, and comprehensible tax system.

Hypothetical Scenario: Applying the UK Tax Rules for the Year 2023-2024

Now, let's examine a hypothetical scenario to demonstrate the practical implementation of the UK tax rules for the year 2023-2024. Take for example an individual named James, a UK resident, earning an income of £150,000 per annum.

Per the UK tax rules for 2023-2024, the Personal Allowance amount (tax-free income) is £12,570. As a high-income individual, James falls within the higher rate taxpayer bracket, where he must pay a tax rate of 40% on incomes between £50,271 and £150,000 annually, and up to 45% for earnings over £150,000.

To calculate his tax obligation:

First, we subtract his Personal Allowance from his total income: £150,000 - £12,570 = £137,430.

Next, we segregate the taxable income within each tax bracket:

Basic tax rate tier: £50,271 - £12,570 = £37,701

Higher tax rate tier: £150,000 - £50,271 = £99,729

Lastly, we total up his tax obligation:

Basic tax rate (20%): £37,701 × 20% = £7,540.20

Higher tax rate (40%): £99,729 × 40% = £39,891.60

Altogether, James is likely to owe HM Revenue and Customs (HMRC) an approximate tax sum of £47,431.80.

It's crucial to note that presenting this in 'simple English' doesn't undermine the complexity of the subject. Rather, it renders this intricate topic more accessible and easier to grasp for a broader audience.

Leveraging Accessible Tools:

For understanding the root causes of tax-related issues, various resources are available for individuals and businesses alike, such as official government publications, websites, tax advisory firms, financial news and publications, industry-focused resources and associations, and academic research and studies. These resources offer invaluable information, providing a wider outlook and expert insights.

Challenging Current Assumptions and Practices:

A skeptical mindset, which questions and challenges existing assumptions and practices contributing to tax-related issues, is also important. This includes critically evaluating existing processes, policies, and strategies. By challenging the status quo, potential flaws, inefficiencies, or outdated practices contributing to tax issues can be identified, spurring innovation and advancements within the tax landscape.

Identifying Systemic Factors:

Identifying underlying causes for tax-related issues involves recognizing systemic factors at play, including economic, societal, and political influences that shape the tax system. Changes in government policies, economic conditions or international tax laws can greatly impact tax issues. Recognizing these systemic factors provides a deeper understanding of the root causes.

Digging Deeper for Insights:

To find the underlying causes, a more profound exploration beyond generic information is needed. This could involve conducting research, discussing with experts, or analyzing case studies. This deeper investigation, coupled with an appreciation of diverse perspectives and different viewpoints, helps individuals and businesses gain a thorough understanding of the issues and possible solutions.

Probing the Depths of UK Tax Laws: Predictive Calculations and Evaluation for 2023-2024

Introduction:

Navigating through the intricate maze of codes, regulations, and annual alterations that make up the UK taxation system can be a daunting task. These complexities are only intensified with every budget announcement, as the Chancellor of the Exchequer implements revisions, alterations, and occasionally reinvents tax brackets, tax relief, or tax credits. In reference to the fiscal year 2023-2024, there are certain subtleties to comprehend, particularly the effects of personal tax allowances and rate bands. However, before examining these repercussions, let's untangle the threads of the UK taxation system with a made-up example.

Consider Mr. James, for instance, a mid-level software developer residing and working in the historical city of London. In the financial year of 2023-2024, he is projected to earn £86,000 from his job. Furthermore, James is not just an employee but also an astute investor. His UK stock and bond portfolio are expected to generate a dividend income of £15,000 in the same fiscal year.

Initially, we'll categorize James's income into two segments - earnings from employment (£86,000) and dividend income from savings (£15,000). According to the UK tax rules for the year 2023-2024, the personal allowance (income one can earn before being subject to tax) stands at £12,750. However, James's total income of £101,000 surpasses the £100,000 threshold. Hence, for every £2 earned over £100,000, £1 of the personal allowance is forfeited. Thus, James's personal allowance will be curtailed by £500 (half of £1,000), leaving him with an adjusted personal allowance of £12,250.

James's employment income incurs tax at three different rates - the basic rate (20%), the higher rate (40%), and the additional rate (45%). His income up to £37,500 over the personal allowance is taxed at the basic rate. Therefore, £25,250 (£37,500 - £12,250) of his income is taxed at 20%, amounting to £5,050. The next band is the higher rate, which would be £60,750 (£86,000 - £25,250) in James's case, taxed at 40% coming to £24,300. His final tax liability from employment income is £29,350 (£24,300 + £5,050).

Let's examine his dividend income next. The first £2,000 is tax-free due to the dividend allowance. However, the remaining £13,000 is taxed at the higher dividend tax rate (32.5%) as his total income surpasses £50,250 (£37,500 + £12,750). Hence, the tax levied on his dividend income is £4,225 (£13,000 × 32.5%).

His overall tax liability for the financial year 2023-2024 amounts to £33,575 (£29,350 + £4,225).

The UK taxation system is undoubtedly intricate and layered, with various elements interacting with each other. James's hypothetical situation sheds light on the functioning of the system and how individual tax obligations might be computed. It is crucial to stay abreast of frequently changing tax rules and rates to ensure accurate and compliant tax calculations and payments. Given the complexities of personal circumstances affecting tax liabilities significantly, professional advice is often necessary.

Relevant Resources:

Various resources can be used to challenge and scrutinize beliefs, affirmations and assumptions in the UK Taxation System. Official government documents and online platforms, tax consultants and professionals, financial news pubs, trade-specific materials and societies, academic research, and case studies can provide beneficial insights. By exploiting these resources, various perspectives can be accessed and evidence to support or challenge assertions can be garnered.

Seeking Justifications:

The process of questioning beliefs, affirmations, and assumptions necessitates the search for justifications to back them up or accept them. This implies that individuals and companies must critically evaluate the logic and evidence behind these claims. By seeking justifications, they can assess the validity, reliability, and relevance of the information shared. This process facilitates informed decision-making and assures that beliefs, affirmations, and assumptions are based on solid reasoning and evidence.

Adequate Evidence Collection:

To accept or dismiss beliefs, affirmations, and assumptions, it's crucial for individuals and companies to gather sufficient evidence. This often involves comprehensive research, data analysis or expert-driven advice. By collecting enough evidence, the credibility and accuracy of the claims being made can be evaluated. This evidence-backed approach ensures that decisions and conclusions are based on reliable information.

Challenging Assumptions:

The practice of questioning beliefs, affirmations, and assumptions involves challenging inherent assumptions as well. This process is about critically evaluating and determining the credibility of these assumptions. By challenging these assumptions, one can reveal potential biases, errors, or limitations in facts presented. This critical examination promotes a more comprehensive understanding of the issues in focus.

Investigating the UK Taxation System for 2023-2024

The ongoing growth of the United Kingdom's tax system exhibits a flexible journey marked by changes and advancements in response to the economy's and society's changing needs. A detailed study of the system for the financial year 2023-2024 reveals significant insights into the rationale behind decisions and their practical effects.

Initial Observations

The UK's taxation structure includes a variety of taxes such as Income Tax, Capital Gains Tax, Inheritance Tax, Corporation Tax, National Insurance, VAT, and others. These taxes are the UK government's chief revenue source, which it uses to finance public services, protect social security, support diverse economic sectors, and maintain infrastructure. However, a profound review is needed to evaluate each tax's execution, administration, and influence.

Example of Income Tax:

Consider an imaginary UK resident, Mr. Brown, with a yearly income of £50,000 for 2023-2024. According to UK tax laws, he is entitled to a tax-free personal allowance of £12,570, so he won't be taxed until his earnings exceed this threshold.

Subsequently, the remaining £37,700 of his income (£50,000 - £12,570) comes under the basic tax rate of 20%, equating to £7,540 in tax. Therefore, Brown's take-home pay is £42,460 (£50,000 original income - £7,540 tax).

Although this system ensures taxes are paid relative to income levels, thus partially preserving fairness, it may deter individuals from exerting extra effort, as a higher income would lead to higher tax bracket.

Perceived Preferential Treatment

Critics have accused the UK tax system of favoring the affluent. As an example, Capital gains tax, which applies to profits from asset sales, is typically lower than income tax. The rich, who are more likely to own assets like shares and real estate, benefit significantly from this. The variance in these tax rates and their effect on income disparity warrant careful examination.

Corporation Tax

Internationally, the UK is recognized for having one of the lowest corporate tax rates among the G20 nations. While this policy invites foreign investments and enhances competitiveness, critics argue that businesses should contribute a substantial part of their profits and environmental impact in taxes.

VAT and Demands of the Public

While the Value Added Tax (VAT) makes a significant contribution to the UK's revenue, it can be regressive, disproportionately affecting the poor more than the rich. There could be a restructuring of the VAT system to correct this, such as lowering VAT on essential goods and raising it on luxury items. Ethical Factors:
Tax evasion and avoidance persist as significant obstacles; policymakers therefore bear the responsibility of curtailing such actions through firm regulations and punishments.

In conclusion, although the UK tax system caters to many public interests, several critical issues need addressing. Uncovering and tackling these matters involves rigorous discussions, feasible policy reforms, and thorough enforcement. The delicate equilibrium between revenue generation and economic justice should be the chief concern of the UK's tax system.

Reference Tools

Individuals and organizations can utilize a range of resources, including government publications and websites, tax consultancy firms, financial news, sector-specific resources, and academic research, to scrutinize and evaluate the UK tax system. Using these resources will provide a variety of viewpoints and valuable insights.

Professional and Ethical Guidelines

The Chartered Institute of Taxation (CIOT) lays out guidelines for professional conduct and ethics that should be considered when scrutinizing the UK tax system. Adhering to the Code of Ethics for Tax Professionals, emphasizing integrity, objectivity, confidentiality, and professional competence, can ensure ethical and professional conduct.

Considering Organizational and Public Interests

Critiques of the UK tax system can be beneficial to the broader organizational and public interests. This could involve examining practices that lead to unfair tax benefits, identifying possible gaps or conflicts in tax regulations, or addressing issues that could undermine public faith in the tax system. By evaluating information and decisions critically, individuals and organizations can promote transparency and equality.

Encouraging Open Dialogue

It's crucial to encouraging open dialogue when disputing information or decisions. Constructive discussions involve presenting well-founded arguments, providing supporting evidence, and incorporating alternative viewpoints. Open and respectful debate can contribute to tax system improvements and foster positive change.

Understanding Assumptions, Restrictions, and Information Gaps in the Analysis

The analysis of the UK taxation system may involve inevitable assumptions and restrictions due to the complexity of the system. Understandably, the nature of such studies to form conclusions based on accessible data and future predictions contributes to these limitations. To fully discern the UK's intricate and multi-layered tax system requires a penetrating study. Therefore, recognizing any potential boundaries that might affect our comprehension of such an analysis and its findings is essential.

A key assumption in this analysis is the stability of tax regulations and policies during the tax year 2023-2024. Tax regulations often change, depending on the country's fiscal health, macroeconomic factors, and political directions. Thus, we assume that the tax laws, benefits, and rates for this tax year will stay unchanged for the duration of the estimated period.

Moreover, this analysis figures that the conduct of taxpayers will stay relatively steady with time. This is, conversely, somewhat of a generalization, as taxpayers' choices, compliance, decisions regarding taxes, and preferences frequently change in response to alterations in tax regulations, fluctuations in personal income, economic situations, and other considerations.

One sizeable restriction is that the analysis is as accurate as the data accessible. There are times when data might be outmoded, incomplete, or contain reporting mistakes, preventing a wholly precise analysis. The absence of thorough data such as taxpayers' income details, demographic information, business earnings, etc., may obstruct our capacity to perform a more detailed investigation of the tax system.

An additional limitation rests on our reliance on predictions and forecasts, prone to sudden macroeconomic changes. Unanticipated worldwide occurrences, like Brexit or the COVID-19 pandemic, can majorly influence tax revenues and taxpayers' actions, possibly causing our forecasts to be less precise.
With respect to gaps in the available information, this analysis may not wholly cover the fluctuating nature inherent in the UK's tax system. There may be special tax laws or benefits that apply to

individual industries, regions, or businesses that aren't addressed. This underlines the call for more detailed and all-inclusive data to attain a more comprehensive examination.

Illustrative Case Study:

To better understand the UK tax system, suppose an average UK taxpayer, Mr. Smith, earns an annual income of £60,000 in the tax year 2023-2024. As per UK tax brackets, he falls into the basic rate band (20%) for earnings between £12,571 and £50,270 and the higher rate band (40%) for earnings between £50,271 and £150,000. When you consider his personal allowance (£12,570), £37,700 of his income falls into the basic rate band, and £9,730 falls into the higher rate band. Thus, his total tax liability amounts to £8,882 (£7,540 from the basic rate band and £1,342 from the higher rate band). This illustration is plain and doesn't consider any other factors like added incomes, special allowances, deductions, etc.

Despite the assumptions, limitations, and insufficient information making the analysis a bit challenging, it stresses the importance of continuously keeping ourselves abreast of the UK taxation system, staying updated on fresh changes and personalizing solutions and strategies correspondingly.

Assumptions Made:

The analysis of the UK taxation system might include certain assumptions due to the system's dynamic nature and intricacy. These assumptions might pertain to the comprehension and application of tax laws, the accuracy of fiscal data, or citizen compliance with tax regulations. Expressly stating these assumptions lead to greater transparency and context for the analysis.

Limitations in the Analysis:

Every analysis contains its restrictions, and the UK taxation system analysis isn't exempt. Restrictions could emerge due to the dependability and accessibility of data, the extent of the analysis, or the competency of the individuals executing the analysis. Acknowledging these restrictions is crucial to ensure that the deduced conclusions are suitably qualified, avoiding making sweeping statements.

Inadequacies in Available Information:

The analysis of the UK taxation system might face hindrances due to insufficiencies in the obtainable information. These could be because of the complexity of tax laws, inadequate access to certain data, or lack of comprehensive and updated info. Recognizing these inadequacies is vital as it stresses the need for additional research, data compilation, or the input of experts to offer a more comprehensive analysis.

Additional Information Required:

For a fuller analysis of the UK taxation system, more information might be needed. This could include specific fiscal data, industry-specific tax regulations, or insights into the political and economic factors affecting tax policies. Identifying this need for additional information will guide future research and ensure that the analysis is as complete and accurate as it can be.

Commercial acumen

The intricate array of rules and regulations that make up the UK tax system is something every citizen, resident, and business entity must conform to. This article highlights the complexities of the tax decision-making process, shedding light on an assortment of organisational and external factors that can potentially influence these decisions. There are a multitude of tax-related and non-tax elements that can significantly alter an individual or entity's overall tax stance, adding layers of complexity to tax planning. It is vital, therefore, to have a comprehensive understanding of these factors.

One key non-tax element influencing decisions is the economic climate. For example, in a phase of economic growth, a company may choose to invest more to capitalize on increased consumer spending, thereby strategizing to optimize tax reliefs on these investments. Conversely, during an economic slump, a business could defer losses to future years in a bid to lower tax liabilities when the economy recovers.

Moreover, the existing political environment can also significantly sway tax decisions. Frequent changes in tax laws and regulations often reflect the policies of the reigning political party. For example, a newly instated government might instigate tax policies designed to boost investment in particular sectors, prompting businesses in those fields to modify their tax planning strategies accordingly.

Let's consider a hypothetical scenario to further clarify this concept. Imagine a UK tech startup, 'Tec Ventures Ltd.', which turned a profit in the 2023-2024 tax year, needing to devise its tax strategy for that year. The firm netted a profit of £250,000 and, based on the UK corporate tax rules for that year (taxed at 19%), would face a tax liability of £47,500. However, the company invested significantly in new software development, an expense that qualifies as capital expenditure.

Under the Capital Allowances Act 2001, companies can claim an Annual Investment Allowance (AIA) on eligible expenditures, allowing for 100% tax relief in the year of investment. During the tax year in question, this allowance was set at £1 million.

Consequently, TechVentures Ltd. can cut down its taxable profits by the funds spent on software development, thereby considerably lowering its tax liability.

In this scenario, the company had to weigh its aspiration for growth (via software development investment) against the potential tax consequences of such an action. The decision was influenced by both external aspects (the economic climate favoring tech development) and organisational elements (the company's profit margins and growth objectives).

External elements strongly affecting tax decisions can include broader economic indicators and trends, the political and regulatory landscape, and factors specific to industry. Market conditions like interest rates, inflation, and market trends are key economic considerations that could impact investment decisions and tax planning strategies. Changes in political policy or new laws can also have significant implications for tax liabilities and incentives.

Organisational goals, strategies, and circumstances are also key in tax decision-making. Every organisation has its distinct goals, whether it involves increasing profits, expanding operations, or fostering a positive public persona. Tax decisions must line up with these objectives and strategies.

Social and cultural factors can also influence tax decisions, particularly around issues like corporate social responsibility and public perception. Businesses might also think about the ethical effects of their tax planning strategies, striving to align them with societal expectations.

Individuals and organisations must consider both tax and non-tax factors to make informed tax decisions. This necessitates studying the interaction between tax liabilities, external factors, organisational goals, and social considerations. By taking a wide-ranging perspective, decision-makers can navigate the intricacies of the UK tax system and ensure their decisions are consistent with broader objectives and values.

Introductory Note

The UK's tax system is often referred to for its complex nature. Even with ongoing efforts for simplification, it often leaves both individual and corporate taxpayers perplexed due to the complex web of direct and indirect taxes. The fiscal year 2023-2024 saw specific tweaks and initiatives within this system. The objective of this article is to demystify these changes and interpret their implications via a hypothetical case study.

Decoding the UK Tax System:

The UK's tax law plays a central role in revenue generation as well as driving the social and economic strategies of the government. The system includes numerous kinds of taxes, like Income Tax, Corporation Tax, Capital Gains Tax, Inheritance Tax, VAT, Stamp Duties, and Excise Duties. Income Tax and Capital Gains Tax are levied based on a person's income and capital gains, whereas Corporation Tax is applied to taxable corporate profits. Inheritance Tax is payable on an individual's estate after their death, while VAT, Stamp Duties and Excise Duties tax consumption.

Tax legislation Alterations in 2023-2024:

The tax legislation for 2023-2024 introduced significant modifications. These adjustments comprised the unification of tax rates for employment and self-employment incomes, adjustments in tax thresholds and reliefs, and alterations to the corporation tax rates. The main attention-grabbing shift was a hike in the national insurance contribution rate to support healthcare and social care expenses.

Illustrative Case Study:

Consider the fictional instance of Mr. John, a self-operating entrepreneur with an annual income of £100,000 and no other source of income. According to the 2023-2024 regulations, John experiences a rise in his National Insurance contributions from 9% to 10% on earnings between £9,569 to £50,270 and from 2% to 3% for income above this threshold.

Calculating his National Insurance for the year:

He will be taxed 10% on income between £9,569 and £50,270, which adds up to £4,070. On the remaining income above £50,270 which, in John's case, is £49,730, he would pay 3%, summing up to approximately £1,492.

Thus, his total National Insurance contribution for the year would be close to £5,562.

Final Note:

The fiscal year 2023-2024 introduced a series of modifications to the UK's tax system. Comprehending the effects of these transitions is imperative for individuals and corporations to plan their finances strategically. Mr. John's case provides an example of how the tax regulation amendments influence liability calculations. Professional guidance becomes indispensable to ensure tax efficiency within legal boundaries in such scenarios.

Identifying Crucial Issues:

To suggest commercially feasible solutions, the essential step is identifying key challenges within the given situation. This may necessitate examining financial statements, tax return files, or other relevant documents to pinpoint troubling areas. Crucial issues could encompass high tax dues, ineffective tax planning strategies, contravention of tax rules, or overlooked tax incentives opportunities. By identifying these issues, decision-makers can direct their effort towards finding suitable solutions.

Using Relevant References:

Identifying key issues and suggesting feasible solutions necessitates using relevant references. These references could be official government publications and websites, tax advisory firms and professionals, financial news and publications, resources related to the particular industry and associations, and case studies. These references provide access to expert opinions, industry standard practices, and real-world examples for decision makers for their proposed solutions.

Exercising Judgment:

Suggesting commercially viable solutions requires exercising judgment to scrutinize the feasibility and efficiency of potential actions. Decision-makers need to consider financial implications, regulatory compliance, and the overall impact on the business or individual's financial objectives. By making informed judgments, decision-makers can examine the pros and cons of different solutions and select the most commercially feasible option.

Ensuring Commercial Viability:

Commercial practicality is a vital factor while proposing solutions in the UK taxation system. The solutions must resonate with the financial capacity and goals of the concerned individual or entity. This may require considering aspects like cost-efficiency, anticipated return on investment, and long-term durability. By ensuring commercial viability, decision-makers can suggest solutions that are practical, achievable, and advantageous for the financial wellness of the concerned party.

A Detailed Review of the UK Taxation System
(2023-2024 Tax Year)

Introduction

The UK taxation system is an intricate economic tool that supports government functions and obligations. Fundamentally, it encompasses four main components, namely: Income Tax, National Insurance, Value Added Tax (VAT), and Corporation Tax. Let's delve into the details and examine how these taxation rules apply, especially in the 2023-2024 tax year.

Income Tax: An Overview

Income tax is the core part of the UK's taxation system, levied on salaries, wages, pensions, benefits, and profits from self-employment and rental income. The 2023-2024 tax year introduces specific changes in income tax brackets and personal allowances that taxpayers need to be mindful of.

Hypothetical Case: Understanding Income Tax Calculations

Consider a hypothetical case of a UK resident, John Doe, who is self-employed and earns £80,000 annually. Under the tax rules for 2023-2024, John is supposed to pay income tax as per the following brackets:

£0 - £12,570: 0% (Personal allowance)

£12,571 - £50,270: 20% (Basic rate)

£50,271 - £150,000: 40% (Higher rate)

Over £150,000: 45% (Additional rate)

John's income tax will be computed as follows:
First, we subtract the personal allowance (£12,570) from John's total income (£80,000) — equaling £67,430.
This amount falls into both the basic rate and higher rate brackets. Thus, we split it accordingly to calculate the tax. For the basic rate bracket, £50,270 - £12,571 equals £37,699. At the 20% rate, John's tax for this portion of his income calculates to £7,539.80.

The remaining amount of his income, £67,430 - £37,699 equals £29,731 falls into the higher rate bracket. At the 40% rate, tax for this portion of income calculates to £11,892.40.

Adding up both amounts, £7,539.80 (basic rate tax) and £11,892.40 (higher rate tax), John's total income tax payable for the tax year 2023-2024 amounts to £19,432.20.

VAT, National Insurance, and Corporation Tax: Brief Overview

Beyond income tax, the UK taxation system also encompasses VAT. This tax is charged on most goods and services sold by registered businesses in the UK. The standard rate for the 2023-2024 tax year stands at 20%.

National Insurance, meanwhile, contributes to an individual's entitlement to certain state benefits. Rates vary depending on an individual's employment status and how much they earn.

Finally, Corporation Tax is levied on pre-tax profits of limited companies and certain other organisations like clubs and societies.

Conclusion

Understanding the UK taxation system, especially in the context of changes introduced in the 2023-2024 tax year, is essential for individuals and businesses. Compliance denotes accurate calculations, timely contributions, and familiarity with exemptions and reliefs. By way of continuing reforms, the system aims to promote both individual prosperity and collective progress within the region.

Determining Main Tax Factors

Main tax factors differ based on each individual or entity's situation. For individuals, these primary factors might be income sources, deductions, tax reliefs, and opportunities for tax planning. For entities, the primary factors might be taxable profits, capital allowances, tax incentives, and compliance obligations. Recognizing these main tax factors helps decision-makers target their suggestions on the most impactful areas on the tax situation.

Examining Tax Aims and Objectives:

Grasping the tax aims and objectives of an individual or entity is vital for providing suitable suggestions. Decision-makers need to determine whether the attention is on reducing tax liabilities, increasing tax incentives, perfecting tax planning methods, or satisfying compliance. By aligning suggestions with the tax aims and goals, specific and relevant advice can be provided by decision-makers.

Utilizing Insight in Suggestions:

Exercising insight in offering suggestions means using expertise, experience, and judgment to reach suitable solutions. Decision-makers ought to think about distinct tax factors, individual or entity's conditions, and the larger tax environment. This could involve suggesting tax planning methods, maximizing deductions and allowances, looking into tax incentives, or tackling compliance problems. By exercising insight, decision-makers can provide insightful, practical, and aligned suggestions with the individual or entity's tax aims.

Case Analysis

Take two hypothetical instances: George, an independent contractor in the world of construction, and ABC Ltd, a mid-sized retail industry business. George's average yearly gross income is £60,000, and ABC Ltd aims to earn £3 million before tax during the fiscal year of 2023-2024.

Calculating Personal Taxes

For the tax year 2023-2024 as set by the UK tax system, George is required to pay Income Tax on his income. The tax-free personal allowance means that the first £12,570 of George's income isn't taxed. The income up until £50,270 is liable to the basic 20% tax, so George will pay a 20% tax on £37,700 of his earnings (£50,270 - £12,570 = £37,700). Any earning above £50,270 is taxed at a higher rate of 40%. For George, this equates to £9,730 (£60,000 - £50,270 = £9,730). Hence, George's year-wise total income tax amounts to £9,014, derived from (£37,700 × 20%) + (£9,730 × 40%).

Computing Corporate Tax

In the tax year 2023-2024, the UK taxes corporations, like ABC Ltd, at a rate of 19%. As a result, ABC Ltd.'s corporation tax amounts to £570,000 (£3,000,000 × 19%).

Suggestions for Tax Planning

To reduce his tax burden, George could ponder investing some income into a pension plan or operating via a limited company. ABC Ltd could reduce their corporation tax by making claims on all allowed business deductions such as goods sold, wages, and overhead expenses. They can also deliberate the reinvestment of profits back into the business or the distribution of dividends in a tax-efficient way.

Given how complex the tax laws and regulations can be, it's vital to seek professional advice to effectively comprehend and navigate the tax landscape, ensuring tax liabilities are managed optimally and in compliance. Keep in mind, this advice is general and its relevance would depend on the specifics of the individual or entity in question. Legislation can always change, affecting the accuracy of this information. A tax consultant or accountant should always be consulted prior to making any plans or decisions.

Employability and technology skills

Utilizing Computer Technology to Effectively Manage Information in the UK Tax System

Introduction:

The vital role of computer technology in gaining and processing relevant data in the UK tax system effectively cannot be overstated. Through the use of various digital tools and sources, both individuals and organizations can traverse through the intricacies of tax norms and regulations, secure current information, and execute computations with precision. This article discusses the significance of computer technology in the efficient management of information in relation to the UK tax system.

Accessing Pertinent Information:

Computer technology aids both individuals and organizations in accessing relevant data effectively. Online resources such as official government publications and websites, tax consultation services and specialists, financial journals and releases, resources, and associations specific to different sectors, and case studies are conveniently accessible. The use of search engines, databases, and online platforms provides a plethora of information to guide tax-related inquiries and inform decision-making processes.

Handling Data and Performing Calculations:

Computer technology supports the efficient handling of data and execution of complex calculations. Tax preparation software, spreadsheet applications, and online calculators offer tools for the input and analysis of financial data, performing tax computations, and producing accurate outcomes. These tools simplify tax planning, compliance, and reporting processes, saving time and minimizing error risks.

Keeping Up-to-Date with the Latest Information:

Computer technology aids in keeping up-to-date with current information about the UK tax system. Official government websites, tax consultation services, and financial news platforms offer real-time updates about changes in tax laws and regulations. Individuals and organizations can stay informed about updates that may affect their tax responsibilities through subscribing to newsletters, following relevant social media accounts, or using RSS feeds.

Utilizing Digital Tools and Resources:

Computer technology provides an ample array of digital tools and resources to support tax-related activities. Tools like online tax calculators, tax planning software, and document management systems simplify procedures and boost efficiency. Cloud storage solutions allow for the secure storage and easy retrieval of crucial tax-related documents. Collaboration tools also enable efficient communication and collaboration among tax experts and stakeholders.

In the modern workplace, employability is heavily dependent on one's ability to leverage technology. To remain competitive, employees must continually advance their skills as technology continues to evolve. Here are some response options for those seeking to improve their employability and technology skills:

Ongoing Training & Certifications: One of the best ways to stay up-to-date in the quickly evolving tech world is to continuously train and receive certificates in new technologies. Many online platforms offer industry-recognized certification programs that can be beneficial.

Engage in Online Learning: There are numerous online resources available to learn new technology skills. Websites like Codecademy, LinkedIn Learning, and Coursera offer courses in everything from coding to data analysis to graphic design.

Attending Tech Workshops and Conferences: These events offer opportunities to learn about the latest developments in technology and network with professionals in the field. They also often offer hands-on workshops where attendees can gain practical experience.

Join Tech-Related Groups or Communities: Engaging with others in the tech industry can provide opportunities to learn about new technologies, receive feedback on your projects, and expand your network.

Experiment with New Tools & Software: Don't be afraid to explore new tools and software that could improve your productivity or enhance your skill set. Trying out new technologies can make you more comfortable with rapid technological changes.

Work on Personal Tech Projects: Working on your own projects can be an excellent way to learn new skills. Whether it's building a website or coding a new app, these projects can serve as tangible proof of your abilities.

Remember, technology is merely a tool. Integrating these tools into your everyday tasks could result in increased productivity and efficiency. However, it is also crucial to have strong soft skills like problem-solving, effective communication, and adaptability. These, combined with robust tech skills, will significantly enhance your employability in the workplace.

Suppose we examine a theoretical scenario involving a small business proprietor named Sarah. She manages a thriving online retail business and aspires to augment her operations by establishing a physical outlet. She wants guidance regarding the tax outcomes and prospective advantages of such expansion.

To offer suitable reply options, we can resort to commonly employed workplace functionalities and technologies. Below are some probable reply alternatives:

Use tax software: Employ tax software tools, for instance, accounting software containing built-in tax components, to evaluate Sarah's fiscal statistics and forecast the likely tax outcomes of inaugurating a physical outlet. This software can compute tax obligations, tax breaks, and allowances in accordance with the prevailing tax rules and regulations.

Seek advice from tax professionals: We can advise Sarah to seek counsel from tax consultancy firms or professionals specializing in small enterprise taxation. These specialists can offer tailored counsel in view of Sarah's individual circumstances, to ensure adherence with tax laws and identify potential tax planning prospects.

Make use of government publications: Guide Sarah towards official documents and websites provided by government bodies like HM Revenue and Customs (HMRC) to avail updated data on tax regulations, allowances, and stimuli related to small businesses and retail operations. This could facilitate comprehending the tax consequences and profits of enlarging her enterprise.

Evaluate case studies: Refer to case studies or practical instances of similar businesses that have grown from online to physical outlets. Reviewing these studies can offer perceptions into the tax considerations, hurdles, and prospective profits that Sarah may meet in her enlargement strategies.

Investigate industry-specific resources: Look into industry-specific resources and associations that offer direction on tax-related matters for retail businesses. These resources can offer insights into industry-wise tax regulations, superior practices and strategies for maximizing tax efficiency.

Keep in sync with financial updates: Urge Sarah to stay updated with financial updates and documents that cover tax-related discussions. This would assist her in keeping informed about any modifications in tax laws, regulations, or incentives that could impact her expansion plans.

By employing these response options and making use of the available functions and technology, we can offer Sarah pertinent guidance and suggestions concerning the tax outcomes and potential benefits of broadening her online retail business to a physical store. This method depicts the use of employability and technological competencies in the workplace, as it necessitates using resources, evaluating data, and leveraging technology to provide informed and practical solutions.

With the advent of digital technology, the need for employers and educational institutions to adapt and utilize these tools effectively has drastically increased. This has led to a significant shift in the skills required for many jobs, which includes not only understanding how to use technology, but also how to navigate through various computer systems and platforms.

The ability to navigate through windows and computer screens is a key component of employability in our modern technological world. This skill involves being able to move through different screens and systems quickly and efficiently, which can increase productivity and make work processes more streamlined.

In the context of exam requirements, this could involve opening multiple windows or tabs to view different parts of an exam, using split screen functionality to view separate documents in tandem, or using various tools and programs to create or amend responses.

The use of appropriate tools is also crucial to successful navigation. This could entail using software specific to the job or task at hand, as well as hardware such as a mouse or a touch screen device. There are also many keyboard shortcuts that can greatly enhance efficiency when navigating through screens.

As an example, for a written exam, a student could employ tools such as a word processor for their responses, while utilizing a web browser to access online resources. They would need to navigate between these windows efficiently, perhaps using the 'alt-tab' keyboard shortcut to switch between the word processor and the browser.

To conclude, developing proficiency in these areas enhances employability and can help individuals thrive in a digitized world. With the appropriate navigation skills, one can excel in their work or fulfill exam requirements more effectively. It's essential to continuously learn and adapt to new technological tools and systems, in order to keep up with the evolving tech landscape.

Hypothetical Scenario Analysis:

Consider the hypothetical scenario analysis of a business, named XYZ Ltd. XYZ Ltd., a manufacturing entity, is contemplating business expansion to an additional location. Our examination prerequisites necessitate that we devise and modify replies to address tax-related aspects and considerations of this proposed expansion.

We can handle the task of formulating/modifying responses using suitable resources like word processing applications, spreadsheets and web browsers. Below are some potential methods to tackle the tax-related aspects of XYZ Ltd.'s proposed expansion:

Initiate a word processing application: Locate the appropriate software on your computer and commence a fresh file to formulate the reply.

Investigate tax-related aspects: Utilize a web browser to access formal government publications and websites, like the ones offered by HM Revenue and Customs (HMRC), and probe into the tax-related aspects of business expansion in the manufacturing sector. Delve into relevant tax statutes, regulations, and guidelines to amass information about tax considerations pertinent to XYZ Ltd.'s sector and expansion strategies.

Formulate an outline: Use a word processing program to construct an outline for the response, collating key points and tax-related aspects that must be highlighted. This aids in organizing the details and ensures a logical progression in the response.

Fill in and modify details: Employ the word processing program to fill in and modify the details compiled during the probe phase. This could involve chatting about the plausible impact on corporate tax, VAT, capital concessions, and any other pertinent tax considerations for XYZ Ltd.'s proposed expansion.

Leverage spreadsheets: If required, launch a spreadsheet program to build financial prototypes or computations connected to the tax-related aspects. Spreadsheets can help to dissect data, carry out computations, and display fiscal details in a lucid and methodical manner.

Revise and correct: After the response are finished, skim through the document to revise and correct the content for precision, lucidity, and consistency. Use suitable tools inside the word processing application to make any essential amendments or enhancements.

By adeptly handling windows and computer displays and exploiting suitable resources, we can formulate and modify replies to address the tax-related aspects and considerations for XYZ Ltd.'s proposed expansion. This signifies employability and technical prowess as it involves using word processing applications, web browsers, and spreadsheets to probe, collate and display details in a mindful and lucid way.

Introduction

In our digital era, both Employability and Technology skills have become critical for job seekers. Being able to effectively present information using appropriate technological tools is a valuable advantage in this market.

Data Analysis and Presentation Tools

Today's vast amount of data requires individuals to possess an ability to sort, aggregate, and interpret it. Some of the popular data analysis and presentation tools include:

MS Excel and Google Sheets: These tools are fundamental for maintaining data and performing basic analysis on it through charts/graphs, pivot tables, etc.

Programming Languages: Languages such as R, Python, and SQL are frequently utilized for data analysis due to their flexibility and efficiency.

Data Visualization Tools: Applications such as Tableau, QlikView, Data Studio, and PowerBI help to convert complex datasets into easily understandable formats through interactive dashboards and reports.

Presentation Tools: Tools like MS PowerPoint, Prezi, Sliderocket, etc., make presenting information easier, more interactive, and engaging.
Examples of Data Presentations
Here is an example of data presentation using the above-mentioned tools:
Pivot Tables in Excel/Google Sheets:

		Sum of Sales
Product		
Product 1		3000
Product 2		2000
Grand Total	5000

In the above-mentioned pivot table, the sales data is aggregated product-wise, giving a quick and easy view of the sales performance of different products.

Bar Graph in Tableau:

Bar Graph showing the number of units sold per product type

A bar graph provides a visual representation of the product performance that is quick to understand and easy to compare.

Using Technology to Enhance Employability Skills

Learning to employ these tools can significantly improve one's employability. Employers value clear and effective communication, and mastering these tools allows candidates to convey complex data in an easy-to-understand, visual manner.

Conclusion

Possessing technology skills and the ability to present data effectively gives job seekers a competitive edge. It not only broadens job prospects but also improves problem-solving ability, decision making, collaboration, and productivity. Hence, these skills are a must in a tech-driven business environment.

Imagine a Scenario:

Let's envision a theoretical scenario involving a firm named ABC Ltd., a tech startup that recently launched a product. In order to meet requirements for both employability and technology expertise, we need to efficiently represent data and information using suitable tools for analyzing and highlighting the firm's financial performance.

Useful tools and techniques are required for effectively presenting data and information. Here are some potential strategies for exhibiting ABC Ltd.'s financial results:

Financial Data Collection: Accumulate relevant financial details, such as income, costs, and profit from the financial statements or accounting software of ABC Ltd. Make sure the information is precise and up-to-date.

Employ spreadsheet software: Use spreadsheet platforms, like Microsoft Excel or Google Sheets, to enter and format the financial data. Generate separate worksheets for various aspects of financial performance, including revenue, costs, and profitability.

Draw charts and graphs: Within the spreadsheet software, employ charting abilities to visually convey the financial information. Graphs, line charts, and pie charts can effectively exhibit comparisons, trends, and ratios. Choose a suiTable chart kind based on the data under presentation.

Data analysis and interpretation: Apply formulas and functions within the spreadsheet software to compute and examine the financial data. Work out critical financial ratios, like gross profit margin or return on investment, to reveal insights into the financial performance of ABC Ltd. Sift through the data to identify potential strengths, weaknesses, and areas of growth.

Create visually appealing slides: Leverage presentation platforms, such as Google Slides or Microsoft PowerPoint, to produce a visually compelling presentation. Insert the charts, graphs, and critical findings from the financial analysis into the slides. Use appropriate fonts, colors, and layouts to augment readability and engagement.
Demonstrate efficient communication: Make sure communication is lucid and succinct when presenting the data and information. Present the financial performance in a logical and systematic way, underlining vital points and insights. Appropriate terminology should be chosen and jargon avoided, to ensure comprehension by a diverse audience.

Rehearse and ask for feedback: Practice the presentation and ask for feedback from mentors or colleagues. Incorporate their suggestions to enhance clarity, flow, and overall presentation effectiveness.

With effective use of excel and presentation software and competent communication, we can efficiently present the financial performance of ABC Ltd. in a concise, visually engaging, and clear manner. This displays both employability and tech expertise, as it involves the efficient interpretation and presentation of data employing the right tools, not forgetting perfecting communication skills.

Milton Keynes UK
Ingram Content Group UK Ltd.
UKHW011518230124
436534UK00001B/108